Media Work

Digital Media and Society Series

New technologies are fundamentally altering the ways in which we communicate. This series from Polity aims to provide a set of books that make available for a broad readership cutting edge research and thinking on digital media and their social contexts. Taken as a whole, the series will examine questions about the impact of network technology and digital media on society in all its facets, including economics, culture and politics.

Mark Deuze: Media Work in a Digital Age
Tim Jordan: Hacking

Media Work

MARK DEUZE

polity

First published in 2007 by Polity Press
Reprinted 2008

Polity Press
65 Bridge Street
Cambridge CB2 IUR, UK

Polity Press
350 Main Street
Malden, MA 02148, USA

ISBN-13: 978-07456-3924-6
ISBN-13: 978-07456-3925-3 (pb)

A catalogue record for this book is available from the British Library.

Typeset in 10.25 on 13 pt FF Scala
by Servis Filmsetting Ltd, Manchester
Printed and bound in Great Britain by MPG Books Ltd, Bodmin, Cornwall

Text design by Peter Ducker

The publisher has used its best endeavours to ensure that the URLs for
external websites referred to in this book are correct and active at the time of
going to press. However, the publisher has no responsibility for the websites
and can make no guarantee that a site will remain live or that the content is or
will remain appropriate.

Every effort has been made to trace all copyright holders, but if any have been
inadvertently overlooked the publishers will be pleased to include any
necessary credits in any subsequent reprint or edition.

For further information on Polity, visit our website: www.polity.co.uk

Contents

Preface

Manpower is a temporary employment agency founded in the United States in 1948, and currently operates over 4,400 offices in seventy-two countries and territories. The company offers permanent, temporary, and contract recruitment, employee assessment and selection, as well as training, outplacement, outsourcing, and consulting services to hundreds of thousands of enterprises.[1] *Manpower*'s corporate slogan – "creating opportunities for all people to participate in the workforce" – sounds like an empowering rallying cry for all who want to be employed, who want to be able to participate in the global economy. At the same time, the enormous success of agencies such as *Manpower* signal a world of work that provides anything but security, stability, or guarantees for participation. This world of work thrives on contingency: whatever happens today has few or no predictable consequences for what will most likely happen tomorrow. One's future – as a contracted employee and thus as a successful consumer – is structurally dependent on something not yet certain. Work is conditional, but the conditions for work are beyond your control. You can excel in what you do today, but if investors pull out tomorrow – you are without a job. You can have a brilliant moment during a meeting on Friday, but if on Saturday the stock of your company collapses, you will find yourself checking *Monster.com* – a jobhunting site with affiliates in twenty-one countries – on Monday.

What people are doing online is a good indicator of how everyday life for a working professional (or those seeking to become one) in today's new capitalist economy has changed. It is not just work that has become contingent – contingency stretches across all walks of life and impacts all social institutions. A growing number of singles – quickly becoming the dominant species in contemporary society – seek, and sometimes find, love online. A popular online matchmaking service, *Match.com*, launched in 1995, currently has more than fifteen million members in more than 240 territories on six continents, and operates more than thirty online dating sites in seventeen local languages.[2] Finding love online gets mediated by simple mathematical formulas linking one's self-reported and constantly tweaked or updated characteristics and preferences to those of millions of others, thereby making the selection process of a mate contingent as well. Other popular sites online combine matchmaking, employment-seeking and other social networking-based services, effectively enacting the convergence of all walks of life. An illustrative example of such hybrid and interconnected online services is *MySpace.com*, a social networking website offering its approximately seventy million registered users blogs, profiles, groups, photos, music, videos, and an internal e-mail system. *MySpace* was acquired by Rupert Murdoch's NewsCorporation in July 2005. By March 2006 the social network was growing by an average of 250,000 new members daily.[3]

Manpower, Monster, Match, and *MySpace* are not examples of a life increasingly lived online – but rather must be seen as case studies of how contemporary life gets expressed through (new) media. Such a life is deeply connected to other people's lives all over the world, yet socially isolated at the same time as life's context has become contingent. Social bonds get expressed through all kinds of networked media at home, at work, and at play. The personal computer, the cell phone and the (portable) game console signify a world saturated by media where age-old ideas of what it means to be part of a community, to have a job or to pursue happiness have become unstable and uncertain. Media are not just pervasive and ubiquitous – we also develop intense relationships with our media. Byron Reeves and Clifford Nass (1996) have shown how people treat and respond to media artifacts (computers, televisions, cell phones, and so on) in just the same way as they treat and respond to other people in everyday social interaction. The rules which people apply to everyday social interaction apply equally well to their interactions with media. These interactions are increasingly shaping and influencing almost every kind of social arrangement: how and where we work, we communicate and socialize, we play. In doing so, we apply to mediated experiences the same rules and conventions as to face-to-face or otherwise "real" experiences.

The seamless and generally taken for granted nature of media in everyday life to some extent explains how our use of media often disappears: when asked, people tend to grossly underestimate how much time they spend with media. Contemporary media usage studies in wired countries such as Japan, the United States, The Netherlands, or Finland tend to reveal that people spend twice as much time with media than they think they do – up to twelve hours a day. Media have become such an integrated part of our lives that most of the time we are not even aware we are using media. American researchers describe this kind of almost constant immersion with media technologies and content from multiple sources simultaneously available through shared or shifting attention as concurrent media exposure, rather than popular industry-terms such as media multitasking or simultaneous media usage, emphasizing how important it is to avoid implying that our engagement with media is necessarily deliberate or atten-tive (Papper *et al.* 2004). It has become automatic.

All of this ultimately means that an understanding of what people do in their everyday lives must take note of the crucial role media play therein. Media do not just influence us in terms of how we spend most of our time, how we organize and give meaning to our social networks, or what we may think about world events; media have also become a crucial part of today's global economy. The industry of media – from the revenues it generates, the ways it manages its workflows to the particular kinds of people employed as culture creators – can be seen as a role model or benchmark of how the globalizing economy is organizing itself. Some of the key elements of what it is like to work in the media today are symptomatic of how people all over the world are increasingly experiencing their work-lives. Understanding media is much more than being able to wield a remote control, to navigate the features of a personal computer successfully, or to get reliable results using an online search engine. It is also more than being able to read between the lines of a newspaper article, or to decode the subtle seductions of a television commercial or soap opera cliffhanger. Understanding media must include a critical awareness of the particular characteristics of making media. This not just to inform and assist those vying for a successful career as a reporter, advertising creative, television producer, or game developer. This to empower anyone entering the current and near future global cultural economy, where media as ubiquitous and pervasive devices, as tools for social organization and as accelerators of everyday experiences provide the dominant frame of reference for what Zygmunt Bauman (2005b) effectively describes as contemporary "liquid life."

The basis of my argument in *Media Work* is the notion that the current lives of people all over the world and most particularly in Western capitalist democracies cannot be understood without an understanding of media – albeit not so much through the content of media, but through the way all elements of work are organized in media as an industry. Following the work of Scott Lash and John Urry (1994) and others, I consider the management of creativity, the culturalization of work, and the processes of giving meaning to one's professional identity in the creative industries (of which media are part) crucial indicators for life as lived in contemporary liquid modernity. This is a time where most people experience their lives as a perpetual whitewater, living in a state of constant flux and uncertainty. In order to get at the heart of the human condition in the context of a life lived through, or rather: *in* the media, I primarily lean on the social theory of Zygmunt Bauman.[4] Bauman was born (1925) in Poland and, since 1971, has resided in Leeds, England. Although he has been a prolific author for most of his career, his works since the late 1990s on the human condition in contemporary late, second or what he calls "liquid" modernity strike at the essence of what it means to live in the world today. During the process of writing *Media Work* professor Bauman was kind enough to see me at his home (on 29 May 2006), which interview significantly helped me on my way. Throughout the book I reference his work as a means to ground my analyses about media and society in the increasingly fluid and unstable character of everyday lived experience – both as a reminder of the fleeting nature of my assumptions and the complex and multiple meanings my concepts and arguments have for the people involved: media workers.

In this book I explain and contextualize the changing nature of media work: what it is like to work in the media today, and how the particular organization of work shapes the professional identity of those employed in the creative industries. I assume how these people manage and give meaning to their life through their work has something to say for all of us, as the current global economy in what most call our information age increasingly turns towards (the production of) culture to reorganize the status quo. Although media work gets carried out in a bewildering variety of contexts, my analysis focuses primarily on those markets, companies, and professionals directly involved in the creative process of making what is called "mainstream news" in journalism, "tentpole movies" in the film industry, and "triple A titles" in computer and video game development. Based on a review of the scholarly and trade literatures, practitioner and journalistic weblogs and e-zines, and in-depth interviews with media workers in five countries (Finland, The Netherlands, New Zealand, South Africa, and the United States), I deconstruct what media work means in

the four key media professions: advertising (including marketing communications and public relations), journalism, film
and television production, and computer and video game
development. The interviews were conducted by the students
in my classes, and in the classes of my colleagues and friends
in these countries: Risto Kunelius (Finland), Addie de Moor
(The Netherlands), Verica Rupar (New Zealand), and Herman
Wasserman (South Africa).

The aim of the book is not only to prepare media students to
become competent media practitioners, but to also enable students to become competent citizens in a media-saturated
"hyper-reality," where meaningful distinctions between public
and private life, work time and non-work time, local and
global, or lived and mediated reality are fading. Studying and
understanding the issues framing the way people inside of the
media industry give meaning to their "work-styles" provides a
window to a world that is quickly becoming culturalized: an
economy in which culture has grown into a vehicle of and for
economic interests. The structure of the book moves from a
broad macro-level overview of the social, cultural, economical
and technological developments currently disrupting and
shaping much of everyday life in (over-)developed nations
around the world to a detailed micro-level analysis of the workstyles of individuals in the games, film, television, advertising,
and game industries.

My work on this book has benefited greatly from the input,
feedback, encouragement, criticism, and'storytelling of many
friends and colleagues currently employed as media workers
or engaged in the academic investigation of media production.
I am extremely grateful for their comments and deeply
indebted to their work. It has been an absolute privilege to
research and write this book and thus be able to connect with
some many amazing and brilliant people. First of all my
thanks to Zygmunt Bauman, whose work – even though he
doubts that I can make such an assertion before I am an old
man – fundamentally influenced and shaped my view of the

world and my potential role in it. Another major source of intellectual stimulation and mentorship is Henry Jenkins, whom I cannot thank enough for his encouragement in engaging with the material in this book. A third colleague I would like to single out is Henk Blanken, who is a constant source of insight and enthusiasm. This book has benefited greatly from our concurrent work on *PopUp* (2007), which book was an absolute joy to co-author with him. Beyond interviews, numerous media professionals made the kind effort to read through critically and discuss my chapters on their respective fields of work: Brian Steward, Joan Johnson, Paul Caine, Hans van Gils, Heather Scott, Tonya Maxwell, Christian Allen, Jason Della Rocca, and Steven Krahnke. On the academic side, I am indebted to the insights and comments from Harmeet Sawhney, David Waterman, Lee Sheldon, Addie de Moor, Jaap de Jong, Verica Rupar, Herman Wasserman, Koos Zwaan, Chase Bowen Martin, Jennifer Johns, Aphra Kerr, Susan Christopherson, John Hartley, Toby Miller, Carlos Volkmer Castillo, Risto Kunelius, and David Domingo. I also would like to thank the people at Polity for their enthusiasm and hard work on this project and the Digital Media and Society series, particularly Andrea Drugan and Susan Beer. Finally my thanks to Betsi and Martha for their patience with my endless rants about all the ways in which our scholarly discipline faithfully ignores, unfairly criticizes, or simply misrepresents the lived reality of media work.

CHAPTER ONE

Liquid Life, Work, and Media

In contemporary society, argues Zygmunt Bauman, work is the normal state of all humans; not working is abnormal.[1] Life has come to mean: work. People spend more time in institutions of higher education hoping to have a better chance in the highly competitive global economy. Work dominates our thinking about life. Choosing not to work is not an option, and the unemployed tend to be seen as people who either need our help (to be schooled or retrained for necessary jobs as defined by current market demand), or deserve our loathing (as those who do not pay taxes, and exploit the welfare system of the state). People's efforts and energy go into developing a blend of work and lifestyle: a workstyle, where life becomes a way of working and a way of being at work.[2] Ulrich Beck (2000) points at the fundamentally ambivalent prospects of current "workstyles" as marked by uncertainty, paradox, and risk. The risk of finding and keeping a job has become a strictly individual risk, as most governments and employers in the world today are retreating from collectively negotiated labor and welfare regulations, instead focusing on keeping a core of experienced employees and outsourcing, off-shoring, or sub-contracting work. Indeed, temporary employment agencies today are among the largest employers in the world. Contemporary workstyles are best understood in a contemporary context where, as Gillian Ursell (2000: 805) writes, the size of permanent staffs quickly diminishes, casualization of the labor force increases, entry to the labor market is more difficult and less well rewarded or supported, average earnings have dropped, and working terms and conditions continue to deteriorate.

People in all sectors of the economy have to come to terms with the challenges and opportunities of contingent employment, precarious labor, and an overall sense of real or perceived job insecurity. Work has become contingent, as the success in keeping a job increasingly depends on developments beyond the control of employee or employer: the fluctuations of the global economy, the unpredictability of the wants and needs of consumers, the rapid shifts in new technologies for the workplace, and in-vogue management styles aiming for short-term innovation and change rather than long-term investment or the cultivation of routine. Labor has become precarious, as it seems to be disappearing fast: it is off-shored to different parts of the world as businesses go global, it gets augmented or automated by sophisticated technologies, and it is temporary as production processes fragment across multiple places and professionals. This does not mean people cannot find solid jobs anymore, nor that everyone must accept that getting fired is an inevitable part of what being employed is all about. It does mean that most if not all people feel their job is continuously on the line (even when such a fear is produced by a manufactured insecurity generated by increasingly market-driven policies and proclamations of prominent politicians). As Joan Greenbaum (2004) argues, since the 1990s the link between jobs and secure employment has been permanently cut.

Fueling people's fear for their career are trends in economic policies around the world, as the governments and employers of the twenty-first century tend to favor a further deregulation or outright cancellation of welfare, benefits, and other types of support for workers. This effectively shifts the provision of these services to external parties, such as commercial companies. Individual employees have become personally responsible for negotiating, securing, and maintaining their own individual support structures. In doing so, individuals cannot turn anywhere else for help – unless they are willing to pay for this help out of their own pocket, and take matters into their own hands. Fueling this trend are policies in for example the United States and Great Britain that transfer welfare into "workfare," where those who cannot find jobs and seek state support are placed in unpaid positions with public agencies. Such practices essentially create free labor for the state in return for benefits, and contribute to a gradual phasing out of full-time jobs by public agencies, hiring workfare participants instead. In countries like Denmark and The Netherlands a notion of "flexicurity" has become a political staple since the late 1990s in an attempt to strike a balance between workforce flexibility and social security. The policy combines unemployment benefits with imposed re-education programs and guided job searches.[3] Contemporary labor laws enable companies to use temporary employment contracts more (and much easier) than they could in the past without being necessarily required to hire permanent workers. Similarly, politicians in developed nations tend to advocate delays in the pensionable age of workers as a solution to the rapid aging of the world population, coupled with what Chris Wilson (2001) considers a global demographic convergence of declining mortality and fertility rates in rich as well as developing countries. Not only do these developments emphasize the centrality of work to a contemporary understanding of life, it also reminds us of how, following Beck, the risks involved with survival in today's society are redistributed away from the state and the economy towards the individual. The relationship between employers and the employed has become based on individualized, short-term, and contingent contracts rather than on companies assuming some kind of formal responsibility for the permanent employment and career development of the worker. This system has increased competition between individual workers for jobs, instead of between companies for laborers, which process keeps average wages down, and increases an overall sense of insecurity among especially younger workers and junior employees.

Individualization in the Information Age

In the information age, the individual carries the brunt of the weight of finding, negotiating, and securing employment. However, it is a mistake to attribute this shift in social responsibility solely to global market forces and government deregulation under the influence of multinational corporations, as much of this trend is also fueled by the ongoing individualization of society. There are two key aspects to this kind of contemporary individualization. First, individualization refers to the fragility, transformation, and even disintegration of traditional social institutions – such as class, gender roles, family, and community. Second, it involves increasing demands being put on individuals by a rapidly globalizing society. One aspect is supercharged by the other, further amplified by the emergence of an increasingly critical and self-aware citizenry. These kind of individualized options regarding work are indeed not just forced upon employees by their managers or employers; the same practice works the other way around as professionals – especially in the knowledge and information industries – are demanding so-called "flexitime" working schedules or other perks particular to their personal demands. Flexitime allows an employee to select the hours he or she will work, within certain limits specified by the employer. Flexitime can be seen as benefiting dual career couples, workers who want to take care of elderly family members, or people working in industries that operate on a transnational scale, thus needing to be flexible regarding the hours they participate working in teams of people in different parts of the world. Other examples of increasingly flexible working arrangements are telework and telecommuting, jobsharing arrangements, and a gradual introduction of on-site daycare. Such increased variability in working hours contributes to the blurring of the boundaries between work and private life. Although the degree to which companies have been able or willing to organize their management practices to fit flexitime demands differs widely, and it is clearly not a type of alternate work arrangement that is preferred by everyone equally, it is important to note here that this trend amplifies the ongoing individualization of work, as well as a rapid decline of any traditional understanding of the stable, lifelong "nine-to-five" career protected by the long-term investment of a company or public agency. In traditional definitions, the organization is seen as a collectivity working towards a common goal according to a formal and rather bureaucratic social structure. This notion of organization today seems a thing of the past. In a critical review of contemporary organization theory, Campbell Jones and Rolland Munro (2005) for example come to the conclusion that the contemporary responsibility for organization – as well as the accountability for its consequences – is increasingly being passed to the figure of the individual.

The global shift towards individual and institutional individualization pervades all aspects of everyday life – where "the way individual people define individually their individual problems and try to tackle them deploying individual skills and resources is the sole remaining 'public issue' and the sole object of 'public interest'" (Bauman 2000, p. 72). The individual has become the center of all things, and the way workstyles have evolved in the course of the last century matches this development. One particularly unfortunate consequence this has is a widening gap between the rich and poor. The global economy has swept up everyone in its wake, providing opportunities for production and consumption for people across the planet, while at the same time increasing the risks for those people in finding and securing employment or sustaining their families as their plight is increasingly dependent on the fluctuations of a worldwide marketplace. For most people life seems reasonably comfortable, moving from job to job and place to place in an attempt to secure and sustain a position somewhere in the middle class. Yet their workstyles have become a delicate balancing act between keeping up with the rest or slipping away into what Bauman sees as a global underclass of "flawed consumers." Bauman refers to the growing numbers of people unable to respond to the seductive expectations of the global marketplace where their individual freedom gets solely defined in terms of consumer choice. It does not seem to take much today to disappear into the void of permanent precariousness, unpaid workfare, and thus flawed consumption; consider for example job destruction because of "de-industrialization" (for instance when factories are relocated from towns in Europe and North-America to cheaper sites in South-East Asia and South America), flexicurity laws that accelerate hiring and firing decisions, and ongoing technology-driven reskilling and deskilling practices that favor the few that can adapt while making others obsolete.

The worldwide shift towards individualized societies has particular consequences for the way people relate to each other. According to Robert Putnam (2004), since the last few decades of the twentieth century people around the world have started to withdraw from participating in social institutions such as political parties, religious institutions, as well as from subscription-based news media, large-scale voluntary associations and organized group sports. This does not mean people do not vote, worship, read a newspaper, or engage in league bowling anymore. It does suggest that if we do, we tend to do it whenever we feel like it – rather than because of our membership of a certain collective. This makes our behavior towards such institutions irregular, sporadic, unpredictable, and ultimately dependent on our personal wants and needs. The individual can thus be seen as the sole reference point for any and all decisions to be made regarding one's life – and living this life now relies on our ability to work. This disconnection between people as individuals and institutions in society as a collective certainly seems to make our world much smaller. Most people live their lives in this context reflexively, directly responding to whatever is happening at home, work, or play without taking (or getting) the time to think and reflect upon their predicament. This has introduced a distinct element of restlessness in our everyday life. People tend to make sense of their lifeworld by reacting to the issues they face on the basis of the know-how of the day, "by what people can do and how they usually go about doing it" (Bauman 2000, p. 56). As Richard Rorty (1999) suggests, whatever the ruling consensus at any given moment in time – it is generally not the best or the only way to go about doing things. The instantaneity in the way people interact and communicate with the world seems to reduce it to their most intimate, direct, and real-time personal environment. Yet the same trend also works the other way around. The world as people experience it not only is getting smaller – it also seems to be getting bigger all the time. The experience of life in the "global village" feels like constantly trying to catch up with what Anthony Giddens (2002) considers a "runaway" world, a world constantly on the edge of swerving out of control. In such a world all the traditional institutions that provided the social cement of modern life – most notably the family, the church, the factory or company, mass media, and the state – are nothing but bargaining chips in our individual negotiations with the forces of change that sweep contemporary life. People cannot simply rely on parents, priests, professionals, or presidents for truth anymore – they have to go out and construct their own narrative, to come up with "biographical solutions of systemic contradictions" (Beck 1992, p. 137). In his more recent work, Beck envisions a new type of cosmopolitan democracy, where people as individuals all over the world will have a more or less equal say in world affairs (such as environmental problems, transnational corporate policies, and worldwide migration patterns), as these affect everyone (2006).

As the contingencies of life, work, and play converge on the shoulders of the individual and traditional social institutions lose their automatic authority, people are at the same time swept up in a world of cosmopolitan politics and a global capitalist economy. As the power of the nation-state to control or protect its individual citizens withers, a new translocal rather than international playground has emerged. Here all kinds of forces and social movements compete for attention, recognition, and cultural acceptance: multinational corporations, cross-border coalitions of social interest groups, globally oriented media, and a growing number of international agencies. These forces increasingly influence interstate decisions and set the agenda of world politics (Archibugi *et al.* 1998). This does not necessarily mean that people as individuals are completely powerless in the face of global market forces – as the worldwide interconnectedness of markets, industries, economies, and social systems also open up numerous possibilities for the entrepreneurial individual. The point is, however, that the ability, skill, and resources necessary to navigate these global waters are beyond the means, capacities (or even wishes) of many, if not most people. We are supposed to increasingly rely on ourselves – which suggested self-reliance has become an endemic property of late twentieth-century policymaking, corporate practice, and public discourse, and it seems to warn people to be reluctant to trust the institutions they used to turn to for comfort or protection.

Reporting on studies in 43 countries, Ronald Inglehart (1997) observed a global shift of people in their roles as citizens away from nation-based politics and institutional elites, towards a distinctly skeptical, globally interconnected yet deeply personal type of self-determined civic engagement. Instead of voting at regular intervals in national elections we temporarily join any of the close to 30,000 international non-governmental organizations (INGO) active in the world today. Rather than subscribing to a so-called "quality" national newspaper or tuning in to the daily evening newscast, we search for news and information online about topics that are only of personal interest to us. We do not form or join unions anymore, we simply move to a different area, city, or country when we become dissatisfied with our working conditions (or when we face permanent unemployment where we live). Although all of these activities may seem beholden to a relatively small group of resourceful financial and cultural entrepreneurs, one cannot forget that blue-collar workers now have become a declining minority in most modern countries, whereas a creative class of professionals in knowledge and information industries increasingly dominate the cultural economies of the contemporary information age. As the rift between the individual and the nation-state widens, Pippa Norris (1998) observes the emergence of a new type of deeply critical global citizen, who is excited about the ideals of democracy but is losing confidence in its national practice. "We are undoubtedly living in an anti-hierarchical age," concludes Beck (2000, p. 150).

Linking the trends of concurrent individualization and globalization with the convergent trends in life, work, and play, a pattern emerges where the conditions of work at the beginning of the twenty-first century are in a constant state of flux. One moment you seem to be doing well, working hard, enjoying relative freedom and creative autonomy in your work – the next moment your company restructures because of a pending merger with a former competitor owned by a group of foreign investors who see new opportunities in different markets as consumer demand for your product seems to have suddenly shifted. Contemporary corporations find answers to these developments by bringing about all kinds of job destruction practices in the context of what Richard Sennett (1998) calls "workforce flexibility," thus rearranging the economy on a working assumption of permanent change. For employees, both young and old, this means that they have to come to terms with structural job insecurity, and a career that seems like an endless accumulation of experiences, ideas, skills, and know-how shaped by the hasty demands of the here and now. In the daily context on the job this suggests that one has to deal with the permanent threat of imminent job loss, which threat may also include the loss of valued job features (such as building a stable community of colleagues), a deterioration of working conditions, or an end to future career opportunities. This kind of anxiety does not stop here, though, as one also has to consider threats to the possibility of future employment for people seeking jobs in a company, industry, region or nation that is experiencing economic difficulty, which can be stressful for both employed people who cannot predict if, or when, they may be laid off, and for unemployed people who cannot foresee if, or when, they will regain employment (Mantler *et al.* 2005). There is no single person, party or group of people responsible for this trend. The operations and management practices of transnational corporations, a growing popularity of *laissez-faire* economics and cosmopolitan politics, rapid innovations in new information and communication technologies, and living in an individualized yet globalizing society: it all contributes to a constant uprooting and repotting of the ways in which workstyles are structured and experienced.

Informational Hypercapitalism

The key to surviving what Sennett (2006) calls the "culture of the new capitalism" is the ability to let go of one's past and develop the confidence to accept fragmentation and permanent change. The worker of today must become an enterprise of her own: perfectly adept at managing herself, unlearning old skills while reflexively adapting to new demands, preferring individual independence and autonomy over the relative stability of a lifelong workstyle based on the collective bargaining power of a specific group, sector, or union of workers. Let us not make the mistake of assuming these survival requirements are particular to those at the bottom of the economic hierarchy; these self-directing competences equally apply to the people in charge: top-level managers, chief executive officers, and directors of big companies or small enterprises all must continuously strike a balance between the opportunities of the new capitalism and the anxieties and uncertainties that come with it.

As it affects all human beings, the economy of the information age is based on what Phil Graham (2005) calls hypercapitalism, where economically productive activities that in many ways are connected to and shaped by a global marketplace consume the entire waking life of people – both at the top and at the bottom of the corporate ladder. This hypercapitalist culture of flexible yet never-ending productivity manifests itself most directly in the notable change of one's career, from a series of more or less predictable achievements within the context of a lifelong contract, to a constant reshuffling of career bits and pieces in the "portfolio worklife," as heralded by Charles Handy in 1989. In the portfolio lifestyle, careers are a sequence of stepping stones through life, where workers as individuals and organizations as collectives do not commit to each other for much more than the short-term goal, the project at hand, the talent needed now. Handy was right in predicting this workstyle to emerge as the preferred organizing feature of work in the new capitalism, for example among those in the knowledge and information industries such as the media. Media workers in their twenties and thirties are more likely to already have had at least three or four different employers, whereas their senior counterparts built their careers largely within one and the same organization. Indeed, people building their careers in the media – in professions as varied as advertising, journalism, public relations, marketing communications, television and movie production, and computer or video game development – are typical examples of this trend. Media professionals in all of these industries are perfect examples of how work, life, and play have converged in the experiences of today's preferred or forced flexible workstyles – which explains the focus on their lives and professional identities in this book.

Most of the jobs in today's information age have moved away from agriculture, manufacturing, and service professions towards so-called knowledge and information work. This trend, largely fueled by the twin developments of market globalization and technological innovations, favors those engaged in what Manuel Castells (2000) conceives as "informational labor": a category of well-educated, resourceful, and innovative workers, who are welcoming the rapid pace of change in contemporary life. People in this category belong to what Richard Florida (2002) has coined as a creative class consisting of scientists and researchers, artists, engineers, designers, architects, educators, writers, entertainers, and professional culture creators in the media. Florida suggests that this group of people makes up almost one-third of the workforce in countries such as the United States and increasingly determines the economic and cultural features of "new urban corridors" rather than cities or countries. Although the professions in the creative class are quite different, all of them are enabled, amplified, and interconnected by information and communication technologies – most notably personal computers and internet.

The ubiquitous nature of technology in everyday life has become a force of social change that is not to be underestimated. As the vast majority of people access the internet from home, computers can be seen as the primary vehicles for the ongoing convergence of work time and leisure time, which means that people use internet time for personal pleasure at the office, for work tasks at home – and vice versa. The humming PC at home allows one to play a game – *Solitaire* is the most commonly played computer game of all time – while its desktop folders remind the user that there is always work to be done. Florida's creative class can be seen as a vanguard of a distinctly individualized class, whose workstyle is highly dependent on information and communication technologies, and who can be considered to be the embodiment of all the trends and developments as outlined above: living an immediate life where work and play are one and the same, which life is completely contingent with the fickle and unpredictable nature of the contemporary global economy for which risks no one but themselves is expected to take personal responsibility.

Media and Everyday Life

The changing nature of work and life at the beginning of the twenty-first century must be explicitly set against the fast-paced innovations in new information and communication technologies that in turn develop as a reflection of new demands of consumption and production. Media have come to be part of every aspect of people's daily lives, facilitated by the worldwide proliferation of the internet and similar services that connect subscribers to a global, always-on, digital information and communication network. The whole of the world and our lived experience in it can indeed be seen as framed by, mitigated through, and made immediate by pervasive and ubiquitous media. This world is what Roger Silverstone (2007) considers a "mediapolis": a mediated public space where media underpin and overarch the experiences of everyday life.

The cell phone can be seen as a case in point for the experience of life, work, and play in the mediapolis: a wireless device, instantanously connected to a regional or even global network, individually customizable through downloadable ringtones and menu interfaces, usable as digital camera, Web browser, instant messenger, e-mail client, television set, gaming platform, music player, and radio tuner – signifying the complex convergence between the telephone, the computer, and telecommunications in a single artefact. Market statistics suggest that the total number of global cell phone sales reached 800 million units by 2006. In most of Europe, wealthier parts of Asia, Africa, the Caribbean, Latin America, Australia, Canada, and the United States, mobile phones are now widely used, with the majority of the adult, teenage, and even child population owning one.[4] The intensive global use of the cell phone puts us, paraphrasing William Mitchell (2003), in a state of continuous electronic engagement. Studies show how people develop deep personal connections with their media, which in the case of cell phones leads to mixed feelings: people seem to enjoy the ability to communicate when and how they want to on the go, while at the same time acknowledging the intrusion mobile and wireless communications have made into their private lives – including their wallets – and in public spaces. The relationship we develop with a device like the cell phone exemplifies and extends the ways we interact with the world and the social environment we have come to live in: inevitably individualized, completely isolated yet instantaneously connected to everyone else.

Today we live in what can be called an "age of universal comparison": by simply switching on the television, surfing the Web or scanning the pages of magazines in a supermarket we are exposed to a bewildering array of different lifestyles, choices, options and challenges. If we can afford it, we can compare ourselves with anyone, anywhere, anytime. In case of the internet one can consider the more than one billion users in 2006, with two billion users expected by 2011 (out of a projected world population of seven billion around that time).[5] Among the top ten countries in internet usage are the United States, China, India, Germany, Brazil, and Russia, where internet penetration reaches about two-thirds of the population.[6] At the same time, researchers in all these and other countries are still reporting increases in the global reach of television. For media conglomerates, the next phase in all of this is the introduction and proliferation of digital television technologies, signaling the (intended) convergence of internet and television into the home, public spaces, as well as the office. This development completes the blurring of the few remaining boundaries between life, work, and play – possibly leading to a kind of "e-topia" that Mitchell envisioned in his earlier (1999) work, forecasting a futuristic living environment where digital communication technologies blend leisure, labor, and family time, and where daily life in cities operates in a 24/7/365 cycle of completely decentralized production. Although we may not be there yet (nor would we want to be, for the prediction begs the question who will be left behind), the underlying assumption is evident in the way we immerse ourselves in globally interconnected yet profoundly personalized media, and in the ways we at times seem to prefer to give meaning to this immersion.

The Network Society

The global explosion of networked information and choice flourishes through the increasingly networked character of economy and society. At the end of the twentieth century, Scott Lash and John Urry (1994) suggest, the world entered a phase of disorganized capitalism, indicating a shift from the manufacturing of endless reproductions of material objects – a Ford factory spitting out the same cars every day – to the flexible customization of products and commodified experiences through the use of signs and symbols – designer jeans, limited edition DVDs, personalized travel packages, television-on-demand. Lash and Urry argue that in this relatively new phase formerly fixed and stable economic properties such as capital, labor, products, information, and services are now flowing across time and space, which process is exemplified by worldwide migration patterns and outsourcing practices, global marketing, branding, public relations and advertising campaigns, and especially the increasing dominance of the industries primarily involved in the production and distribution of all those signs and symbols: the media. As different sectors of the economy get caught up in this phase of disorganized capitalism, the production process gets integrated in a global network of businesses, corporations, and markets. This for example means that companies increasingly seek alliances across national borders and across the traditional boundaries of the firm, that services are marketed across time and space, and that the way an organization operates has become reflexively interdependent with all kinds of related sectors of an economy that is at once local and global. The production of goods and services – whether it is clothing, electronics, or ideas and information – is progressively more driven by a type of company that serves as a cog in the machine of the network society. Manuel Castells (2000) defines a network society as a society where the organizational arrangements of humans in relation to such crucial everyday life-issues as production, consumption and experience are made of networks. Of course, complex social networks have always existed, but recent technological, economical, and cultural developments have made networks the dominant form of social organization. Such networks connect people to other people across traditional borders of time and space – advertising creatives in Soho who work with video producers in Milan, South Korean gamers who play online with friends in Iowa, Indian software programmers working with computer engineers in Germany. The physical infrastructure of the internet would be an excellent representation of such networks, where people are at once connected to others across the globe while at the same time functioning in increasing social isolation.

The network society can also be understood as a logical next step in the evolution of the global market economy from perfectioning production to understanding consumption – as figuring out how to get people to buy or use goods and services is the prime mover of today's cultural and information industries. Labor in this digitally networked personal information economy is organized around the principle of reflexive production, where constant monitoring of consumer habits and patterns serves to flexibly adjust existing production processes. Work in a digital age thus becomes contingent on constant and immediate communication with local and global markets of infinite variety, and is to a significant extent premised on the effective management of large amounts of information, which trend towards a "cybernetization" of work can be considered to be typical for the way media industries operate.

Society in a digital age has become increasingly organized around the various ways to organize and diversify the intertwined or networked processes of production and consumption. Again one has to note the importance of technology in this historical trajectory; governments, businesses and researchers tend to adopt the expectations embedded in Jacques Ellul's (1967) "Technological Society," intrinsically linking technologies to the promises of efficiency, automation, self-augmentation, rationality, and artificiality. Yet these values, often reproduced through the celebratory marketing and management mantras of contemporary capitalism and politics, are also shaped by the profoundly "human" characteristics of the global network that is internet: its virtual communities, weblogs, chatrooms, podcasts, online multiplayer games . . . if anything, the logic of computers and cyberspace must be seen as increasingly dissolving the distinctions drawn all too easy between humans and machines, or, as Lev Manovich (2001) explains, between culture and computers. Applied to the workstyles of people in the network society, Michael Hardt and Antonio Negri argue how "the computer and communication revolution of production has transformed laboring practices in such a way that they all tend toward the model of information and communication technologies [. . .] the anthropology of cyberspace is really a recognition of the new human condition" (2000, p. 291).

The new human condition in the network society certainly seems much more dynamic than it used to be. People move constantly in and out of all kinds of networks, both physical and virtual, and these networks thus never stay the same. The contexts of these networks vary widely – from such traditional social institutions as the neighborhood, the (extended) family, and the work environment, and including electronic mailing lists, *Usenet* newsgroups, and so-called "clans" in online multiplayer games. In a network society each and everyone of us is connected with everyone else through dense networks of strong or loose but generally temporary affiliations, and such networks are enabled and amplified by new media like internet. The relationships of capital and labor in this at once global and local network society, argues Castells, are increasingly individualized, as they are organized around the network enterprise form of production. This type of post-industrial production practice integrates the work process globally through digital telecommunications, transportation, and client – customer networks. Workers find themselves collaborating or coordinating their activities with team members in different parts of the company, sometimes located in different parts of the world. Sometimes a company only develops a certain part of the product, service or user experience, and has to rely on other firms and partners to supply the next step in the productivity pipeline. The planning and management of such increasingly commonplace practices relies on, and is based on, the facilities and functions offered by global communication networks. As industries expand across time and space, the level of sophistication in information technologies increases exponentially – extending James Beniger's earlier (1989) thesis of a control revolution taking place in the development of a vast information sector especially after the Second World War. Beniger has argued that the industrial production of huge flows of goods led to a crisis of control at the end of the nineteenth century. This crisis was resolved by the professionalization of bureaucracy to deal with the logistics of it all, and with a rapid expansion of investments in computer technologies to manage the flow of information between businesses, markets and consumers, leading to what today can be called the information age. Andrew Shapiro (2000) updates Beniger's analysis by showing how this control today has shifted in two seemingly opposite directions, as social institutions (such as corporations or governments) as well as individuals have to come to terms with the management of an endless supply of online information, goods and services. Corporatization and individualization go hand in hand, which convergence must be seen in a context of what Dan Schiller describes as the hallmarks of digital capitalism, where "the internet is bound up in a profound threefold shift of the greater media system, from "mass" to "class" marketing, from national to transnational marketing, and from what we might call probabilistic to individualized marketing" (2000, p. 135).

The worldwide integration of producers and consumers enabled and supercharged by communication technologies introduces a fundamental aspect of unpredictability to the nature of work, as the success or failure of the local production process becomes almost completely contingent on fluctuations in the global network – and vice versa, as "any individual capital is submitted to the movements of the global automaton" (Castells 2000, p. 18). It all contributes to a worker's heightened sense of employment insecurity, as the quality of one's work seems to bear little or no consequences on one's future employment perspective. Now that most if not all companies in the knowledge and information sectors of the economy have established online business-to-business and business-to-consumer networks, the interaction between company and customer – and thus their interdependency – has intensified. This also means that any sudden change in market demands can mean new projects and employment opportunities, just as much as it can instantly put jobs on the line. Facing the need to be able to adapt quickly to local as well as global shifts in consumption and production trends, many parts of the industry are choosing to casualize labor, which means that a significant part of a company's workforce today consists of underpaid, insecure, low-status, short-term jobs with little or no benefits or opportunities for promotion. To some, this predicament seems liberating, as it promises freedom of movement within the labor market – a freedom, however, that is ultimately dependent on uncontrollable market forces and a constant demand on each and everyone's individual adaptability to permanently changing circumstances. Here, adaptive behavior, structural change, casualization of labor, and continual innovation are all expressed in the executive credo of flexible production which according to Bauman (2002a, p. 24) has turned from something to be avoided into a virtue to be learned and practiced daily. This flexibility for many means living in constant fear of real or perceived job insecurity. Sennett signals how even affluent, successful, and highly educated young professionals are "on the edge of losing control over their lives. This fear is built into their work histories" (1998, p. 19). Society today, argues Sennett, uses the feverish development of flexible productivity against the "evils" of routine. Unlike Handy, he sees little promise in this re-interpretation of uncertainty as the corporate strategy of choice: "Revulsion against bureaucratic routine and pursuit of flexibility has produced new structures of power and control, rather than created the conditions which set us free" (ibid., 47). This flexibility stretches out into both work time and non-work time, which distinction has blurred for many, if not most, people. Adapting to changing management practices, new technologies, and cultivating creativity and talent cannot be necessarily tied to a nine-to-five working weekday, especially considering the general lack of corporate investment in employee training. With the slow demise of lifelong full-time employment, continuous searching for jobs, preparing for potential future jobs, as well as managing multiple careers more or less simultaneously have become core elements of the workstyle in everyday life for many.

Precarity

Work comes in many different shapes and sizes – paid and non-paid, voluntary and employed, professional and amateuristic – and we seem to be engulfed in it all of the time. Working increasingly includes (re-)schooling and training, unlearning "old" skills while adapting to changing technologies and management demands, moving from project to project, and navigating one's career through an at times bewildering sea of loose affiliations, temporary arrangements, and informal networks. This perception and experience of working has come to define life in late modern society. Additionally our understanding of contemporary workstyles by definition includes structural uncertainty and risk, thus framing every aspect of our lives within that context. In a critical assessment of the labor market in the United States, Jacob Hacker (2006) for example shows how the responsibilities for managing economic risk continue to shift from government and employers to individuals and

their families, increasing the pressures on individuals to perceive, plan for, and secure themselves against the most threat-
ening risks to their welfare. The key to understanding this
"brave new world" of work is its precariousness, characterized
by endemic uncertainty and permanent change (Beck 2000,
pp. 22–3). The nature of work is changing rapidly in our runaway world – some even foresee an end of work in the nearby
future, as technology supplants human labor. However real or
perceived the insecurities experienced in our everyday workstyles are, its *precarité* bleeds into every understanding we have
of ourselves and who we are. As colorfully described on the
British activists' website *Precarity.Info:*

> What is precarity? Precarity stretches beyond work. It
> includes housing, debt, general instability, the inability to
> make plans. We can talk about the subjugation of life under
> capital, not just the subjugation of labour under capital.
> Precarity is an instrument of control; it is enforced by those
> with power upon the powerless. We can't choose how we
> want to live. It engenders competition in social life. It forces
> us into a Darwinian "struggle for existence" on a social level.
> Precarity is the basic condition of individuals in capitalist
> society. It divides us, and limits opportunities to get
> together. People are disempowered and social relations
> break down."[7]

Jonathan Gershuny (2000), after comparing time-use datasets
from twenty different countries (including Australia, Finland,
The Netherlands, and the United States), summarizes the
characteristics of modern industrial societies in terms of a continuous growth in the numbers of skilled workers as a proportion of all employment, and a growth of time allocated to the
production and consumption of sophisticated products and
services. Even though we tend to spend more time consuming
products and services of the information age, and technologies
increasingly augment and automate human labor, this does
not mean we are spending less time working. Quite the opposite: new forms of work organization in fact entail intensified

demands on the work-time of both permanent and temporary employees. The trend towards flexible work started in the 1970s, and has accelerated in the late 1990s, coinciding with the rush of an increasingly information-based global economy to the internet. It is particularly in this sphere of information- and knowledge-based work where the culture of flexible capitalism has taken root as the dominant mode of labor organization – and where researchers have found both employers and employees in fact preferring a precarious condition of so-called "boundaryless" employment. A boundaryless career reflects a career path that goes beyond the boundaries of single employment settings, and involves a sequence of jobs between different companies and different segments of the labor market. This changes the way one should understand how people in firms and organizations operate, and must include an awareness of the strategies workers today use to manage and develop their careers. As from the late 1980s, Michael Arthur (1994) signaled a rapid decentralization of work and a shift in job creation away from large firms to small companies with 500 or fewer employees. At the time Arthur suggested that having a boundaryless career might be the best if not only way to survive the unpredictable, market-sensitive world. "As job security and promotional opportunities within larger organizations decline, individuals may view multiple employer experiences in a positive light because it supports skill development, increases marketability, shifts career control to the employee, and perhaps results in better matching career and family life-cycle demands. As such, boundarylessness represents a different conception of job security" (Marler *et al.* 2002, p. 430). In other words: it is important to note how the portfolio worklife can be seen in different lights as providing both benefits as well as significant threats. Pierre Bourdieu (1998) has been one of the fiercest critics of this increasing precariousness of work in the digital age, suggesting that living under precarious conditions prevents rational anticipation and, in particular, the basic belief and hope in the future that one needs in order to (individually or collectively) rebel against intolerable working or living conditions.

Whereas for most workers in traditional temporary and contingent settings their employment situation is far from ideal, many in the higher skilled knowledge-based areas of the labor market seem to prefer such precarious working conditions, associating this with greater individual autonomy, the acquisition of a wide variety of skills and experiences, and a reduced dependence on a single employer (Kalleberg 2000). The portfolio workstyle of the self-employed information or "cultural" entrepreneur can thus be characterized by living in a state of constant change, while at the same time seemingly enjoying a sense of control over one's own career. Bauman warns against overtly optimistic readings of the relative freedom these prime beneficiaries of inevitably unequitable globalization claim to enjoy: "We are called to believe today that security is disempowering, disabling, breeding the resented 'dependency' and altogether constraining the human agents' freedom. What is passed over in silence is that acrobatics and rope-walking without a safety net are an art that few people can master and a recipe for disaster for all the rest" (quoted in Tester 2001, p. 52). Indeed, research among freelancers and teleworkers in the media by Susan Baines (1999) shows that for many, their workstyles are marked by histories of redundancy coupled with a structural and unsettling insecurity about the future and one's success or failure on the market, and a dependence on single client organizations including former employers. Freedom and security, often seen as mutually exclusive, thus become ambiguous in the context of how different people from different walks of life deal with, and give meaning to, the consequences of not having either. It is perhaps the perfect paradox of contemporary liquid life: all the trends in today's work-life quite clearly suggest a rapid destabilization of social bonds corresponding with increasingly disempowering effects of a fickle and uncertain global high-tech information economy, yet those workers caught in the epicenter of this bewildering shift also express a sense of mastery over their lives, interpreting their professional identity in this context in terms of individual-level control and empowering agency.

Conditions of real or perceived job insecurity thus do not necessarily mean the workers involved are suffering in silence – nor that the anxiety that comes with a boundaryless, contingent, and portfolio worklife necessarily must be seen as a blessing in disguise. The convergence of the time and effort we invest in both production ("work") and consumption ("life") as signaled by Gershuny does suggest that our most common solution to the increasingly anxious and sometimes exciting developments in society is an endless individual and professional remixing of the cultures of working and living. Again it must be noted how the blend between work, life, and play is not necessarily nor exclusively mixed by changing market conditions, by shifting government and corporate policies, or by networked technologies – next to such economic, political, and technological explanations lies an equally valid social explanation: people are also doing it to themselves. This is a crucial insight framing my argument in this book, one that is premised on the ongoing convergence of all elements of life – Bauman would argue that the traditionally separate cups of life, work, and play are spilling over, leaking and flowing into one another, creating the conditions of a liquid life (2005b). Bauman's concerns are similar to issues voiced in the field of management, where Peter Vaill (1996) for example has advocated strategies for corporate survival in a world of "permanent white water" – referring to the frothy water appearing when a river current becomes rapid, agitated and unstable. According to Vaill, personal and professional life today are beset on all sides by a myriad of crises, which require new strategies of lifelong learning to cope with conditions of constant and accelerating change.

If work and life are increasingly indiscernible in the play of the everyday, the key institutions linking their practices to modernity – jobs and the family - must also be seen as undergoing a fundamental shift. Martin Carnoy (2002) in particular has argued how the practices of workforce flexibility and decentralized management disrupt traditional social integrators like the family, the long-term job, and the relatively stable neighborhood community. This is exacerbated by the continued movement of women into paid work, which puts a greater strain on the family's ability to care for and rear children. Carnoy makes it clear that all this happened both before and independently of globalization and the arrival of new information and communication technologies like the World Wide Web. Considering the more recent trends, Carnoy sees "a serious social contradiction: the new workplace requires even greater investment in knowledge than in the past and families are crucial to such knowledge formation, for adults as well as for children. But the new workplace destabilizes the child-centered nuclear family, degrading the very institution crucial to further economic development" (p. 414). With the increasing precariousness of labor, the further technologization and deterritorialization of work, and the exponential entry of women into the workforce both "work" and "family" have not only changed; these core institutions of modern life have merged. As Catherine Hakim (2003) notes, this social convergence produces adaptive or work-centered (instead of home-centered) lifestyles among middle class families and young urban professionals in modern societies. Marriage and the family have become what Anthony Giddens (2002: 58–9) calls shell institutions: people and policymakers alike still refer to the family as the primary unit in today's society, even though in its traditional connotation of the nuclear family – two married parents living with their own children – it has all but died. In a report on the 2003 census, the United States Census Bureau for example concluded that the most noticeable trend was a decline in the proportion of married-couple households with their own children from 40 percent of all households in 1970 to 23 percent in 2003. In England, the Office for National Statistics reported in 2004 the number of married couple households with dependent children at 38 percent, and projected this percentage to fall quickly – much like most countries in Western Europe. The Australian Family Characteristics Survey, conducted in June 2003, found that of all couples with children aged 0–17 years, 12 percent were in a de facto marriage. In a country like South Africa the number of marriages tends to be even lower and differs widely across different population groups, many of whom live under cohabitation circumstances unrecognized by traditional marriage law. All of this does not mean there are no "families" anymore – on the contrary, family life still makes up for the majority of lived social experience today. A 2005 survey among American adults by the Pew Research Center for example showed how people have more regular contact with family members today than ten or twenty years ago. However, this increased family time is primarily facilitated by new media such as cell phones and e-mail.[8]

Families perhaps must be seen as transitory units similar to what Georges Benko (1997) describes as "non-places" like shopping malls or airports. Such spaces primarily exist for temporary convenience and the more or less anonymous exchange of goods, services, and information. No one is really expected to stick around very long. The family as a traditionally celebrated safe haven from the uncertain world outside, seems to have turned itself against the values of domestication and "settling in" – it has become the place and space for deliberate coupling and uncoupling (Bauman 2003). With a divorce rate between twenty and fifty percent in most capitalist economies, a growing normalization of unmarried or same-sex cohabitation, an increase of predominantly childless peoples like recent immigrants, aging babyboomers, and empty nesters, and with singles forming forty percent or more of the total population of countries in North America and Western Europe, it must be clear that the experience of family life as a social institution has changed.

In his assessment of the personal consequences of the changing nature of work, personal character and social bonds,

Richard Sennett (1998, p. 21) laments how no one becomes a long-term witness to another person's life anymore. Indeed, most of us, rich and poor, are constantly on the move – either as economically and politically desperate migratory *sans-papiers* or as highly skilled cultural entrepreneurs in an globally networked marketplace where knowledge and information have become the primary form of capital. People are not just on the move from part-time job to flexible contract, nor just from one type of family to some other form of temporary social situation; in the particular urban settings of flexible capitalism one also moves from "pink-slip party" to yet another network-ing event, from rented apartment to leased living space, from a single-issue vote to project-based volunteer work, from fling to affair. Our only shared condition increasingly seems to be the lived experience of being "permanently impermanent" (Bauman 2005b, p. 33), which in turn disables us to bear wit-ness to anything other but our own plights, to be solely solved deploying our individual skills and personal resources. In the beginning of the twenty-first century we are seemingly becom-ing blind to each other, getting to know others only in passing, which social fragmentation is exacerbated by the undeniable primacy and individualized nature of work in everyday life.

The Consumer and the Citizen

Crucial to understanding how work, life and play have come to mean more or less the same thing is the realization that not only are we spending more and more time producing – infor-mation, knowledge, products, stuff – we are also increasingly engaging in acts of consumption. The values, ideals, and practices of consumerism tend to be framed in an extremely negative light – focusing for example on the increasing infan-tilization, mainstreaming and materialism of contemporary consumer cultures. The sometimes devastating consequences of unbridled consumerism are documented extensively, such as a worldwide widening gap between the extremely rich and permanent poor, excesses of waste produced by a "throwaway" society, and the uprooting of millions of people to provide cheap labor for insatiable multinational industries.[9] In a comprehensive study of individual tax returns data in North American and European countries throughout the twentieth century, Emmanuel Saez (2006) shows how while the income of the few working rich has surged over the last few decades, the salary growth of just about everyone else has grinded to a halt. Although this growth in income disparity is much sharper in the United States than elsewhere, Saez and other economists foresee more wealth concentration in the (near) future. It is clear that the successes and failures of a global market economy are not equally or even equitably distributed. However, in the context of people's everyday lives in developed nations as they try to balance work, life, and play, consumerism should also be seen in terms of its transformative potential regarding elitist, top-down, mass-oriented, and otherwise non-responsive social institutions such as the political system (cf. the emergence of the "citizen-consumer"), the economy (cf. the "conquest of cool" and the marketing of resistance), and the media.

The meaning of citizenship has changed in the last few decades. Michael Schudson (1999) argues how most people still tend to be seen by politicians, scholars, and journalists alike as citizens that need to inform themselves widely about all political parties in play, so that they can make an informed decision come election time. However, Schudson also shows how this model of citizenship is a thing of the past – an unrealistic and rather elitist notion of how people should make up their minds, and what political representation means to them. Today's citizen is not only skeptical and anti-hierarchical, she is also what Schudson calls "monitorial": scanning all kinds of news and information sources for the topics that matter to her personally. People are not necessarily disengaged from the political process – they just commit their time and energy to it on their own terms. This individualized act of citizenship can be compared to the act of the consumer, browsing the stores of the shopping mall for that perfect pair of jeans – it is the act of the citizen-consumer. The distinctly anti-hierarchical character of our time also comes into play in the consumptive world, where advertisers cleverly market to people's desire to be different, to be critical, to be cool. Bauman reminds us that under conditions of a consumerist culture people can never really achieve difference, nor should they, for at that moment the act of consuming would stop. On the other hand, once settled in carefully target-marketed brand communities – whether the brand is *Shell* or *Greenpeace*, *CNN* or *Indymedia* – citizens achieve some kind of collective identity similar to the one achieved by voting (as an act of political allegiance). Mark Poster (2004) stipulates that consumer activity is central to society, as it is the domain where the individual is realized. Considering the act of consumption as productive and creative, Mitzuko Ito (2005) takes this argument even further. In the various ways people engage with each other via the products they consume – whether that product is a political candidate, TV show, or a T-shirt – their consumption becomes a creative and meaningful act. Stated another way, under conditions of liquid life consumer culture and civic engagement seem to be interconnected and co-creative rather than opposing value systems, and as such function to make the daily remix of work, life, and play just a little bit easier.

The consumptive trend has been particularly visible in the sphere of knowledge and information-related leisure services provided by the cultural industries. We spend more and more time and money on entertainment experiences – which vary from acquiring consumer electronics to attending multimedia shows, from collecting technological toys to participating in social media online, and from navigating between "high" cultural (cf. art house movies, classical music, non-fiction literature) to "low" cultural (cf. reality television, videogames, tabloids) forms of expression. Indeed, our collective quest towards increasingly compelling and diversified mediated experiences has turned us into cultural omnivores: attending a local school play one day, renting a Bollywood movie the next; reading the latest installment in the *Harry Potter* (or Russian equivalent *Tanya Grotter*[10]) book series this week, spending the following weekend building a personal hobby website. It certainly seems people have a lot of spare time on their hands if we add up all these activities. However, Gershuny found evidence of what he calls the "end of leisure": "each year we have to work harder in our free time to consume all those things that we have been working harder to produce in our work time" (2000, p. 51). Status in society today thus comes with a price: time outside of work (whether at home, on the road or in the office) has become a scarce commodity, even though we seem to spend more of it all the time.

Personal Information Spaces

The paradox of more time spent simultaneously at productive and consumptive activities can be resolved taking into consideration how both spheres of activity have converged in the contemporary mediapolis, further facilitated by advancements in information and communication technologies. Next to engaging in all kinds of leisure activities to compensate for strains and other drawbacks of professional life, work and leisure can increasingly be seen as extensions of each other – especially for professionals in the informational sectors of the economy. One particular effect this spillover has had on everyday experience is the ongoing retreat of people into what can be called "personal information spaces" at home and at work. These spaces can be seen as particular physical environments such as turning parts of the house or apartment into a "home theater" and "home office" filled with all kinds of consumer electronics used to consume and produce media content. Other examples of such personal information spaces include the ensemble of mobile media technologies people carry with them everywhere they go – devices that seem to socially isolate and at the same time connect people to the rest of the wired world (using a cell phone, laptop, Personal Digital Assistant, digital camera, walkman, and other more intricate forms of wearable computing that truly put the "personal" in Personal Computer).

Personal information spaces can also be experienced as disembodied – as in our ongoing immersion in persistent online environments varying from virtual workspaces (for example through videoconferencing capabilities and company intranets) to massively multiplayer computer games (ex.: *World of Warcraft*), virtual worlds (ex.: *Second Life*), and social networking services (ex.: *MySpace*). Although different, all three are examples of personal information spaces, where people carefully cultivate their identities through the creation and development of virtual representations of themselves, called *avatars*. The avatar is a term derived from Hinduism, where it refers to the incarnation of a Supreme Being. In the popular online multiplayer game *Ultima* the avatar is the embodiment of a set of ethical guidelines and virtues. The key to one's avatar is its customization to suit individual preferences – an avatar thus can be seen as an extension or even augmentation of someone's offline identity. It is quite normal to have and maintain multiple avatars in everyday mediated life, where this part of one's identity can consist of a buddy icon in Instant Messaging, a profile picture used in company intranets, and a character in three-dimensional (3D) computer role-playing games like *World of Warcraft* or *Everquest*, or in non-gaming environments such as *There* or *Second Life*. As an example, Blizzard Entertainment (a Viacom-owned company that produces and maintains *World of Warcraft*) claimed in February 2006 to have more than six million players, defining these customers as "individuals who have paid a subscription fee or purchased a prepaid card to play World of Warcraft, as well as those who have purchased the installation box bundled with one free month access."[11] In such virtual, persistent and continuously expanding environments people roam alone or in groups called clans or guilds, complete quests, trade goods and services, or just hang out and lurk – all for a monthly fee. The cultivation of such personal information spaces does not stop online – the companies behind these virtual environments regularly organize "real world gatherings," where the people behind the avatars meet in person.

The various ways in which ever-growing numbers of people both young and old engage with each other through media is sometimes taken as a new form of community. The promise of online communities tends to be seen as either to bridge existing social divides, or to bond people with already similar beliefs. Drawing from various international projects, Pippa Norris (2002) suggests that most online groups serve both functions – which she terms "hyper-pluralism" and "over-specialization" – at the same time. Although it may be too early to draw conclusions, the results from these and other studies suggest people who use the internet regularly feel it both widens and deepens their experience of community. People's intensifying exchanges and interactions in everyday life online can be seen as an emerging form of "hypersociality" where the social consists of networked individualism "enhancing the capacity of individuals to rebuild structures of sociability from the bottom up" (Castells 2001, p. 131). Earlier, Pierre Lévy (1994) envisioned how people would produce new social bonds through the ongoing development of sophisticated systems of networked intelligence such as internet. Scott Lash (2002) similarly suggests that in today's world previously long-lasting and proximal social bonds – such as the neighborhood community, the extended family, the employee and his co-workers - are giving way to distanced "communicational bonds". Instead of social relations mediated by space and time, such bonds must rather be seen as forms of communication that are increasingly short-lived, transient, and mediated by new, super-fast technologies. Lash sees this development as inevitable and not necessarily detrimental to new forms of community in an information age. Bauman is more pessimistic about these observations: "in my view, both Castells and Scott fall victims of internet fetishism fallacy. Network is not community and communication not integration - both safely equipped as they are with 'disconnection on demand' devices."[12]

The social bonds between personal information spaces as mediated by information and communication technologies are particularly visible in all kinds of social networking services, of which *Myspace* is perhaps the best-known example. Next to such international virtual meeting places, all kinds of topical, regional, or national social networking sites operate quite successfully as well (some examples are *Hyves* in The Netherlands, *Facebook* in the United States, *Q-Zone* in China, or *Cyworld* in South Korea). Other similar social networks include sites where people upload, exchange, and interact using pictures (*Flickr*), video (*YouTube*), music (*Last.fm*), and all kinds of other both commercially and user-generated media. Some of this distributed media use is strictly private: connecting and staying connected with friends and family, meeting potential partners, forming fan communities. Some of it is related to work: discussion groups for engineers, or game developers, or medical professionals. Some of it lies somewhere in between, as businesses browse online social networks to find information about job candidates, or start their own blogs, profiles, and groups to give their business a Web-savvy face. Although the scholars of the World Internet Project[13] faithfully assess a digital divide in many countries, and suggest many people – especially senior citizens – opt out of computers and the internet, it is impossible to ignore what growing numbers in the populations of wired nations seem to be consistently doing with their time: they use digital media to network.

Connected

Both online and offline, at work, at home or at play, human beings tend to connect and get connected to others all the time, to which kind of social networks media organizations cleverly tap into. In order for such media to be successful, they need the "work" of consumption that we all do every time we turn on the television, log in, and play - because what media industries do is sell their consumers as audiences to advertisers. The emergence of all kinds of new and improved yet temporary and distanced communities – whether based on clan, guild, brand, professional, or otherwise collective identities – thus serves networked sociability and commercial viability at the same time. Sennett's act of witnessing (or perceived lack thereof) seems to have moved online, where people move in and out of interactive networked environments, managing their multiple virtual selves in persistent gaming, chatting, instant messaging and otherwise digitally connected contexts.

The way we understand ourselves and get to know others increasingly develops in the context of mediated environments, which process loosens – but not destroys – what John Thompson (1996, p. 207) has described as the connection between self-formation and shared locale. Indeed, Barry Wellman (*et al.*, 2001) suggests that access to new media like the internet enhances people's participatory capital, and supplements their social contacts – even though in doing so, we are less likely to feel committed to traditional forms of community. Wellman and his colleagues stress how none of these trends are necessarily new or particular to media: "Even before the advent of the Internet, there has been a move from all-encompassing, socially-controlling communities to individualized, fragmented personal communities. The security and social control of all-encompassing communities have given way to the opportunity and vulnerability of networked individualism. People now go through the day, week, and month in a variety of narrowly defined relationships with changing sets of network members" (2001, p. 455). An example of this is the website *Meetup.com*, a "convening" or "rendez-vous" technology that aims to physically bring together people (in different parts of the world) with shared interests.[14] Indeed, sites that serve as nodal points for connecting people are among the most popular on the Web: *Yahoo* (including its "groups" service), *Microsoft Network* (generating most of its traffic through instant messaging), *MySpace*, *Orkut*, and *Blogger* (both online communities owned by *Google*).[15] The way people use new media suggests something profound about the contemporary human condition: it seems to be increasingly interconnected and networked, yet socially isolated and fragmented at the same time.

People use the internet overwhelmingly for interpersonal communication, whether it is in the context of work, love, or play. And yes, these distinct domains of everyday life dissolve in our deepening interactions online. The most successful businesses on the internet – such as auction site *eBay*, internet portal *Yahoo*, *Google*, and *Amazon* – share one fundamental characteristic: the product these companies deliver is connectivity, bringing people together to trade, communicate, interact, and exchange knowledge, information, goods, and services. However, not only businesses thrive on interaction and connectivity online. The most often used reference guide on the World Wide Web is *Wikipedia*, a multilingual free-content encyclopedia, which started in 2001. The encyclopedia is based on the so-called "wiki"-concept, which means it is written collaboratively by volunteers, allowing most articles to be changed by anyone with access to a web browser and an internet connection. Such sites bring people together to communicate, exchange, trade, co-create and collaborate, which processes are primarily regulated through reputation metrics: on *Wikipedia* everyone can check the historical trajectory of each entry's editing process to see who did what in the past, and on *eBay* and *Amazon* people can check customers' previous ratings of third party sellers. Although these kind of reputation systems tend not to be portable across different websites and social networks, research suggests that as long as a large numbers of individuals participate, trust and credibility within a certain virtual community accumulates simply by operating effectively over time (Resnick *et al.*, 2000).

Weblogs are another excellent example of how witnessing has become an increasingly virtual, yet also deeply personal act. Weblogs first appeared in the mid-1990s, becoming popular as simple and free publishing tools became available. Since anybody with internet access can publish their own weblog, there is great variety in the quality, content, and ambition of weblogs.[16] Estimates on the total number of these online journals vary widely and generally run into tens of millions, whereas studies suggests that the "blogosphere" doubles about every half year.[17] Indexing research shows how the vast majority (70 percent) of weblogs are highly personal vehicles for self-expression and empowerment, written almost exclusively by individuals (Herring *et al.* 2005). However, this kind of individualism in weblogs is in fact quite connective, as bloggers include comment and feedback options with their posts, put up their blogs for free syndication (cf. Really Simple Syndication feeds), reference and link to other blogs when creating posts, and cut and paste all kinds of content – including moving and still images, text, and audiofiles – from all over the Web as well as their own original work onto their weblog.

The area online where the convergence of connectivity, content, creativity, and commercialism reaches its pinnacle is in the realm of computer games. At the time of writing more than five million active subscribers participated in massively multiplayer online games, and many more millions connect irregularly, temporarily, or otherwise sporadically.[18] In a massively multiplayer computer game like the immensely popular *World of Warcraft*, players connect to game servers via the internet and interact in real time with other users worldwide. A significant part of this gaming experience consist of "meta-gaming": in-game communication between gamers, using all kinds of devices such as headsets, chat commands, and in-game player signals. The playing of multiplayer games both reproduces and challenges everyday rules of social interaction, as the game environment can be seen both as an extension of real-world experiences and as strictly virtual space. Yet, meta-gaming is not just about the game: it includes any type of social interaction such as talking, loving, and trading. Ted Castranova (2005) for example has shown how we buy, sell and exchange goods and services in online games to the extent that such synthetic economies of scale have come to resemble those in "real," offline worlds – if only because of their sheer size. Analyzing online game culture, T.L. Taylor (2006) shows how social relationships begin to extend from in-game to real life, which type of social spillover she sees as contributing to living in a fluid landscape where people's existence has become plural. She additionally develops the argument how gamers can be considered to be central productive agents in game culture, stressing the importance of considering the consumers of computer games as participants in their design, governance, and product innovation.

All of these activities must be seen in terms of their concurrence, as people simultaneously engage in them through for example the windowing of computer screens: pressing "alt-tab" gets you from a job resume to a weblog, from browsing the information in a *Wikipedia* entry for a presentation to contributing a book review to *Amazon*, from a purchase on *eBay* to an exchange in *World of Warcraft*. It is important to note how through these interactive, interconnected and networked devices and environments our work- and lifestyles further converge, not only facilitating but rather accentuating the blurring of modern life's traditional boundaries. It is even possible to argue that the introduction of the personal computer into the home has not only enabled us to plug and play in a persistent worldwide networked environment – it also acted as a Trojan Horse, as the device serves as a powerful and constant reminder that there is still work to be done.

Because of the omnipresence of computer-mediated communication one would almost assume that people spend less time watching television. Quite the opposite is true: international market research companies like Nielsen, Jupiter, and Forrester report every year how television viewing worldwide keeps growing steadily. The number of televisions per household continues to go up, the number of available channels keeps rising, and so does the average number of hours households reportedly spend watching TV. Indeed, the same can be said of the money and hours dedicated to all other kinds of digital devices, such as cell phones, laptops, digital video recorders, video game consoles, satellite radio receivers, and portable music players. Simply adding up the time spent with all these media does not seem to make sense as people multitask, continuously switching between all kinds of mediated consumption, production, and communication, more or less deliberately remixing their activities related to work, life, and play along the way. Contemporary changes in society and technology thus get expressed in our increasing concurrent immersion in all kinds of media, which immersion in turn amplifies the convergence of the different spheres of activity in everyday life, dissolving the lines between work and leisure as well as between production and consumption.

Participatory Media Culture

At the heart of most if not all of today's new media technologies saturating our work-life environments is their distinctly commercial and networked character, which profitable interconnectivity has woven itself into the fabric of everyday existence among the majority of the population in European, Australasian, and North-American countries. In whatever shape or form, media bring the world to our doorstep – and we bring our world into media. No one is "outside" anymore, whether by choice or necessity. It is perhaps necessary that we stop referring to our behavior towards media as either consumption or production, instead acknowledging that we are working and living *in* the media.[19] This also means that the precarity of contemporary life through media within a

global capitalist consumer culture extends to each and everyone of us, and cannot be said to be beholden to any particular
group, race, class, or gender – even though life's current precariousness means different things for different people in
different settings.

In this context it is both fascinating and indeed hopeful that
what characterizes most of the ways people engage with media
and worldwide-networked technologies – whether commercial, state-owned, non-profit, or alternative – is the extent to
which human beings seem to be doing so through cooperation. It can be through the online collaboratively authored
encyclopedia *Wikipedia* credible enough to challenge the
Encyclopedia Brittanica, the open source software movement
potent enough to ruffle the feathers of *Microsoft*, the networking portal of *Meetup* powerful enough to propel US presiden-
tial hopeful Howard Dean into the public eye, the search
engine based on treating links as user recommendations
Google, or the free-for-all online classifieds listings of *Craigslist*
successful enough to eat away the profits of corporate newspapers: the bottom line of all of these practices is collaboration,
the flourishing of a "collective intelligence" particular of cyberculture, as Pierre Lévy (1997) suggests. When asked to explain
the worldwide success of *Craigslist*, founder Craig Newmark
hints at collaboration as the key value embedded in the way we
use, design and give meaning to networked information and
communication technologies: "my experience has shown me
that most people are essentially good and trustworthy, and
want to help each other out. I have been reminded that the rule
about treating others the way you want to be treated is a good
one."[20] Similarly, the founders of *Google*, Sergey Brin and Larry
Page, base much of their company's success on letting individual employees and users co-develop new and existing applications like *Google Scholar* or *Google Video*, which are made
available in so-called "beta" versions first to solicit sugges-
tions.[21] Yochai Benkler (2006) considers all these forms of
commons-based peer production examples of powerful new

ways of thinking about the economic wealth of networks, advo-
cating that commercial firms and especially mass media corporations increasingly should find ways to interact, collaborate,
and in essence work together with all kinds of non-market
types of cultural production emerging online. "It is this combination of a will to create and to communicate with others, and
a shared cultural experience that makes it likely that each of us
wants to talk about something we believe other will also want
to talk about, that makes the billion participants in today's
online conversation, and the six billion in tomorrow's conversation, affirmatively better than the commercial industrial
model" (p. 55). Although we must not forget that much of this
collaboration occurs within distinctly commercial contexts,
an evitable sidebar to the emergence of collective intelli-
gence-based media experiences is the challenge this poses to
the traditional authority of "expert" systems such as governments, organized religion, universities, and news media
organizations. As noted earlier, the popularity of a participatory yet highly individualized media culture must be understood in a context of an emerging cosmopolitan, voluntarist,
and critical citizenry.

Considering the commonly voiced concerns of an increasingly fragmented society and a general decline in traditional
social capital as defined by people's trust in politics, institutions such as church and state, and to some extent their fellow
human beings, it may be counter-intuitive to claim that
a more engaged and participatory culture is emerging.
Considering the interactive, globally networked and increasingly participatory nature of new media, it is inspiring to consider a different kind of social cohesion emerging on the basis
of the earlier mentioned notions of hypersociality, networked
individualism, and communicational bonds particular to digital culture. In other words: perhaps people are finding new
ways to connect with each other, collaborate, and participate in
social life that move beyond traditional notions of collectives
and communities. Sennett and Wellman are among those

who have argued that what we commonly understand as "community" has increasingly become synonymous with an oppressive notion of living in a place where there are no strangers – where the community is characterized by an absence of difference. Examples are sprawling exurban neighborhoods in the United States and Australia, gated communities in countries like South Africa, Brazil, Mexico, and China, or gentrified urban centers in Europe. Through media these and other kinds of otherwise enclosed and divided communities get linked in again, becoming part of an increasingly networked, mediated, and digital living environment, exposing all participants to the volatility and persistent open-endedness of the world today. The communities we work, live, and play in may have become fragmented and segregated (by class or lifestyle), they are more integrated at the same time. It is the secluded individual clicking through an endless list of user profiles in online dating databases, combined with her extended social network of hundreds or even thousands of people engaging in ongoing dialogue using instant messaging, chatrooms, discussion forums, and virtual meeting places: through media people have become more isolated yet connected at the same time.

It must be clear that people are endlessly fascinated with media, as with all acts of mediation. Media have become central to our understanding of ourselves and the world in which we live. However, as David Croteau and William Hoynes argue, "in the twenty-first century, we navigate through a vast mass media environment unprecedented in human history. Yet our intimate familiarity with the media often allows us to take them for granted" (2003, p. 5). The enormous extent to which this is true can be exemplified by looking at how people from all walks of life talk about and give meaning to their media use. We get up in the morning to the sound of the radio-alarm, switch on the television for breakfast, make our first calls using the hands-free set on our way to work, spend most of the day at our desks in front of a computer screen with fax and phone at hand, surf the Web for the latest news, blog-posts and shopping deals during lunch hours, watch our favorite sitcoms and sometimes news shows over dinner, and spend the remainder of the day chatting, e-mailing, and instant messaging online. All of this only consists of the kind of media we ritualistically or routinely choose to use, ignor-ing advertising and marketing messages, simultaneously reading a magazine or newspaper when zapping or zipping past television channels or commercials, reading billboards along the highway, browsing the headlines of a free daily newspaper while in transit, thoughtlessly scanning through radio stations or songs on our walkman, downloading, upgrading, tweaking, installing and uninstalling software, and so on, and so forth. Our media environment has thus become a key site of how we give meaning to the converging context of how we live, work, and play, as media connect us to each other, to our entertainment, and to our work – all at the same time.

Conclusion

In short, the modern categories of life and work at the begin-ning of the twenty-first century must be seen as spilling over, converging, making each of these key aspects of our human condition subject to the conditions of the other. Bauman (2005b) shows how this increasing fluidity of the everyday, coupled with a prevalent sense of permanent flux, has created the conditions of contemporary liquid life as a precarious life, lived under conditions of constant uncertainty. Living a liquid life involves a complex dance between work, play, and life in the context of a rapid-changing "glocal" environment, which life gets enacted in and through media. Living and working in the media is inherently confusing, as mediated experience blurs what is private and what is public, what is local and what is global, what is work and what is play. This continuous blur-ring of the boundaries between all aspects of everyday life through media creates a bewildering global complexity, as John Urry (2003) for example acknowledges. A life in media is a life constantly on the edge of chaos, confronted on all sides by ambiguities and contingency – while it is also a life where new media create endless affordances for people to seek out alternatives, yet also to remain behind the walls of homophilious social networks. The key to understanding our increasing opportunity, tendency, or even necessity to more or less collaboratively remix our "glocal" lived reality is too see this kind of behavior as a way for us to make sense of the growing complexity and uncertainty of the world around us (and in ourselves). Paraphrasing Bauman, our global mediated remix culture can be seen as a coping mechanism for dealing with the absurdity of life in today's liquid modernity. Bauman defines a liquid modern society as "a society in which the conditions under which its members act change faster than it takes the ways of acting to consolidate into habits and routines. Liquidity of life and that of society feed and reinvigorate each other. Liquid life, just like liquid modern society, cannot keep its shape or stay on course for long" (2005b, p. 1). A liquid modern society is one where uncertainty, flux, change, conflict, and revolution are the permanent conditions of everyday life. Bauman makes a compelling argument how this situation is neither modern nor post-modern, but rather explains how the categories of existence established and enabled by early, first, or solid modernity are disintegrating, overlapping, and remixing. It is not as if we cannot draw meaningful distinctions between global and local, between work and non-work, between public and private, between conservative and progressive, or between mediated and non-mediated experiences anymore. It is just that these and other key organizing characteristics and categories of modern life have lost their (presumed or perceived) intrinsic, commonly held, or consensual meaning. Whether it is information, entertainment, advertising, news, work, politics, sports, or a computer game, the meanings and messages become a blur, leaving no separation between formerly distinctive parts of society. Bauman extends these and other ideas to his notion of a liquid life, which I use as a framework for looking at the people working in the industry that serves as the most important guilty party of reflecting as well as directing the remix, convergence, instantaneous integration, and overall liquefaction of life, work, and play: the media.

CHAPTER TWO

Creative Industries, Convergence Culture, and Media Work

Economies are increasingly about the production, distribution, and consumption of items that are cultural and informational in character. Indeed, economic processes are cultural phenomena in and of themselves, as markets, products, and productivity are best understood as lived realities, rather than as abstract concepts. Culture, on the other hand, is both manufactured and managed: it is produced and experienced by people, in specific social and organizational contexts, with certain purposes (which in the case of commercial media organizations are also economical in nature). Culture is increasingly important to do business in the contemporary world, as more and more goods become cultural commodities – containing information that people use for identification, representation, belonging, and difference. We wear clothing with all kinds of logos, customize the appearance of our digital toys such as cell phones and portable music players, and in doing so engage in the "mass personalization" of every device we use to organize and experience our everyday life.

In this context, Allen Scott signals how "an ever-widening range of economic activity is concerned with producing and marketing goods and services that are infused in one way or another with broadly aesthetic or semiotic attributes" (1996, p. 323). This process of omnivorous production and commodification of culture is what Mike Featherstone (1992) considers consequential to the aesthetization of everyday life. People like individually and collectively to experience and express culture across and between traditional cultural hierarchies of taste, and do not essentially consume or produce culture grounded in a meaningful context, which is a trend commercial organizations in, for example, advertising and marketing successfully exploit. Lived experience thus becomes similar to the aesthetic experience of a song, a painting, or a book: people move from event to event, consuming and evaluating each and every event on the spot, perhaps, but not necessarily, reflecting on its impact (or lack thereof), but quickly moving on to the next event. Cultural products – ranging widely from clothing, jewelry, and perfume, via advertising and tourism to music recordings and live concerts, movies, videogames, or magazines – have multiple and sometimes contradictory functions at the same time: to inform as well as to entertain, to display socially as well as to escape individually. It would be too easy to argue that cultural production has become unduly commodified by this trend in Sennett's new capitalist culture, as commodities and the organization of work that produces these goods and services themselves are increasingly invested with symbolic value. Whether it is your car, your favorite video game, or the professional identity of your job: these things have meaning beyond their instrumental functionality as things that take you there, let you play, and earn you a living. In the contemporary cultural economy, boundaries between economy and culture are particularly blurred in the way markets are organized and experienced by the people participating in them: producers and consumers.

In today's economy, the buying and selling of products and services has become culturalized, for example through branding and design, as well as through practices of customizability, user co-creation, and mass personalization. Consider for example the key source of revenue for cell phones: downloadable ringtones. According to the US *Billboard* magazine – which offers a "Hot Ringtones" chart as part of its most popular music listings – global ringtone sales were $4,4 billion in 2005, up from $3,7 billion in 2004. However, this economic success was not part of the original planning of the developers or marketers of the original cell phone. As Sumanth Gopinath

(2005) writes: "The great irony in this flurry of financial activity to make ringtones increasingly profitable is that initially they were not predicted as potential means of accumulation by capitalists. The technology was essentially conceived as a novelty, but young consumers creatively used ringtones and similar mobile entertainments to 'personalize' their phones." The enormous popularity of the downloadable ringtone as an unintended side-effect of corporate strategy is a fascinating example of the complex context of an increasingly culturalized experience economy. The culture economy is riddled with similar examples, where the behaviors and passions of consumers have become more likely to propel businesses into action, steering product development, innovation, and differentiation. Scott Lash and John Urry (1994) have argued how the late twentieth-century individual has become more aesthetically reflexive and semiotically literate. People are increasingly (made) aware of what matching colors for clothing are by reading up in the relevant popular magazines; how to critically evaluate a movie by comparing it to previous ones; how to negotiate ten, thirty, or a hundred television channels and programs in one evening's zapping and zipping. People seem to be quite comfortable choosing brands, logos, and designs that somehow mean something to them (and their social networks), although without necessarily always choosing to buy the best or most useful product. One of the best and earliest examples of this global trend was the advertising slogan "It's a Sony!", introduced by Sony in 1982: "When launching such products as the Betamax VCR in 1975, the Walkman headphone stereo in 1979, and the 8mm camcorder series in the 80s, Sony sought to create new markets and lifestyles. Because such products often presented completely new concepts, they had to be advertised in ways that effectively explained what they were and how they should be used. Therefore, Sony advertising staff was involved in product planning so that product names, marketing slogans, and advertising strategies were created in tandem with the products themselves."[1] This integration of cultural intermediaries – such as advertising creatives and marketing planners – in the production process of all kinds of hardware and software has become a staple for the way businesses operate today.

The culturalization of the new economy, when coupled with the aesthetization of everyday life, has also produced a consumer increasingly willing and able to modify, design, and innovate products herself. This is what Eric von Hippel (2005) considers a democratization of innovations, showing how in an individualized society people not only look for something on the market that meets their needs – they also engage in tailoring and adapting the acquired products or services to fit exactly with what they want. In turn, companies in several fields – and particularly the media and cultural industries – have begun to incorporate the productive activities of consumers in their business strategies. New media technologies have accelerated these trends, transforming customer co-creation into what Tiziana Terranova (2000) sees as "free labor" for the new media industry: "In the overdeveloped countries, the end of the factory has spelled out the obsolescence of the old working class, but it has also produced generations of workers who have been repeatedly addressed as active consumers of meaningful commodities. Free labor is the moment where this knowledgeable consumption of culture is translated into productive activities that are pleasurably embraced and at the same time often shamelessly exploited." The liquefaction of the cultures of production and consumption undermines a major structure of the social division of labor between firms and industries on the one hand, and consumers on the other. Yet it also opens up all kinds of ways for commercial organizations to harness the voluntary work performed by "atomized" and therefore powerless individual customers. This is a powerful dynamic in the contemporary cultural economy, greatly enabled and amplified by the affordability of new information and communication technologies, by liquid life increasingly lived in and through media, and by the need for capitalist markets to expand and differentiate products continually, keeping all of us on our feet as perpetual customers and collaborators.

Media Life

Media, in the broadest sense, can be seen as the key drivers and accelerators of a global culturalization of economies. Our engagement with media is a broad social and collaborative process of making meaning, as media connect each and every individual (through the newspaper, a magazine, radio, television, or internet connection) to ideas and events experienced by other individuals – who in a contemporary age of talk radio, reality TV, weblogs, and *MySpace* have become just like us. It is through our uses of media that the complexities of contemporary culture get articulated, as media have come to pervade every aspect of life. This in turn makes the media as a business, as in those companies that work to create the content of our media, of central importance to an analysis of the human condition (Silverstone 2007). Indeed, part of what makes media as an industry so special, is the fact that – paraphrasing Bauman (2002, p. 161) – whatever media does to the world we inhabit, it seems to be a perfect fit between the two. If media lead the world, it is because media follow it; if media manage to disseminate new patterns of life, it is because media replicate such patterns in the media's own mode of being. Media are our window to the world, yet also function as its mirror; media reflect and direct at the same time.

The work of Allen Scott (2000) on the cultural economy of contemporary cities suggests another reason why it is important to consider the media as the prime focus for studying and understanding liquid modern life: cultural and creative industries tend to cluster close to certain city regions – such as Los Angeles, New York, Vancouver, Milan, Wellington, Munich, and Manchester – and thus catalyze a flurry of economic, cultural, and social activities in those regions, reinvigorating those areas. This in turn has led many local and regional governments to invest in public relations campaigns, profiling themselves as "creative" or "media" cities, as in the case of, for example, Dubai (United Arab Emirates), Singapore, Islamabad (Pakistan), Leiden (The Netherlands), Lille (France), Tampere (Finland), and Bristol (England). These trends may seem counter-intuitive, considering the global proliferation of new information and communication technologies that would facilitate teleworking and other forms of fragmentation of cultural production. Scott argues that one would expect "a sort of universal deterritorialization/liquifaction of world capitalism" (2000, p. 24), but shows that quite the opposite is occurring – especially in media industries like cinema, music, and multimedia. Those industries are attracted to, and attract, investors and generate business for restaurants, clubs, theaters, galleries, and other ingredients of cultural and economic life. Media thus are not only central to an understanding of everyday life in terms of the aesthetic quality and utility they bring to information and communication – as industries, media are also key to analyzing the changing economic and cultural environment of the world's urban spaces and the social shaping of technologies.

Whatever we do with our media – what we read, watch, listen to, participate in, create, or use – is much more than the tightly corporate-controlled substance offered through cable television, dot-com websites, or frequency modulation (FM) radio. It is also the bewildering array of community and "alternative" media, pirate radio, our use of the office photocopier as "the people's printing press," letters we write, Short Message Service (SMS) texts we send to participate in a TV show or to ask someone for a date, pictures taken with the built-in digital camera of our cell phones and uploaded to photosharing social networking sites like *Flickr*; postings we make to our own or someone else's weblog . . . and so on, and so forth. Media companies increasingly make use of this incredibly varied and complex media ritual we go through every day, which means that the cultural production taking place within such organizations is becoming increasingly complex as well. Media companies are both pioneers and benchmarks for what Lash and Urry (1994) call a reflexive productivity typical of post-industrial industries. This for example means that media work is often not only organized informally in ways that enable instant adaptation to changing consumer demands, but also that the media enterprise must be understood in radically different terms than traditional industrial-era factories.

In terms of the management and organization of work, media organizations can indeed be considered to quite special, partly because of the delicate and contested balance between the creative autonomy of culture creators, and the scientific management of commercial enterprises. Zygmunt Bauman considers the relationship between commerce and culture a sibling rivalry, as "management's plot against the endemic freedom of culture is a perpetual casus belli. On the other hand, culture creators need managers if they wish [. . .] to be seen, heard, and listened to, and to stand a chance of seeing their task/project through to completion" (2005b, p. 55). Media contribute to the culturalization of economic life through a constant remix of commercially viable yet generic work, next to or combined with innovative, flexible, and highly creative production processes. This is an unique blend of what Bryan Turner (2003, p. 138) describes as a dialectical and unstable process between "linear" and "liquid" differentiations. Examples of linearity in cultural production are predictable iterations of the same franchise, such as the *James Bond* movies, a soap opera like *Eastenders*, or the *Legend of Zelda* video game series. Liquid differentiation occurs in the production of groundbreaking, unconventional new media formulas, hybrid genres, and unexpected or otherwise experimental storytelling formats. It is important to note here that the same companies or indeed the same professionals tend to be engaged in both types of production. Following Turner, this dialectical production process makes the media as an industry the core culprit responsible for cookiecutter-style McDonaldization, as well as a key agent in introducing social, technological, and economical innovation and change.

It must be clear that in a creative economy the role of media industries is extremely important, and not just because of the clustering of these industries in certain city regions, or because of the significance of cultural intermediaries in the manufacturing of ideas, signs, images, and symbols that help human beings give meaning to their lives. Indeed, the fact that the media above all else deal in ideas, information and culture has been used to set them apart in studies of their organization and structure. However, as Nicholas Garnham (2000, p. 86) notes, studies of the media tend to fetishize their existence as institutions, content, and audiences. Such an approach all too often limits one to instrumental explanations of media production, focusing on the complicity of media industries in the commodification and mainstreaming of culture, or on the resistance by increasingly savvy audiences to the inscribed and preferred meanings of media messages. On the one hand it makes sense to look at media industries strictly in terms of the commercially successful transnational enterprises they are. As such, argues Yochai Benkler, the commercial mass media environment has created two important effects on society: the Berlusconi and Baywatch effects. The Berlusconi effect refers to "the disproportionate political power that ownership over mass media outlets gives its owners or those who can pay them," while the Baywatch effect refers to a "displacement of public discourse by the distribution of commodifiable entertainment products" (2003, p. 8). On the other hand, studies of how people engage their media suggest that a notion of passive, hapless, or apathetic consumption does not do justice to the complex ways in which we consume, produce, and generally give active meaning to whatever we see, hear, read or click on when multitasking our media. What both of these important views omit, then, is an understanding or respect for the moment of cultural production – the complex process of making media, the organization of work, the role of new technologies, the interdependence of issues such as creativity and commerce, and the translation of increasingly precise market orientations to the differentiation of productivity in media organizations large and small.

Media as Creative Industries

The social process of work in the media industries is a fascinating object of study, as the production of culture is in itself a cultural process. This for example suggests that the social process among people within and between organizations in which cultural goods and services (such as news, advertising, movies, television shows, and video games) are produced will influence their content. At the same time, corporate structure, strategy, management, and behavior likewise impact the nature and supply of content. As economic life in general has become culturalized, the creative as well as commercial process of cultural production today extends beyond the walls of media organizations, providing additional ground for analyzing the social conditions that shape creative industries. This does not mean that media production exclusively takes place within, and under the unique control of, archetypical media megacorporations such as Rupert Murdoch's NewsCorp.[2] The contemporary media marketplace must rather be seen as shaped by the individual and collective professional identities of artists, writers, directors, editors, designers, and the hundreds of thousands of other creatives employed, subcontracted, or otherwise engaged by this what Jeremy Tunstall (2001, p. 1) introduces as an "extremely variegated, fragmented, and unstandardized" industry.

Although the definition of the media as an industry is a matter of ongoing academic debate, for the purposes of this book it is important to note the distinct emphasis on media production as the more or less exclusive domain of firms, companies and corporations of an endless variety in size and structure. Media work can be seen as a particular (and popular) set of professional values and practices within a wider context of cultural production, which would include theater, painting, philosophy, architecture, and other examples of a contemporary "culture industry." This culture industry tends to be criticized for its role in packaging people's experiences into commercial commodities that are produced in factories of cultural goods.[3] In a sweeping review of the field, David Hesmondhalgh (2002) advocates a much broader view of media as part of the *plural* cultural industries, suggesting how cultural production has become more, rather than less complex, diverse, and contested than one would perhaps expect in the course of the twentieth-century era of mass media. Part of this complexity and ambivalence of cultural production as it pertains to media industries is the fact, that much of the work is done by individuals, or by teams and groups of people that generally only temporarily bundle their talents and skills for a specific project – such as a film, a video game, or one season of a television show. Considering the consequences of the culturalization of everyday life and the individualization of people's workstyle, it becomes especially relevant for a deep understanding of media work to adopt a definition of the field that allows for an uniquely blended perspective on the industrial and commercial context of cultural production coupled with an appreciation of the individual creativity, passion, and vision of its practitioners.

Since the late 1990s policymakers, industry observers, and scholars from around the world have sought to reconcile the emergence of increasingly individual and small-scale, project-based or collaborative notions of cultural production – be it for commercial or other purposes –with traditional notions of media work as it takes place within the cultural industries. The contemporary concept of choice has become: creative industries, a term introduced by the Creative Industries Task Force (CITF) of the British Department of Culture, Media and Sport in 1998. The CITF defines creative industries as "those industries which have their origin in individual creativity, skill and talent and which have a potential for wealth and job creation through the generation and exploitation of intellectual property. This includes advertising, architecture, the art and antiques market, crafts, design, designer fashion, film and video, interactive leisure software, music, the performing arts, publishing, software and computer games, television and radio."[4] The concept has been taken up and extended in the scholarly literature as a new way to look at cultural industries, focusing on the combination or coming together of creativity and commerce in cultural work. The popularity of this term among policymakers as well as academics suggest a growing significance of culture and creativity in all aspects of industry.

The creative process in this context not only refers to the development and production of goods and services – it also refers to the ways in which consumers make their choices for certain products. Referring explicitly to the media, John Hartley defines creative industries as an idea that "seeks to describe the conceptual and practical convergence of the creative arts (individual talent) with cultural industries (mass scale), in the context of new media technologies (ICTs) within a new knowledge economy, for the use of newly interactive citizen-consumers" (2005, p. 5). Hartley's definition suggests a hopeful, perhaps even utopian outcome of the merger between individual creativity and cultural entrepreneurialism, as it certainly seems to open up new avenues for consumer choice and producer creativity. On the other hand, Brett Neilson and Ned Rossiter are among those who warn against an overtly optimistic or uncritical acceptance of the concept, arguing it consists of "an oxymoronic disingenuousness that wants to suggest that innovation can coexist with or become subordinated to the status quo. In this context, innovation becomes nothing other than a code word for more of the same – the reduction of creativity to the formal indifference of the market" (2005, p. 8).

A critical perspective is certainly warranted, given the emphasis in this book on the changing nature of media work. Rossiter (2006) in particular warns against the celebration of digital culture by drawing attention to the exploitation of labor in the creative industries. An intellectual as well as practical shift towards creative industries affects traditional notions about the status, security, and function of jobs, as the creative work that takes place both within and outside of the cultural industries becomes ever more contingent on global market conditions and producer–consumer relationships. The concept thus presumes that any and all people involved in creative work see themselves and their talent, skills, and ideas in commercial terms too – which can be a "hard sell" for the self-perception of professionals in media industries, who tend to cherish creative autonomy and peer review as most important indicators of the quality of their work. On the other hand, the creative industries approach resolves two particular tensions maintained throughout the literature on media industries, media use, and everyday life: the binary opposition between the social identities of "consumers" and "producers" (as these activities can be seen as mutually enabling and constitutive), and it considers whatever acts and practices emerge from this convergence as potentially commercially relevant and viable – a necessary precondition for any consideration of the legitimacy, nature, and possible future of professional media work. The creative industries approach to sites of cultural production reminds us of the seminal role (the management and organization of) creativity *and* commerce play in any consideration of media work.

Media as Work

Although many occupations in the different areas of the media started out quite distinct from each other, media work has become increasingly comparable and similar across the industry in the course of the twentieth century. Enrique Bustamante

(2004) analyzes the key trends contributing to the emergence of a singular model for cultural industries in the digital age as: the ongoing international deregulation of formerly protected media markets, increased concentration and conglomeration of media companies, and a globalization of forms and principles of media management. As these trends must be seen as further supercharged by innovations and developments in new information and communication technologies, "media work has become more similar and also more similar to office work in general" (Tunstall 2001, p. 22). Although Bustamante rejects the notion of a move towards a single global model of media, with Néstor García Canclini (1999) he does conclude that a global reconstruction of "world culture" and "local creativity" is taking place under the paradigms of technology and the market.

Media organizations tend to be a combination of public service and for-profit companies dealing with the industrial and creative production and circulation of culture. In terms of media work, this "culture" refers not only to the production of spoken and written words, audio, still or moving images, but (and increasingly) also to providing platforms for people to produce and exchange their own content. In contemporary definitions of what the work within these industries involves, four elements tend to get mixed up, which to some extent makes an adequate assessment of media work rather difficult: content, connectivity, creativity, and commerce – which all translate into the production of culture (see Figure 2.1). Media industries produce content, yes, but also invest in platforms for connectivity – where fans and audiences provide free labor. Media work is culture creation, yes, but tends to take place within a distinctly commercial context.

In economic terms, the media serve a dual product market: media are sold as newspapers, magazines, movies, CDs, and so on to audiences, while at the same the attention of that audience – expressed as ratings, circulation figures, unique site visitors, et cetera – is sold to advertisers. This is a fascinating area

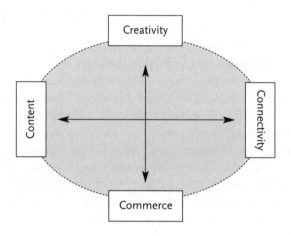

Figure 2.1   *Modeling Media Work*

of tension within the industry, as the wants and needs of audiences, creators, and advertisers may not always be the same, and in the current digital and networked media ecosystem the roles played by advertising creatives, media producers, and content consumers are increasingly intertwined. This networked character also reveals the often translocalized nature of the media production process (or "pipeline"), as many industries – such as computer and video game development, film, and television – offshore, subcontract and outsource various elements in the production process to save costs and redistribute risks. Examples are securing international financing for television projects, shooting a movie at several locations (often in different countries), moving an online division or marketing department of a newspaper to another part of the world (a practice called "remote control journalism"[5]), mixing music recorded in Los Angeles in a studio outside of London, localizing game titles set in one regional, cultural, or national context in another part of the world, adding local soundtracks and hit songs to generic advertising campaigns generated for global brands, separating out the marketing and distribution of titles, and so on. Such "supranational forms of market-based cultural production" (Schiller 1999) primarily benefit and in part result from structural trends characterizing the media industries in recent years: growth, integration, globalization, and concentration of ownership. The media industry has been moving from a primarily national to a global commercial media market, currently dominated by seven oligopolists: Sony, Viacom, Bertelsmann, News Corporation, Vivendi, Disney, and Time Warner. Although it is tempting to see these companies as efficient risk-averse monoliths, research on the relationship between international strategic management and firm performance of global media conglomerates shows otherwise. Analyzing the product and geographic diversification strategies of these conglomerates, Sylvia Chan-Olmsted and Byeng-Hee Chang (2003) for example conclude that although these companies initially expanded and diversified to reduce overall risks, the increased complexity of international operations and exposures to uncertainties, coupled with risk in consumer tastes, regulations, and investment in distribution, in fact leads to performance declines. Research on synergy management, global – local relationships and intracorporate cooperation in media conglomerates such as Bertelsmann (Schulze *et al.* 2005) and News Corporation (Marjoribanks 2000) furthermore suggests that the organization of work in these companies is far from streamlined, uniform, or necessarily successful, as much depends on particular values, behaviors and beliefs of individual actors in the creative process.

Although each field, genre or discipline in the media has its own peculiarities and distinctiveness, the trends towards business integration, technological convergence, and the mutually reinforcing developments of localization and globalization ("glocalization") have made working experiences the media industries increasingly similar. It becomes possible to discuss "the" media according to a couple of key distinctive trends and features. David Hesmondhalgh includes as the core cultural industries: advertising and marketing, radio and television (broadcasting), film, internet (including Web design, portal providers), music (record labels, press and promotion, publishing), print and electronic publishing (including books, magazines, and newspapers), video and computer games (2002, p. 12). All of these industries interact and interconnect with each other in complex ways, sometimes as competitors (for audience attention, investors, and for skilled creative and technical labor), sometimes as albeit temporary collaborators – for example when the British record company Earache Records in 2006 entered in a joint partnership with video games publisher Metro 3D, and the games developer Data Design Interactive to create, publish, and market a game called *Earache Metal Racing* featuring the music and in-game avatar renditions of international Earache artists like Morbid Angel (from the US), At The Gates (Sweden), and Mortiis (Norway).[6] These kind of project-based inter- and intracompany strategic alliances are typical for work the creative industries.

Chris Bilton (2007) typifies the cultural geography of the creative industries as a range of informal networks of collaboration, expertise and influence. "These networks extend in two dimensions, horizontally, through peer-to-peer relationships with organizations and individuals, and vertically, through supply chain relationships which contribute to different phases of cultural production and distribution" (p. 46). Bilton emphasizes the informal, collaborative and intangible nature of the creative process. A second crucial contextual aspect of media work for the negotiation of commerce, connectivity, content and creativity is the largely project-based nature of production. The organization of work in projects with a limited lifespan occurs both within certain companies – as in temporary teams assembled for particular clients in an advertising or integrated marketing communications firm – as well as between companies. In short, it is possible to summarize that informal networks among generally short-term (and often freelance) employed professionals within a broader industry structure dominated by project-based work are what epitomizes workstyles in the media today. The various ways in which media professionals and managers alike strive to give structure and meaning to their workstyles in this context are premised on what Eric Louw (2001, p. 65) calls "communicative complexity," befitting a global networked form of enterprise in the culture industry.

The current structure of core sectors within a broad conceptualization of creative industries grows out of two simultaneous developments: the number of media outlets and products has been growing at a rapid rate, while media corporations are getting much larger, often merging or partnering with competitors. A diagrammatic overview of organizations and businesses in the media industries therefore reveals an "hourglass effect" in the distribution of employment, with people working in either a relatively small number of large companies, or in the growing multitude of small firms – with some employed at the few medium-sized businesses in between (Keith Hackett *et al.* 2000). Large, often multinational media conglomerates tend to strive towards some kind of horizontal and vertical integration. Horizontal integration is achieved by expansion through mergers and acquisitions of firms offering similar products and services. In the advertising industry this for example means that in recent decades the majority of well-known agencies has been bought by large strategic holding groups like Omnicom, Interpublic, Havas, and Publicis. Conglomeration has become the norm across the publishing, broadcasting, film, and music industries, indicating the practice of horizontal integration by combining related or complimentary businesses. On the other end of the hourglass one finds tens of thousands of small enterprises, ranging from individual cultural entrepreneurs to smaller companies and loose networks of collaborating professionals – generally working in part-time, freelance, for-hire, subcontracted, and otherwise contingent capacities. According to Hesmondhalgh, "most creative workers exist in a vast reservoir of underused and under-resourced talent, picking up work here and there. In many cases, production will actually take place under the auspices of a separate, independent company" (2002, p. 22). The major film, game, and music companies for example have always operated a deliberate balance with so-called "independent" production houses, development studios, and record labels to discover, cultivate, and promote new talent. In the game industry there is an important role for third-party developers, or independent development studios, who develop their own projects and try to sell them to a publisher, or market their games directly to gamers online. In arguably the "oldest" media industry, journalism, this balance has been established throughout history by a strong tradition of so-called "alternative" or citizen's media appearing alongside their larger corporate counterparts. Often, the reporters of such newspapers and local community radio or television stations originally came from the larger media companies in the area – opting out because of job insecurity, corporate encroachment of editorial autonomy, or the prospect of job rotation: circulating reporters and editors around the various departments and titles part of the same newspaper chain across the country.[7] A second crucial aspect of the strategic management in media companies is vertical integration, which has for example contributed greatly to the power of Hollywood movie studios, as these companies not only control the production process, but also the distribution of films to theaters, video stores, and television. As Janet Wasko explains in How Hollywood Works (2003), the US film industry is dominated by a handful of companies that through vertical integration draw much of their power from film distribution. This control not only allows Hollywood to set the agenda for movie production and release schedules in the US, but also extends its reach to much of the world's film business. A crucial aspect of the media's tendency to integrate vertically – gobbling up businesses facilities, products, and services across the entire industry pipeline – is the fact that these acquisitions go hand in hand with disintegration and media deconcentration, as the expected benefits of such mergers often fail to deliver.

Key Trends in Media Work

Working in the media industries, both large and small, means coming to terms with a couple of related and overlapping trends. It must be clear that media industries to some extent are faced with issues similar to those by any other commercial enterprise, such as global and local ("glocal") competition, and corporate concerns over sales, advertising revenue, and profits. However, as Richard Caves (2000) and others effectively argue, the business of creative industries is to some extent unique. I therefore focus on those trends that can be considered to be particular to the professional identity of media work: the tendency of cultural companies to cluster in specific urban areas; the risky and unpredictable nature of the media business; the complexity of controlling and collaborating with creative individuals in the context of project-based labor and commercial enterprise; and the pervasive nature of technology and information management in all aspects of the creative process.

Risk, Trust, and Clusters. Media companies are attracted to the city, and the development of what Allen Scott (2000) calls the cultural economy of cities is bound up with the presence of clusters or geographical networks of cultural firms and media industries – ranging from large vertically integrated corporations to micro networks of cultural entrepreneurs. Clustering is primarily motivated by a strategy to counter the risky nature of the media business. The key risk in media work lies in the paradoxical nature of the media product. In some ways, a cultural commodity – a film, a video game, an ad campaign – is just like any other commercial product in that it is made to appeal to a certain audience. On the other hand, the success or

failure of the media product relies on its novelty and difference, and on its ability to meet the inherently volatile, fickle,
and therefore difficult to predict sensitivities and tastes of
people. The first trend signifies an economically sound strategy of producing the kind of content that has proven itself in
the marketplace – what Turner (2003) describes as a certain
linearity in cultural production. The popular reality television
show *Big Brother* for example premiered in The Netherlands in
1999, and was sold as a franchise all over the world (as from
2000 the show came to the US, from 2001 also in
Australia/New Zealand and South Africa, and in 2005 a
Finnish version premiered for a franchise total of almost seventy countries).[8] After it became such an international success, television stations from all over the world started to
develop or commission more or less similar reality shows,
leading to a proliferation of sub-categories and genres within
the overall framework of reality-based gameshows.

The linear homogenization process in the production and
development of cultural commodities can be set against a concurrent need for diversifying and differentiating production,
as the public's tastes, preferences, and attention spans rapidly
(and continually) change. Focusing on diversifying ("liquefy-
ing") the production portfolio is thus an equally smart thing to
do for media industries. This tactic leads to a glocalization of
popular franchises – as in the case of South African reality
show *The Apprentice* with former political leader Tokyo
Sexwale, a Dutch version called *De Nieuwe Moszkowicz*, the
Finnish *Diili*, and the American original with Donald Trump
that share many similarities, but are also notably different and
informed by local circumstances. Yet this tactic also stimulates
the development of a wide-ranging repertoire of cultural products for niche markets and specific target audiences. All of this
contributes to the industry's masochistic need for innovation
and constant change – masochistic, in that its commercial
impetus for mass appeal and a steady stream of advertising
revenues in fact demands market stability and low-cost formu-

laic production (as for example in the case of newspaper journalism or blockbuster movie production).

Linearity and liquidity are rather different production styles and market strategies. The tension this creates can be seen as typical and indeed fundamental to the creative process of making media. Opting either way always involves taking great risks, as the outcome of both strategies is unpredictable – and increasingly so in the contemporary media-saturated cultural economy of liquid modernity. Risk and its counterpart, trust, are constitutive in the organization and management of media work. In cultural industries, "risk is managed and trust is negotiated in informal contexts, social networks and social spaces [. . .] new ties of trust, whether they be strong or weak, help break down industry boundaries and themselves become part of the creative process leading to unforeseen collaborations and/or new cultural product" (Banks *et al.* 2000, p. 463). It is therefore quite common for professionals to work with different employers in the same industry, which companies are often physically located in the same block of streets and office buildings, whose employees frequent the same restaurants, bars, and clubs for lunch, after-work activities, and networking parties. All the time, these professionals may subsequently or simultaneously work on projects that fit either linear or liquid production styles.

Management of Creativity. Professionals in the creative industries are somewhat different from their colleagues in other fields of production in that they often care deeply about their work. The difficulty of media management is underscored by the combination of this rather unique element of media workers' sense of professional identity and a structural sense of risk and unpredictability at the heart of the cultural production process. Writing about cultural entrepreneurs, Charles Leadbeater and Kate Oakley (1999) argue that the creative process is sustained by inspiration and informed by talent, vitality and commitment, which makes creative work volatile, dynamic, and risk-ridden, shaped by crucial tacit skills that are often vague and remain unspoken. "In media organizations, you have a rapidly changing, dynamic atmosphere where people within the organization frequently see themselves more as independent contractors than employees. They see the organization as merely a conduit for their work" (Redmond and Trager 2004, p. 59). Caves (2000) adds that as a result of this, there are many more people wanting to work in these industries than there are jobs available, and most of them are willing or forced to accept below-average salaries, contingent wages, and temporary contractual arrangements without benefits or any kind of guarantees for future employment.

The management of media industries is, by all accounts, special. It not only involves the supervision and facilitation of creative individuals in the context of project-based labor and commercial enterprise – it also entails managing contacts and contracts with outsourced and subcontracted labor, as well as with all kinds of auxiliary industries, such as reproduction facilities, licensors, vendors, distributors, and retailers. Some of the people in these fields are internal to the media company, but most of them are not. Often every single project – a game, a movie, a special section of a magazine or newspaper – gets produced by a team of people specifically assembled for that purpose. Interestingly, just as consumers tend to choose products primarily for their sign-value rather than their use-value, the putting together of a team does not necessarily involve choosing the best people for the project at hand – it also means getting people together who trust each other, who have earned the trust of a manager or client in the past, or who are known to be able to work with each other without too much conflict. In other words: project- and teamwork-based media production, just as media consumption, tends to be done within a cultural context of what it means to the people involved, more so than according to rational, scientific, objective, or strictly economical principles.

Teams in media work have a limited shelf-life, and their performance tends to be limited to the immediate demands of the project at hand. Sennett laments that teamwork "is the group practice of demeaning superficiality" (1998, p. 99), suggesting that the short-lived super-adaptive culture of such a group is emblematic of the modern flexible political economy. Teams can be considered to be the organization of work particular to the network society, as they are cooperative, instantaneous, and the key competence the individual members are expected to bring to the job are so-called "soft" skills. At the beginning of the twenty-first century several schools and departments of journalism, in collaboration with the news industry, initiated studies of the changing market for journalists, focusing on what skills are needed for newcomers to be successful. Analyzing such reports from organizations in The Netherlands, South Africa, and the US one common theme emerges: a perceived need for new newsworkers to have excellent social, communication, and people skills (Deuze 2004a). The 2004 report by the International Labour Organization (ILO) on the organization and future of work in the media, culture, and graphical sector similarly signaled an increasing need for communication and teamwork skills for newcomers in these industries.[9]

The organization of teamwork in the media centers on meeting a series of deadlines of deliverables and milestones – an installment in a series of stories, a set of photographs for a magazine spread, a specific asset like the soundtrack of a video game–forcing cooperation among project participants with different skills and perspectives on the project outcome. Team-based labor also tends to be portable, in that workers move from project to project rather than carrying out a continuing set of tasks. This means that employers are continually faced with re-composing a workforce, while workers are always looking and preparing for their next job (Christopherson and Van Jaarsveld 2005).

Technology and Information. Employees in the media are engaged in what Maurizio Lazzarato (1997) defines as immaterial labor, deploying in their work a set of skills primarily involving the gathering, selecting, organizing, and communicating of information. All this immaterial labor ultimately serves the interests of a type of industry that aims to be flexible, reflexive, and extremely versatile when it comes to answering the demands of a global marketplace. Again, the media as part of the creative industries can be seen as the key examples and drivers of this economic and cultural shift, as Lazzarato argues: "Immaterial workers (those who work in advertising, fashion, marketing, television, cybernetics, and so forth) satisfy a demand by the consumer and at the same time establish that demand."[10] The key to understanding this symbiotic process of cultural production and consumer demand lies in the enabling role technology plays in media work.

Throughout all accounts of the structure, management, and work in the media the pervasive and ubiquitous role of technology stands out. The media industries are among the key accelerators of the development and innovation of new information and communication technologies. Print journalism is a media profession that has contributed to increasing demands on the efficiency, cost-effectiveness, and quality of printing presses, digital reproduction and distribution methods, and desktop publishing tools. The computer and video game industry supercharged upgrades to processor speeds, memory compression, three-dimensional graphics, and screen pixilation technologies for home computers and game consoles. The film industry contributed to the development of digital surround sound and widescreen projection systems in theaters and, increasingly, at home, whereas the music and recording industries greatly facilitated the introduction and advancement of portable music players.

In the daily work environment and practices in the media, technology plays a crucial part in the creative process. A significant concern regarding this trend is the standardization of work practices implied by an omnipresence of technologies. In order to facilitate technological convergence and the corresponding managerial expectation of a synergy between different practices and processes, media companies increasingly rely on content management systems (CMS), which are sophisticated software packages generally acquired on the commercial market, further developed using open source applications and finally customized in-house. As different media formats – audio, moving and still images, text – become increasingly standardized regarding their translation to the digital, the exchange, and repurposing or "windowing" of multimedia content becomes more manageable. Yet this lowering of the threshold for technological convergence can at the same time be considered to be problematic for media practitioners, who like to see themselves as creative workers, not as "slaves" to the relatively limited range of options offered by preprogrammed templates, shells, and formats offered by technologies like CMS. The earlier mentioned ILO report additionally signals how technological standardization in the media might undermine multilingualism, cultural diversity, and local languages.

Concerns regarding the efficient ordering, standardizing, and streamlining promises and effects of technology can be read next to more techno-optimist notions, celebrating their digital, networked, interactive, and easy-to-use potential. New media networks make all kinds of reorganizations possible and tend to contribute to a shift from more hierarchical to networked structures and decision-making processes. Bar and Simard (2006, p. 360) make the case that control over the configuration and application of technologies in organizations is flexibly separate from ownership of the underlying network infrastructure. This, they argue, creates opportunities for individuals and teams using these technologies to shape them in different ways. However, this expectation of some kind of collaborative social shaping is not given to all – as Stanley Aronowitz and William DiFazio (1995) for example warned against the deleterious effects of computerization, and signal increased opportunities for exploitative labor practices enabled through cybernetization of the workplace. On the other hand, observers such as Jeremy Rifkin (2004) who also signal an

"end of work" enabled by technology are in fact cautiously optimistic about the creative freedom this would generate for an
admittedly small elite of knowledge workers.

Although different technologies are used in different contexts throughout the different areas of the creative industries,
today media professionals are first and foremost expected to
come to terms with technological convergence in their work.
Technological convergence refers to the coming together of
audio, video, telecommunications and data onto a common
platform, enabled by the digitization of all these formerly separate technologies. The crucial nature of information and communication technologies in the creative process of media work
gets supercharged in a converged environment, where multiple technologies are integrated. People increasingly use the
same device for multiple functions, making the computer (as a
standalone device, or as integrated into other hardware like a
cell phone) a truly "universal machine," that we use to work
and play simultaneously, which activities are enabled yet con-
strained at the same time by the parameters and implications
of technology. As these purposes can be served both from
home and the office, the boundary between those kinds of
places begins to lose significance. Convergence in media work
thus relates to two intertwined processes: the convergence of
place – as in the workplace and the home office – and the convergence of *technology* – as in the digital, networked hardware
and software available to set the parameters of creative endeavors, and to further the means for managerial control over
media work. Such control takes place through workflow standardization, workplace surveillance, and decentralization of
work through for example telework, and the outsourcing of
specific segments ("deliverables") of a project to external
agents. As such, convergence directly affects four key aspects
of mass media industries: the content of communication, the
relationships between media producers and consumers, the
structure of firms, and ultimately how communication professionals do their work.

The convergence of different media and technologies now enables media workers to tell their stories using different platforms, engaging consumers on different levels, using different media at the same time. These opportunities offer journalism, public relations and advertising new challenges in thinking about their content: using multiple media to repurpose or window the content of one medium, to stimulate the production of original content for each medium, or to come up with a strategy that would simultaneously produce content across all media at the same time. Whatever creative process chosen, it has direct consequences for the kind of content produced, and for the way the production process can be organized. A key element in this process is the relationship between the media worker and the (intended) audience. In an "always on" digitally networked media environment, the audience can be more visible and said to be disappearing at the same time. Because of decades of audience research, consumer surveys and focus groups, media organizations – especially marketing and advertising firms – are acutely aware of changes and consistencies of market trends and tastes. People have become "glass consumers" in what Greg Elmer (2004) maps as a global personal information economy, facilitated by the proliferation of more or less integrated digital pay and registration systems and feedback mechanisms. Examples of such "profiling machines" are websites' use of cookies (small text-files automatically stored on someone's computer by a company or organization, documenting user behavior for future reference), credit card purchases and age verification, mail-in rebates and coupons, and customer discount cards distributed by retailers, petrol stations, and supermarkets. All these strategies serve to store consumer behavior in databases that can be mined to monitor closely trends in the wants and needs of potential audiences. Although this would suggest an omnipresent "dataveillance" of each and every move we make as consumers, it must be noted that much of this surveillance is reciprocal, as audiences not only give away their personal information voluntarily, people are also becoming more actively involved in the production of media content.

In journalism, people contribute feedback and comments to news stories online, in advertising people participate in playing games (as in ordering a guy in a chicken suit to dance on a website as part of an ad campaign for Burger King), and in the film industry US-based Participant Productions (behind such films as *Syriana*, *North Country*, and *Fast-Food Nation*) solicits audiences to get engaged and participate in all kinds of activism target-marketed around the topics of their films. In a 2003 rapport, television industry analyst Monique van Dusseldorp shows how companies such as MTV Europe, The Music Factory – TMF (the Netherlands), RTL (Germany), YLE (Finnish Broadcasting Company), and others generate revenue on top of advertising through SMS-television: offering viewers a chance to participate in a program through voting, gaming, and chat options using the Simple Message Service protocol of cell phones. Van Dusseldorp suggests that in doing so, television producers satisfy their viewers' desire to publish messages, influence programming and communicate with each other.[11] Such practices would suggest that the audience becomes more visible than ever before – yet the exact opposite is true as well. Because of their active behavior, audiences are becoming co-creators of content – ranging from putting increasing demands on the creative process to generate personalized and customizable products to engaging in productivity on their own, especially online. Such activities and demands raise the profile of the audience as a consumer as well as a producer, which trend is key to the adoption of the creative industries approach to cultural production and media work by policymakers and industry observers alike.

What these examples of the role of technology in media work show, is how new media, information and communication technologies influence and are influenced by the way creative industries operate. Additionally it must be said that technologies are not "cold machines" – these are devices and associated practices that have certain meanings for the people involved. A photojournalist can for example see the omnipresence of digital camera-enabled cell phones as a threat to her livelihood when editors increasingly rely on lower quality pictures taken on the scene of a news event by bystanders rather than the professionally produced shots after the fact. It could mean that reporters and editors of news organizations are all of a sudden expected to cooperate with colleagues working elsewhere (and with other media) facilitated by an economic merger and technological convergence. In game development, radio and television production, and advertising, new media technologies contribute to the increased outsourcing of specific parts of the creative process to companies or individuals located all over the world.

The introduction of all kinds of content management systems, company intranets, and desktop publishing software in newsrooms, advertising agencies, film and television, (post-) production houses tend to mean two different, but important things for the professionals involved: it speeds up the creative process, and it contributes to a sense of having to do and learn more on top of one's existing competences, skills, and talent. New technologies force people to learn new skills and unlearn old ones, while the work process accelerates at the same time. Technologies are also developed and implemented differently across different organizations or even parts of a single organization, leading to a constant reshuffling of adaptation processes and experiences. In order to see completely the pivotal role technologies play in media work, one has to consider the broad definition offered by Leah Lievrouw and Sonia Livingstone about new media as "information and communication technologies and their associated social contexts, incorporating: the artefacts or devices that enable and extend our abilities to communicate; the communication activities or practices we engage in to develop and use these devices; and the social arrangements or organizations that form around the devices and practices" (2006, p. 23). It is in the combination of equipment, hardware and software, the incorporation of these artefacts into one's everyday workstyle, and the new ways of doing and organizing work that follows out of these activities that the role of new technologies in media work becomes apparent. Technology is indeed central to media work, but its role is neither unproblematic nor inevitable.

Convergence Culture

In today's increasingly digital culture, media work can be seen as a stomping ground for the forces of increasingly differentiated production and innovation processes, and the complex interaction and integration between work, life, and play, all of which get expressed in, and are facilitated by, the rapid development of new information and communication technologies. The new human condition, when seen through the lens of those in the forefront of changes in the way work and life are implicated in our increasingly participatory media culture, is convergent. This convergence is not just a technological process. Media convergence must also be seen as having a cultural logic of its own, blurring the lines between production and consumption, between making media and using media, and between active or passive spectatorship of mediated culture.

Henry Jenkins (2006) sees in the merger of media production and consumption the emergence of a global convergence culture, based on an increasingly participatory and interactive engagement between people and their media, as well as between professional and amateur media makers. "Convergence is both a top-down corporate-driven process and a bottomup consumer-driven process. Media companies are learning how to accelerate the flow of media content across delivery channels to expand revenue opportunities, broaden markets and reinforce viewer commitments. Consumers are learning how to use these different media technologies to bring the flow of media more fully under their control and to interact with other users. They are fighting for the right to participate more fully in their culture, to control the flow of media in their lives and to talk back to mass market content. Sometimes, these two forces reinforce each other, creating closer, more rewarding, relations between media producers and consumers" (Jenkins 2004, p. 37). As concrete examples of this trend Jenkins considers the significant role so-called online "spoiler" forums play in the production of reality TV shows like *Survivor*, and how transmedia storytelling franchises like the combined *The Matrix* movies, animation series, and video games encourage consumers to assemble their own version of the overall narrative. Similarly, producers of popular television entertainment – such as soap operas or police dramas – are developing innovative ways to collect audience feedback, and then applying this information to the development of new characters and plotlines, as well as to include the most current social issues in their shows.

Indeed, the role of the customer as co-creator of the media message increasingly finds acceptance throughout the cultural industries. Among creatives and brand managers in ad agencies the contemporary focus is on interactive advertising, defined by Leckenby and Li (2000) as the paid and unpaid presentation and promotion of sponsored products, services, and ideas involving mutual action between consumers and producers. Marketers brainstorm about the potential of "upstream" marketing, which refers to the strategic process of identifying and fulfilling consumer needs early in product development, up to and including end-users in the product innovation cycle. In journalism, editors of news publications actively consider adding what is called "citizen journalism" to their websites, allowing members of the audience to respond, comment, and submit their own news. Convergence culture has been particularly part of the organization of work in the computer and video game industries. Game publishers often consider their consumers as co-developers, where product innovation and development largely depends on online consumer communities – such as for example in the modifying of games by players, which so-called "mods" are then integrated in new commercial versions of the original computer or video game (Deuze 2007).

The extent to which this convergence culture plays a significant role in the entire media ecology, and therefore in the development of a professional identity among media workers, can be illustrated by a November 2005 survey by the Pew Internet and American Life Project among teenagers in the United States, which report concludes: "Some 57% of online teens create content for the internet. That amounts to half of all teens ages 12–17, or about 12 million youth. These Content Creators report having done one or more of the following activities: create a blog; create or work on a personal webpage; create or work on a webpage for school, a friend, or an organization; share original content such as artwork, photos, stories, or videos online; or remix content found online into a new creation."[12] Studies among teenagers in other countries including Iran, The Netherlands, and New Zealand reveal similar findings, showing how the use of media for the majority of people – and especially for those who grew up with game consoles, cell phones, and internet – has become an active act of remixing, bricolage, and "media meshing," which according to a 2005 study commissioned by Yahoo! among teenagers in Chicago, Mexico City, London, Berlin, Seoul, and Shanghai is "a behavioral phenomenon that occurs when people begin an experience in one medium, such as watching television, then shift to another, such as surfing the Internet, and maybe even a third, such as listening to music. The explanation for this behavior is the constant search for complementary information, different perspectives, and even emotional fulfillment."[13] Media meshing is similar to the multitasking behavior researchers find among people of all ages when using media, but includes a distinct element of media co-creation, ranging from the customization of media devices (ringtones, wallpapers, screensavers, channel programming) to the production of fan movies, citizen journalism sites, advertising clips, and computer game modifications.

It is important to note that much of this culturally convergent content not only dissolves the distinctions between the producer and consumer of media, but in many cases also the line institutionally drawn between the professional and the amateur. In this context, using British examples, Charles Leadbeater and Paul Miller (2004) describe the emergence of the "Pro-Am": people pursuing amateur activities with professional standards, using their leisure-time to enthusiastically engage in commercially viable activities in fields as diverse as computer programming, astronomy, technical research, and now, increasingly, cultural production. In 1980, futurist Alvin Toffler predicted the rise of a prosumer economy, considering the release of do-it-yourself pregnancy tests in The Netherlands during the late 1970s the earliest example of such a mixed economy (1980: 275ff). Prior to that, Marshall McLuhan foresaw in 1964 how increasing computerization and automatization would not just affect the production, but also the consumption of media, arguing how the consumer would become a producer in the automation circuit. Citing numerous online examples such as *Wikipedia* and *Ohmynews*, Axel Bruns (2005) goes on to introduce the concept of the "produser" as people who, when online, continually combine some kind of using and producing of information. Such people, for instance, browse and publish websites, read and submit news, receive and process it in private and to their own ends. The key here is a "not only, but also" perspective on media use – people consume and produce information and communication while connected to many others involved in similar media meshing behaviors. Beyond the quest for compelling media experiences people seem to be increasingly willing to participate voluntarily in the mediamaking process to achieve what can be called a networked reputation. By generating discussion and comments to their voluntary work on websites such as Amazon (book reviews) or YouTube (user-submitted videoclips), people are recognized – which indeed at times can lead to a book contract or the chance to work professionally in television. These kind of reputation-based publication mechanisms can be a benefit to the individual, as small business proprietors, independent cultural entrepreneurs, freelancers and aspiring writers or moviemakers can quickly gain an audience and build a positive reputation that hopefully they can translate into actual business opportunities.

The emerging new media ecosystem inspires and is inspired by networks of more or less collaborative end-users – what Von Hippel (2005) calls "user-innovation communities" operating in a media ecosystem that Benkler (2006) describes as "commons-based peer production." There are two types of social networks at work in the media environment today: on the one hand, groups of people create, collaborate, and exchange all kinds of products and information, both online and offline, emphasizing the more or less free sharing of ideas and knowledge. Most contemporary commentators celebrate these kind of communities, seeing in them new hope for the loss of social cohesion and connection experienced in society's traditional institutions. On the other hand we find the commercial media organizations: giant multinational corporations using international copyright legislation to put limits on the free flow of cultural works, benefiting from government deregulation to merge into even larger conglomerates, and exploiting the "free labor" that excited consumers are doing to promote and forward their intellectual property. The culturally convergent practices of media industries, remixing professional content and user-generated content in the creative process, led the *Economist* (of 20 April 2006) to ask the fundamental question: what is a media company? Traditionally, media companies would be seen as audience aggregators: engaging in the production of content aimed as mass audiences. Considering the sketched social, technological, and economical trends, such a definition has become problematic. Instead of "audiences" businesses talk about "networks," emphasizing media work as a practice that would (or should) generate endless opportunities for people to form communities of interest around content. On the one hand this creates interesting dysfunctional family-effects within large media corporations, where some parts of the firm are actively restructuring to meet the demands of what *The Economist* describes as a race to become "the most liquid media marketplace,"[14] while other sectors of the company are still very much in the process of developing intricate Digital Rights Management (DRM) software intended to prevent all this audience activity from actually taking off.

Although it is certainly true that the economic trend in the media industry of the last few decades has seen an exponential increase in the number of media outlets, owned by an ever-declining number of media corporations, that picture is too simple since much of the community-oriented and at times participatory content production in fact takes place within the walls of commercial media conglomerates. Indeed, the social trends and developments emerging in the second half of the twentieth century as outlined earlier – individualization, globalization, hypercapitalism, and the rise of the network society – are implicated in people's increasingly participatory media use, as well as in the gradual embrace of the consumer as co-creator of content by media firms. A participatory media environment fits with our highly individualized workstyle within a networked form of enterprise, where the unpredictable nature of everyday existence demands media that enable people to timeshift, control, and customize their work, life, and play. It also fits with an industry-wide trend towards greater flexibility in production, intensified relationships with consumers, and finding new ways to foster customer loyalty and engagement. This participatory media environment has been further supercharged by the widespread proliferation of networked computers with broadband internet connections at home and in the office, and increasingly the migration of such technologies to handheld mobile devices. Convergence culture thus takes place on both sides of the media spectrum – production and consumption – within which spectrum the distinctions between the traditional roleplayers in the creative process are dissolving.

Conclusion

Pertinent to the concerns in this book are the ways in which media workers are affected by the redrafting of their professional environment as creative industries operating within a globally emerging convergence culture. If convergence is a cultural logic that at its core integrates users and producers in the process of creating mediated experiences, how do the professionals involved give meaning to their productivity, creative autonomy, and professional identity? One way of looking at this focuses on the political economy of multinational media conglomerates, emphasizing their role in rationalizing and routinizing production for the (glocal) masses. Holdings across different media industries have indeed become giants through horizontal and vertical integration, and an ongoing technological integration of different production processes into systems that yield and cross-promote content for different media. The symptomatic business strategy of these multimedia enterprises is, as Espen Aarseth (2006) suggests, to deploy market-driven strategies to redistribute the risk of producing content across multiple media instead of investing in costly stand-alone titles. In this context one could argue that convergence culture plays into the hands of corporations that seek new ways to intensify customer relationships, and cultivate consumer loyalties by captivating people's media use across multiple platforms at the same time. In doing so, the structure and organization of work in such industries effectively constrains the creativity and autonomy of media workers, reducing their labor to the production of more effective means of control over hapless audiences. Although this is a valid concern, it bypasses not only the dominant self-perceptions of media workers, it also ignores the chances an increasingly liquid media marketplace offers to the talent, skills, and resources of individuals or (temporary) teams in the creative process.

This is not to say that commercialization and corporate control do not play a significant role in the lives of media workers – indeed, the necessity of success on the glocal market is a constant element in the decision-making and deliberation processes within media organizations large and small. It must be noted, however, that the creative industries conceptualization of media work does not see business, management, and commerce as necessarily hostile towards creativity, quality, or culture. I would like to acknowledge the inevitable yet potentially stimulating role the symbiosis of creativity and commerce can play in an assessment of contemporary media work. Such an approach recognizes the goals and ideals of corporate management of global enterprises, but draws our attention more specifically to those people directly involved in the process: the media workers. "Being environmentally conscious, showing a social conscience and being a good corporate citizen are viewed in modern management theory as benefiting the bottom line. But this management-speak hides the growing focus in the media professions – the cultural boundary spanners – on genuine links between modern organizations and the different individuals and groups in society that deal with them" (Balnaves et al. 2004, p. 193). Terry Flew (2004) argues how the mass reproduction and distribution of culture is just as much tied into creativity as the seemingly authentic, original, and commerce-free production of the individual artist. To that I would like to add the perspective of media work as creating content as well as connectivity: the creative process in today's media industries not only produces content such as games, movies, shows, and newspapers, it also generates platforms for debate, exchange, and communities. Some of that process serves to reproduce the commercial success of the industry, while other aspects of media work can indeed be seen as new ways of fostering social networks.

If the media in the broadest possible sense are the sites of the struggles over meaning and symbolic exchange in global society, it becomes essential to understand the working lives of the people within the creative industries. It is in these media industries that Simon Cottle describes how "a growing army of media professionals, producers and others work in this expanding sector of the economy, many of them in freelance, temporary, subcontracted and underpaid (and sometimes unpaid) positions [. . .] They are also often at the forefront of processes of organisational change including new flexible work regimes, reflexive corporate cultures, and the introduction of digital technologies, multimedia production and multi-skilled practices" (2003, p. 3). Media professionals – those employed in journalism, marketing communications, advertising, public relations, game development, radio and television production, and the film industry – embody in their workstyles all the themes of social, cultural, and technological change in liquid modern times as expressed in this book. To some extent this has opened up the creative process in the media for technological and economical interventions, particularly regarding the flexibilization of work and the individual autonomy of media professionals.

According to James Curran, "for the vast majority of those employed in the cultural industries, even more than in other industries, flexible specialisation has meant little job security, depressed wages, few employment rights and long hours" (2000, p. 34). Yet the liquid character of today's transnational labor market tends to be seen by some professionals in the cultural and media industries as a plus, supposedly freeing them from the constrains of working for a single employer, on a single project, utilizing a single skill. The cultural field of media production, when seen from an individual workers' perspective, is clearly not an autonomous sphere, devoid of external pressures, influences and constraints – but it should also not be seen as a domain of activity wholly determined, standardized and controlled by the structure and organization of industry, nor by the increasingly prosuming activities of people when using media. It is through the daily interaction of creativity, commerce, content, and connectivity media practitioners give active meaning to their work and professional identity, which in turn shapes the meaning and significance of the various influences on content as it is produced by journalists, advertising creatives, public relations officers and marketing communicators, game developers, and professionals in the radio, television, and film industries.

CHAPTER THREE

Media Professions in a Digital Age

In the constant remix of time spent on work, life, and play in and through media the differences between these spheres of activity get lost. Through the redistribution of risk away from the state or employer to each and every worker, people as individuals become solely responsible and uniquely accountable for running their own lives. The individual, not the firm, has become the organization – a company that needs to be run efficiently and smoothly, where order and control can only be individually established and disciplined to lead one into a supposedly productive and secure future. According to Ulrich Beck, people in this labor context are muddling through as one-man or one-woman businesses, trying to mould a life of their own full of breaks and contradictions, a workstyle supposedly where "everything would be woven together into a quite individual web of activities and employment situations [. . .] forming the basis of a precarious new culture of independence" (2000, p. 55). The media as creative industries – emphasizing individual creativity as a catalyst for commercial cultural production – are the prime example of a sector where its professionals actively manage these kinds of "independent" lives. This does not only refer to the growing numbers of freelancers, part-timers, flexiworkers, or otherwise contingent employees in the media – even though this group of people by all accounts is the dominant force in the media labor market. Even those currently employed fulltime by large and small media firms alike are affected by the shift towards the individual for the responsibility and accountability of the organization of work, as they must also balance the competing demands of creativity versus commerce, of producing content versus exploring opportunities for connectivity, and of translating the accelerated demands of a competitive, technology driven, and liquefied work environment into meaningful actions, values, and ideas that combined would constitute one's professional identity as media worker.

Maurizio Lazzarato (1997) suggests that creativity and productivity in postindustrial societies reside in the dialectic between the forms of life and values they produce, and in the activities of subjects that constitute them. In doing so, Lazzarato points towards a key consideration for a respectful understanding of the role of the individual in today's media industries: the crucial importance of agency and choice for individuals facing a vast array of influences, pressures, pleasures, and constraints. Are the attitudes, behaviors, and choices of an individual simply a product of socialization into the existing order of things, or can her goals, ideas, and actions be considered to be more or less independent of the way things work in existing companies or organizations? To opt either way would be too easy, as it would ignore the enormous diversity in organizations, companies, workstyles, and practices available in the industry today. To argue, as Anthony Giddens (1984) does, that all human social activities are recursive – simply put: whatever people do in a certain way produces routines, rules and norms that in turn inspire people to do things in a certain way – seems fruitful. Research on how journalists make editorial decisions in newsrooms or how project teams in advertising agencies organize the creative process for particular clients provides evidence for this approach, showing how people in such organizations over time tend to commit to patterned behaviors, thereby "routinizing the unexpected" as Gaye Tuchman originally argued in 1973. Tuchman's seminal work among journalists at a local independent television station and a daily morning newspaper showed how they based their decisions and actions on the way work was patterned and structured within the news organization, rather than on individual or collective deliberations unique to every decision that needed to be made. Even though Tuchman's research has been repeated in other media institutions with similar results, it seems to fit rather awkwardly with the current dogma of flexible production, increasing precariousness of employment arrangements, a globally emerging convergence culture, and an all-consuming shift of responsibility and accountability towards the individual.

Paul du Gay (1996) noted how in the field of cultural production managers and employers increasingly stress the importance of "enterprise" as an individual rather than organizational or firm-based attribute. This does not mean that such a notion of the enterprising self is simply or unproblematically accepted by workers. Shifting the notion of enterprise – with its connotations of efficiency, productivity, empowerment and autonomy – from the company to the individual employee, it becomes part of the professional identity of each and every worker, however contingently employed or not. John Storey and colleagues see this shift as a deliberate managerial attempt to regulate professional identity as a form of organizational control, with the intent "to reconstitute workers as more adaptable, flexible, and willing to move between activities and assignments and to take responsibility for their own actions and their successes and failures" (2005, p. 1036). As noted in the first chapter, this shift towards an individualization of labor counters the historical trend towards socialization and salarization, instead favoring more fluid and flexible notions of work – ushered in through rapid developments in technologies of communication, a decentralization of management practices, and the fragmentation of markets. These trends are arguably experienced most directly by professionals in the various media industries. This does not mean that newcomers in the media are not asked anymore to adapt themselves to existing ways of doing things, nor that professionals are not expecting regular salaries for their work. It does suggest, however, that socialization today is quite different from the industrial master–apprentice model, where the aspiring practitioner would dutifully observe and copy an existing consensus-driven creative process.

In the contemporary setting – where media work gets done primarily in the context of temporary teams, outsourced or subcontracted assignments, using contingent labor – socialization functions through one's effective participation in informal networks, whereas one's fee is largely determined by the successful completion of the job at hand, using a skill that is unique and particular to for example the deliverable or asset one is asked to produce. Research throughout Europe during the late 1990s in the context of the Information for Cultural Industries Support Services (ICISS) program for example suggests how participation in (in-)formal, local and global, dynamic, strong, and supportive networks is crucial for employment and survival in the media.[1] However, researchers also found that this kind of networking is not an inclusive practice, where women and ethnic minorities in particular tend to get excluded or marginalized through elitist, nepotistic, and cliquish networking practices with high (and informal, therefore hard to articulate or challenge) barriers of entry.

Considering this individualized, informal, and contingent context of media work, we have to rethink the notion of "organization" as the operational framework for analyzing what it is like to work in the media. In recent years, scholars in the fields of organization science have gradually shifted their emphasis on explaining the behavior of organizations as entities in themselves, embracing organizations as "open systems" of interdependent activities linking shifting coalitions of participants in interorganizational networks (Baker and Faulkner 2005). On the one hand, such an open approach enables us to look at organizations as loosely integrated units of individuals working together temporarily – which seems to fit the realities of the contemporary character of media work – while on the other hand it allows for the equally necessary acknowledgement that still much of the work in the media gets done within the context of large, hierarchical, and bureaucratic businesses. Although much of the work in the media takes place within the walls of media organizations, using the organization as an operational definition of the context of media work would miss the lived realities of contemporary workstyles: media work takes place on an individual level, often within the context of a team, a group or department of a larger organization – which teams or groups increasingly are not necessarily located in the same building, city, or country. Considering the contemporary trends of increasing casualization of work and the globaliza- tion of markets for cultural and symbolic goods, a coherent conceptualization of media work has to look outside the his- torical boundaries of the organization to adequately address the working lives of its professionals. With the globalization of distribution and marketing of media has come a transnation- alization of cultural production, supercharged by outsourcing and offshoring management practices.

The New International Division of Cultural Labor

In a sobering recapitulation of worldwide developments in the creative industries, William Uricchio writes that: "In the US, as in the rest of the world, (commercial) creative industries are more concentrated than ever, steadily sharpening their under- standing of the possibilities of convergent media systems [. . .] Consistent with this, expansion (globalization) has been the rule [. . .]" (2004, p. 83). Thomas Eisenmann and Joseph Bower (2000) call this the emergence of the entrepreneurial "M-Form," describing the pitfalls and opportunities for either top-down or bottom-up management in increasingly large, complex, multidivisional (M) global media firms. The conse- quences of this increasingly global operational space of media conglomerates for the professionals involved are quite funda- mental. The creative industries production system, much like the rest of the media ecology, is becoming more individualized and globally integrated at the same time. In an attempt to understand and map the connections between globalizing processes, as embodied in the production networks of multinational corporations and development in specific cities and regions, British economic geographers use a Global Production Networks (GPN) approach (Coe *et al.* 2004).[2] Using this approach, the media are seen as part of a globally organized nexus of interconnected functions and operations by firms and non-firm institutions through which goods and services are produced and distributed. For the purposes of this book, it is important to note how the GPN approach both acknowledges the importance of looking at media work from a cross-national perspective, as well as framing an analysis of media work from the perspective of the individual professional in the creative process. Jennifer Johns, for example, identifies three key elements in the GPN framework: "how value is created, enhanced and captured, how power is created and maintained within the production network, and how agents and structures are embedded in particular territories" (2006, p. 153).

Although useful for a macro understanding of the trends and development influencing the structure and organization of creative industries, the GPN perspective leaves something to be considered when it comes to specific analyses of the lived realities of media workers. It is in this context that Toby Miller and Marie-Claire Leger (2001) developed a critique of the emerging global production workflow in creative industries, terming this approach The New International Division of Cultural Labor (NIDCL). Of particular interest for the NIDCL perspective is the central role flexible cultural labor plays in the global cultural economy. The NIDCL approach suggests that we critically consider what issues such as rampant globalization, the rise of the entertainment economy, the triumph of popular culture over civil society and the dominance of the neo-liberal discourse of market-driven "free trade" might in fact mean for the people directly involved. Basing their analyses primarily on the international production system of the film and television industries, Miller and Leger (2001) show that co-production arrangements are now well established between US firms and French, British, Swedish, Australian, and Italian companies, with connections to television, theme parks, cabling, satellite, home video, and the internet. In each instance they address the crucial role government deregulation, tax cuts, and subsidies play in attracting media production, marketing, and distribution to particular locales all over globe. In a critical assessment of the global Hollywood production system, Miller and colleagues for example note that within this context, "workers and bosses strike complex, transitory arrangements on a project basis via temporary organisations, with small numbers of diverse hands involved at each stage other than production, when sizeable crews function both together and semi-autonomously" (Miller *et al.* 2005, p. 114). This complex international division of cultural production continues to increase the distance between creative labor and the final product, Miller argues, creating a disconnect – both creatively as well as financially – between the work media professionals do and the final fruits of their productivity. Simultaneously, the production of culture in the creative industries cannot be separated anymore from the work of individuals, in particular in terms of what media work means to the professional identities and workstyles of the people directly contributing to the creative process.

The solution to the recurring dilemma of institutional structure and individual agency in the production of culture lies in understanding media conglomerates, organizations, and even temporary project-based collaborative networks as "inhabited institutions," where people do things together and in doing so continuously struggle for symbolic power within their respective fields of work. Tim Hallett and Mark Ventresca (2006) describe this inhabited institutions approach as on the one hand accepting that institutions provide the raw materials and guidelines for social interactions, and on the other hand, that the meanings of institutions and the work taking place in (and for) institutions are constructed and propelled forward by social interactions. Organizations, whether seen as enterprising individuals or multinational corporations, are dynamic entities, within which people constantly move in and out of their roles as consumers and producers, and where the production of culture is built on the particular workstyles of media workers.

The Production of Culture

It must be clear that the media worker operates in a complex environment, somewhere between the splendid isolation of one's individual creative endeavors and a constantly changing transnational context of ties, relationships, demands, and pressures of colleagues, consumers, employers, and clients. This must be the point of entry to discuss the infrastructure, trends and developments affecting individual practitioners in (and outside of) media companies. The creative process of work in the media industries refers to patterns of behaviour – not so much the acts in themselves, but the characteristics and meaning of these acts. This means that neither the individual, nor the big corporation completely controls the production of culture – elements of social structure (the organization of work, the parameters set by time, budget and space, media ownership, and so on) and the norms, values, and ways of doing things of the professionals involved mutually influence each other. Indeed, cultural and economic concerns are not necessarily different, but in the context of media work rather must be seen as what Liz McFall calls "constituent material practice" (2004, p. 18): the combination of specific technical and organizational arrangements as these influence and are shaped by the generally idiosyncratic habits of individual media practitioners. An emphasis on the individualistic and idiosyncratic nature of media workers suggests that contemporary trends such as workforce casualization, technological and cultural convergence, and flexible productivity not only mean different things to different people, but are also differently articulated in the context of specific media products, genres, and organizations because of the ways in which departments, teams and individuals work together.

Surveying the landscape of cultural production, David Hesmondhalgh (2002, p. 171) concludes that a rather loose control of creativity is at the core of managerial practices in media companies. James Curran on the other hand signals how "individual autonomy has in fact declined for many people working in the media industries" (2000, p. 33). It must be clear, that autonomy is an important, individual-level and thus particular concept in media work: it both refers to the level of control over one's career, and the (real or perceived) ability one has in making more or less independent decisions in the creative process of producing media. McFall (2002) argues how in this way the meaning of media work can be understood as based both in semantics and pragmatics – in what certain ways of doing things mean to the professionals involved, and how things are done in certain ways to achieve specific goals and objectives. Considering these remarks I thus describe, analyze, and interpret media work from the perspective of the individual media practitioner, looking at the organization of the creative process in the media industry in terms of how this determines the workstyle of each person within that industry.

In general, media work can be seen as a particular instance of the production of culture as it takes place both within and outside of institutions, by both professionals and amateurs, both within and across particular media. In the following chapters, I offer detailed reviews of the production of culture in the domains of journalism, advertising, public relations and marketing communications, film and television production, and game development. As an initial mapping tool I use the production of culture perspective as developed by Richard Peterson and Narasimhan Anand (2004). Such a production of culture perspective considers the various ways in which the professionals of culture and creative industries use, innovate, and give meaning to technologies, laws and regulation, industrial and organizational structure, their occupational careers, and the markets (or: audiences) they intend to serve. This approach underscores the argument that the social process among people and institutions through which cultural goods and services – such as news, advertising, movies, television shows, and video games – are produced influences their content. The production of culture perspective also makes it possible to draw comparisons across the diverse sites of culture creation. My investigation of the structure and contemporary trends and issues in the different media sectors follows their "production nexus," discussing how similar changes in the role of for example new information and communication technologies and the relationships with consumers affect (and are influenced by) the work of media professionals.

Technologies. Regarding the significant role of technology in media work, it is important to understand how technology automates as well as augments media practitioners' abilities to communicate, create, interact, and distribute. In doing so, the work done in media industries further supercharges the developments of new technologies – the necessity to accelerate the copying of books (especially the Bible) inspired the development of the printing press, the expanding market for television increased the need for smaller video cameras, and the success of video games in conjunction with the emerging market for desktop personal computers spurred the design of sophisticated video graphics cards. On the other hand, technologies also influence the work professionals (can) do, such as the ongoing convergence of different media formats due to digitalization, the opening up of new markets and modes of interaction by disseminating media products online, and overall a directly felt acceleration of work practices as the use of new technologies such as sophisticated content management systems in media organizations speeds up creative processes.

In 2004, the International Labour Organization (ILO) released an extensive study and report on the future of work and quality of life in the Media, Culture and Graphical sector, particularly focusing on the role and impact of information and communication technologies in the sector.[3] Among the many conclusions drawn in the report, the ILO addresses the consequences of technologies for jobs and employment in the media in detail: "In relation to jobs, there have been major shifts in the composition of employment across the sector as a result of technological change – including growth in some areas and occupations, some relocation of work to other countries or sectors, and cutbacks in employment in specific segments and occupations" (p. 14). The report also signals how because of the growing concentration and specialization of media and entertainment businesses – a trend in part facilitated by new, internationally networked information and communication technologies – some workers may accept contracts with lower pay and poorer conditions than in the past, rather than have no work at all. The rapid advances and developments in Information and Communication Technology (ICT) also introduce a fast-paced reskilling, deskilling, and multiskilling practice to media work, as employees have to adapt and retrain themselves continuously to meet the new or changing technological requirements on the job – a need for training that only few employers effectively address, according to the ILO report. It is certain that the introduction of new technologies has disruptive effects on established ways of doing things, and that technology has the potential both to augment as well as automate human actions in the contemporary enterprise (Dutton *et al.* 2004). It is crucial to note here that the role of technology in media work is significant, but cannot be seen as exclusive to further the cost-efficient exploitation agenda of employers and managers – nor should it be uncritically heralded as ushering in a new era of collaborative, networked and flexible productivity. It remains important, as Rob Kling (1996) in particular has noted, to focus on the ongoing computerization of society as it is actually practiced and experienced.

In recent years, new media technologies like the internet have made visible what was practically hidden from the sight of media professional producers: the participatory engagement of people with their media as, for example, shown through the popularity of social software and personal media production through weblogs, fan communities, and mashups (websites or web applications that use content from more than one source to create a completely new service). As media companies are beginning to integrate the emerging creativity of producing consumers this in turn changes the ways of doing things for media professionals, who now have to find ways to incorporate their audiences as colleagues in the creative process. One has to conclude that people are using more media than ever before in history, yet this intensive engagement with media does not translate into more attention paid exclusively as consumers to the content and storytelling experiences generally offered by the typical media professions (such as journalism, advertising, and television production). Inspired and armed with new, digital, networked, and easy-to-use technologies, people are either making their own media, or claim their agency in customizing, modifying, and remixing existing content. This is a problem – at least for media companies who traditionally based their income and profit margins on the selling of content to audiences (or the selling of audiences to advertisers), and for those media workers whose rationale for doing what they do has been entirely based on the assumption of a (mass) audience existing somewhere "out there."

Laws and Regulation. The work of the creative industries has always been shaped, influenced, enabled and to some extent restricted or censored by laws and regulations. Consider for example the different rating systems for violent or graphic movies and videogames in Japan, Europe, and the United States – influencing the decisions made by the companies involved about what kind of products to release in the various international markets, and increasing the need for careful localization of such products. As argued earlier Miller (*et al.* 2005) in particular shows how local, regional, and national governments actively intervene in the production of culture by cutting taxes for media firms outsourcing work to their locales, by introducing all kinds of subsidies to protect their respective media industries, and by including media into cultural policies aimed directly at bolstering the economic output of a country (such as film and television in EU countries, or computer and video games in South-East Asian nations).

Intellectual property is the crucial element in the production of culture. Intellectual property rights protect as well as limit the range of possible markets and applications of cultural products. The current system of copyright protection tends to be favored by transnational corporations and Western governments, as it provides incentives for corporations to invest in artists and franchises with the certainty of control over the marketing, distribution, and consumption of the products. Restrictive copyrights allow artists and publishers (or their investors) to collect revenue on each song played on the radio, and each game or movie sold. Several legal and media scholars argue that such a system is flawed, in that it restricts the emerging practices of collaborative production and "prosumer" type co-creation. Lawrence Lessig (2001) is among many law scholars who call for a new form of international intellectual rights legislation – expressing the need for a new copyright system that would enable and protect all kinds of collaborative cultural production – from folklore via fan fiction to remixed music and video mashups. Such a positive intellectual rights would shift the focus from restricted usage to enabling societal exchange, a process actively advocated by Yochai Benkler (2006) and others. On the other hand, Henry Jenkins observes how in today's global media environment "every important story gets told, every brand gets sold, and every consumer gets courted across multiple media platforms" (2006, p. 3), both through at times equally powerful corporate strategies, or via tactics of grassroots appropriation. Again, it is important to note how the same element in the production of culture facilitates different and sometimes paradoxical interpretations and effects on the way media professionals (can) do their work, underscoring the need for looking at what these issues mean to the people directly involved in the creative process.

Organizational Structure. As Robert McChesney and Dan Schiller (2003) remind us, the same communication technologies that enable interactivity and participation have been deployed throughout the 1980s and 1990s to foster the entrenchment and growth of a transnational corporate-commercial global media system that can be said to be anything but transparent, interactive or participatory. Ben Bagdikian (2004) goes as far as to argue that only five huge corporations control most of the media industry in the United States. This "control" must not be exaggerated however, and Ben Compaine (2005) among others presents compelling evidence that world-wide media consolidation and increased diversity of choice and competition in the production and distribution of content are not anathema. These trends must be seen as co-existing, mutually enabling, and symbiotic. The organizational structure of the creative industries tends to include both a few vertically integrated oligarchical firms as well as many small competing firms producing a diversity of products, services and applications. The parameters for opportunities and constraints for media companies large and small either to merge, collaborate, or go more or less "independent" (such as is the case in the film and music sectors) are set by national governments.

The dominant regulatory trend worldwide has been an ongoing relaxation of laws prohibiting the concentration of media ownerships, thus enabling the vertical integration of big media companies. However, the rapid developments in flexible production and new communication, creation, and distribution technologies also facilitated the proliferation of many smaller companies and cultural entrepreneurs able to provide customizable and niche services to the more rigid and bureaucratically structured multinational media businesses. In order to make the transition towards a more flexible type of production large conglomerates in recent years have tended to reorganize themselves into multiple smaller units, or have shifted towards a more decentralized, team-based managerial and working style – significantly flattening the existing hierarchies in the company. At the same time recent case studies suggest that within many of these conglomerates the sharing of knowledge or cross-fertilization of ideas and projects is in fact quite minimal, and tends not so much to depend on structural intra-firm relationships (in business jargon: "synergies"), but rather on personal, informal, and indeed emotional personal networks (Grabher and Ibert 2006).

Media work tends to get caught between two oppositional structural factors in producing culture within media organizations: on the one hand, practitioners are expected to produce, edit, and publish content that has proven its value on a mass market – which pressure encourages standardized and predictable formats using accepted genre conventions, formulas, and routines – while creative workers on the other hand can be expected (and tend to personally favor) to come up with innovative, novel, and surprising products. Following Peterson and Anand (2004), this structural ambiguity and uncertainty in media work gets translated in two institutional logics that govern organizational decisionmaking either way: an editorial logic and a market logic. Working in an organization using an editorial logic, media professionals tend more or less to ignore the shifting wants and needs of the audience in favor of producing content that holds up to peer review, wins trade awards (such as the Oscars in the film industry, a Pullitzer Prize in journalism, the Game Developer Choice awards, or the Golden Lion in advertising), and builds prestige and acknowledgement throughout the industry. A market logic on the other hand embraces a competitive way of doing things, creating content for as wide an audience as possible, and thus favoring a strictly commercial – Turner (2003) would say: linear –

mass audience approach to making decisions in the creative process. Richard Caves (2000) suggests that a market logic – which is more typical of the few integrated multinational companies in the creative industries – generally produces the most lucrative content, whereas an editorial logic – more particular to smaller businesses – results in the most innovative content.

Considering the work by Henry Jenkins (2006) and others on the increasing role of the consumer as collaborator or co-creator of media content, I have to conclude that a possible third institutional logic is emerging next to, and in a symbiotic relationship with, editorial and market logics: a convergence culture logic. Work done following this logic includes the (intended) consumer in the process of product design and innovation, up to and including the production and marketing process. The work of authors in fields as varied as management theory, product design, journalism studies, and advertising define media content in this context interchangeably as: consumer-generated, customer-controlled, or user-directed. According to Jenkins, this shift towards a more inclusive production process makes perfect sense for media companies, as they can use the increasing participatory nature of media use to foster consumer loyalty and generate low-cost content. In a July 19, 2006 post to his weblog, Jenkins shares his experience and research on the different responses of the creative and business sides of media companies to the idea of user generated content in an increasingly participatory media culture: "For the creative, the fear is a corruption of their artistic integrity as they turn over greater control over the shape of their work to its future consumers. This reflects [. . .] an editorial logic. For the business side, the greatest fear is the idea that consumers might take something they made and not pay them for it. That's the extension of the market logic. Both may need to rethink their position if media companies are going to benefit from the work of [consumers as co-creators of content, MD], who can both appreciate the value of an intellectual property and extend its shelf life. And it is the neat fit between the

Editorial and Market Logics which insures that many media companies will adopt prohibitionist rather than collaborationist approaches in the short term."[4]

Occupational Careers. Peterson and Anand identify two typical careers of professionals in the media. The first is a top-down career, largely established through lifelong participation in vertically structured institutions, where seniority, experience, and a transparent system of salaries guide the professional towards higher positions in the office hierarchy. In more competitive environments where the organization of work is tailored towards flexible production, "careers tend to be chaotic and foster cultural innovation, and career-building market-sensing entrepreneurs enact careers from the 'bottom up' by starting from the margins of existing professions and conventions" (2004, p. 317). As argued earlier, the workstyles of contemporary media professionals are consistent with a portfolio worklife, where the everyday reality for most media workers and especially newcomers consists of a rather restless combination of network socialization, deskilling (unlearning old skills), reskilling (training on-the-job skills) and preparing for the (potential) next job, coupled with an all-encompassing emphasis on creating, sustaining, and mining personal knowledge networks of colleagues, clients, and customers.

Following the work on global trends in flexible labor of Alan Felstead and Nick Jewson (1999), the key to understanding occupational careers in knowledge-intensive creative industries is the practice of workforce flexibility, which flexibility in the workplace has four main variants: functional, numerical, temporal, and financial. Functional flexibility relates to the division of the workforce in a multi-skilled "core," consisting of privileged professionals enjoying greater job security and career development performing many different tasks throughout the organization, and a "periphery" of professionals. The peripheral group tends to be temporarily employed in subcontracted or outsourcing arrangements, and consists mainly of freelancers. In broadcast production (of news and entertainment television shows) such a peripheral group can be quite substantial, where professionals compete with each other for assignments. This in turn shifts the control over labor to the company, as workers compete for employment rather than employers compete for talented, skilled workers. International figures and estimates by the International Federation of Journalists (IFJ) suggest that such a rotating core group of newsworkers is increasingly supplemented by a growing group of so-called "atypical workers" – freelancers, casuals, short-term workers on rolling contracts, and temporary workers – who supply stories, leads, and ideas on a contingent basis.[5] In print journalism functional flexibility is primarily achieved through job rotation, where reporters move from department to department, or even from newspaper to newspaper – especially in the current situation around the world where the vast majority of newspapers in a country are part of large group holdings. Job rotation in newspaper chains and broadcast networks in the United States has led to the situation, that a majority of reporters for local media in fact do not come from the communities they report on. Another consequence of the concentration of media ownership and increasing functional flexibility of media work is the clustering of professionals in a few urban centers – a tendency especially felt in journalism, as the number of foreign or regional correspondents dwindle and reporters for newspaper chains, magazine publishers, and television networks converge in the major cities of their home countries.

In other businesses job rotation – the systematic movement of employees from one job to another within an organization or between organizations, usually to a new position for a fixed period of time and then back to the former position – has led to increased stress among the workers involved, as well as for the co-workers with which the rotating employee has to build a new network. On the other hand, research among converging newsrooms – where formerly distinct news operations in broadcast, print and online media are expected to come together and collaborate – shows that participants feel the experience can provide a broader perspective on the profession, stimulates their careers, and gives them a sense of agency in where the industry is heading (Singer 2004; Silcock and Keith 2006). In the course of the twentieth century, advertising agencies have seen a comparable trend towards becoming full-service companies, offering expertise to clients that ranges across disciplines as varied as account planning, management, media buying, creative work and production, sales promotion, public relations, and marketing communications across multiple media (in recent years increasingly including viral marketing and interactive advertising primarily using cell phones and internet). Within such full-service and often international agency conglomerates teams consisting of professionals with a wide variety of skills (such as copywriters, art directors, media planners, database technicians, and marketing designers) are continually assembled, disassembled and reassembled to meet the needs of certain clients or specific projects. Such integrated communications tend be heralded as the "next big thing" in solving some of the advertising business' problems. On the other hand, as Joep Cornelissen (2002 and 2003) argues, there exists a wide gap between integrated marketing communications theory and the "theories-in-use" by practitioners in the field. Cornelissen concludes that in real-world, everyday working practices a supposedly seamless transition towards integrated, multi-disciplinary and flexible teamwork is a great deal more complex, unruly, and uncertain, thus effectively showing how the discourse of functional flexibility in media work primarily serves ideological purposes that benefit owners (and theorists) of the advertising, marketing, and public relations industries.

Numerical flexibility is associated with the creative use of workforce numbers to manage more effectively the organization, which in media companies primarily means assigning the creative process to teams, mainly consisting of a combination of specialist temporary employees and a couple of core workers with flexible, individualized contracts. Caves (2000) for example shows how demand uncertainty shifted the Hollywood film industry from organizing teams under long-term contracts within a firm to per-project contracts. Such limited life project-based work supposedly harmonizes and coordinates team members' interests, and sequences product stages. The status of these temporary teamworkers – generally hired in periods of high demand of a specific skillset – tends to be less privileged and protected as their colleagues. However, trade unions have been quite successful in organizing the self-employed – such as specific technicians, programmers, correspondents, actors, musicians, and writers. This has meant that freelancers have long been able to demand certain guarantees and securities in dealing with a highly volatile and competitive industry, such as movie production studios. However, trade unions in the media are in a difficult position, often ending up negotiating forced retirement, pay cuts or benefit-reducing packages for their members in situations where companies undergoing managerial shifts try to minimize the numbers of core employees, and increase opportunities for flexible productivity.

Temporal flexibility in media careers refers to a lack of dependable, well-organized working schedules. The "nine to five" office is a thing of the past – not just because the market for media products and services is always on, or local and global at the same time, but also because of the dependence of these industries on creativity, which is a talent that generally resists imposed or neatly structured working hours. As one poster on *Gamewatch* – an online discussion forum for professionals in the computer and video game industry – exclaimed (in a post dated April 30, 2006): "Everyone making games does highly creative work, even programmers, and you could liken all of the games-related work to art. How do you treat an artist? Do you sit him down, take away all distractions, give him 8-hour day with set hours, and say 'paint the next Mona Lisa'? If you do, you have no understanding of what it means to do art."[6] On the other hand, it can be argued that the relaxation of nine-to-five working hours in favor of working overtime and weekends, as well as working at home benefits further exploitation of the workforce, encouraging a flexibility and efficiency-driven remix of the work–life balance (Perrons 2003).

If one couples the sometimes enforced, sometimes voluntary arrangement of work-time with the largely informal, dispersed, and networked nature of organization throughout the creative industries, it becomes clear that temporal flexibility is a staple of all occupational careers of media workers. In the workplace this translates, for example, into debates about unpaid overtime and compensatory time: getting some time off upon completion of a certain project (such as a videogame). The interdependent issues of corporate pressures, unpaid overtime, creative work, and intense producer–consumer relationships bears upon all media industries, but are particularly prevalent in the work game developers do. In April 2006 a two-year legal story came to conclusion involving quality of life issues for gameworkers. Industry giant Electronic Arts (EA) settled two lawsuits regarding unpaid overtime for millions of dollars. These lawsuits are the tip of an iceberg that not only involves EA, but stretches across the game and indeed the entire media industry to some extent. EA is one of a number of game companies hit with lawsuits in recent years for demanding gruelling hours without paying overtime. What makes this case especially relevant is the fact that EA is the industry's biggest publisher, developer and distributor, with studios in Redwood Shores, Los Angeles, Orlando, and Chicago (all in the US), Vancouver, Montreal (Canada), Chertsey (UK), and Tokyo (Japan). The company claims to employ more than 4,100 people in its various development teams.

The game industry has its own benchmark case regarding temporal flexibility of work: the so-called "EA_Spouse" case. On November 10, 2004, Erin Hoffman – using the pseudonym *EA_Spouse* – posted a long comment on the group weblog

LiveJournal about what life was like for her and her husband as game developers working for EA, citing 90-hour workweeks, no comp time, and no paid overtime: "No one works in the game industry unless they love what they do. No one on that team is interested in producing an inferior product. My heart bleeds for this team precisely *because* they are brilliant, talented individuals out to create something great. They are and were more than willing to work hard for the success of the title. But that good will has only been met with abuse."[7] After the court rulings in April 2006, Hoffman signalled a turnaround at EA (and indeed at other game studios) on the *Gamewatch* forum: "I've been trying to poke around and talk to people and I was really, really glad to hear that things have turned around at EALA. I meant every word when I said that you guys were way too freaking brilliant and wonderful to continue suffering like you were. It wasn't smart and it wasn't fair. Kudos to EA indeed for turning it around, and here's hoping that they stay on track."[8]

Finally, occupational careers in the media industries can to some extent also be characterized by a high degree of financial flexibility – a move away from single and uniform payment systems towards more individualized and performance-based systems of rewards and remunerations. An increase in wage-inequalities coupled with decentralized decision-making in (transnational) networked enterprises emerged in most of the "overdeveloped" capitalist world during the 1980s and 1990s, and can be particularly observed in the (new) media and telecommunications industries (Katz and Darbishire 2000). Media companies have been described as rather typical "meritocratic" organizations, stressing talent, networking skills and knowledge-intensive competences, rather than traditional benchmarks such as seniority or experience, as markers for success. This in turn builds upon and reinforces the aggressively competitive nature of the media industry as a whole, leading to large inequalities of income and wealth among its workers as a function of merit.

In this context it is important to note how studies among media workers in various professions consistently suggest that pay is one of the weakest predictors of job satisfaction, as for example David Weaver (1998, p. 461–464) reports in an overview of surveys among journalists in twenty-two countries. Indeed, most reports show how intrinsic motivators – peer acknowledgement, status, prestige – are valued mostly by workers in the creative industries. On the other hand, studies among media professionals as collected by for example James Curran (2000) and Jeremy Tunstall (2001) signal a general lack of evaluative discussions or feedback in the work environment. Richard Sennett (1998), when briefly describing the advertising industry in New York, also notes the absence of clear indicators suggesting to employees that they have done a good (or bad) job. Sennett thus considers the ways the advertising firm – and indeed the media business as a whole – operates as "mysterious" (p. 78) and "unusually fluid and superficial" (p. 80). The literature on journalism and advertising suggests that ultimately these media workers seek recognition and acclaim from their colleagues and not necessarily from citizens or consumers. This would suggest that the formal and informal management of interpersonal and collegial communication and collaboration is among the most important assets of running a media company – which is anything but true.

In a study among ninety newspapers in the United States, researchers found that the vast majority of reporters and editors said their newspapers did not have in place good people-management practices, citing a lack of training and upgrading opportunities, the exclusion of employees in decision-making processes on the future of the company, and low retention rates (especially of younger journalists, women, and minorities).[9] Industry observers furthermore like to point to the managerial fiasco's of the mergers of giant media and telecommunication companies, such as America On-Line (AOL) and Time-Warner, or between Vivendi and Universal as additional indicators of how badly managed media businesses can be. This sentiment is echoed throughout the various literatures on different media enterprises, where for example Eric Mower, in writing about the management of advertising agencies, concludes that "the agency business has become increasingly demanding and stressful [. . .] Even though this increased level of difficulty is not only manageable by competent people but often welcomed as stimulating and beneficial, it still takes an unnecessary toll. Much of the burden borne each day by those at every level of the agency organization comes as the result of management's inability to deal effectively with forces that buffet people, process, and, ultimately, individual and organizational perform-ance" (1999, p. 22). A comprehensive 2004 report by the International Game Developers Association (IGDA) on the organization of work in the computer and video game industry overwhelmingly registered complaints about quality of man-agement. As the authors of the report remark regarding the lack of management training in the industry: "all too often do we see very good developers become unhappy leads, or profes-sional managers/producers whose very useful skills are sneered at by non-developers who feel that the managers don't know what they're talking about because they have never pro-grammed a game" (p. 49).[10]

Financial rewards are, if anything, less of an issue for media workers than less quantifiable– and some would say, there-fore easier exploitable – notions of "feeling good" on the job. It is striking to witness how especially newcomers in the media industries often take low pay and lack of benefits for granted when seeking employment. As reported by the International Labour Organization (ILO), it is important to note that the acceptance of lower pay is not necessarily a vol-untary act, but can for example in the broadcasting and film industries also be attributed to the power of multinational conglomerates. The internationalization and networked form of enterprise in cultural production allow such companies to bypass local union agreements or national regulatory frame-works regarding the rights and benefits structures for professionals in the creative industries, thus further undermining the collective bargaining powers such unionization may have offered in the past.

Markets. Applying the "Pareto Principle" or "80–20" rule, Richard Caves signals how a major problem in the creative industries is the huge failure rate: the vast majority of all cultural products fail to recover their costs.[11] Caves emphasizes that in the creative industries nobody knows what will be successful, and that everyone accepts that few products will end up paying the bills for the rest. In recent years, Chris Anderson (2006) has been among those who indicate how the digital networked form of production and distribution challenges such business models. Anderson calls this "The Long Tail" of the new economy, arguing how in a world where people can download or use media products from anywhere the cumulative sales and uses of the 80 percent can outnumber or outweigh the initial 20 percent portion, such that in aggregate they comprise the majority. The business model of Web-based retailer Amazon is a clear example of this, where little-known authors, obscure movies, and alternative music artists together sell more products than the latest instalment in the Harry Potter franchise or a new album by U2. Anderson argues that "we have historically looked at the market at the head of the curve in isolation, and we can now shift our gaze to the right and see that the tail is another market."[12] For media workers in different industries this has opened up many new opportunities for exploring and exploiting their creative potential, as there might be a market for even the most marginal taste or interest. On the other hand, the production process of media work has become even more unpredictable than it already was. This is not to say that major motion picture studios are not able to produce huge international blockbuster hits anymore, nor that advertising companies cannot seem to generate campaigns that have a tremendous effect on people's memory and recall. It does mean, that such successes are much more temporary, unpredictable, and few and far between than in the past, and require increasingly flexible and market-driven production processes.

A second important aspect of the role of the market in media work is the external evaluation of success or failure in terms of ratings (film and television), sales figures and subscriptions (print media and games), and attention or "eyeballs" (advertising, marketing, and public relations). All of these aspects of media work are strictly determined by the market and tend to be despised, denounced, ignored, lamented, or criticized by practitioners involved in the creative process (see for example McManus 1994). This indicates a deep rift in the industry, as top-level management tends to work according to a market logic, whereas creative professionals seem more comfortable embracing an editorial logic in their work. This is, as argued earlier, an all-too-easily embraced model of the production of culture as an ongoing conflict between the "suits" and the "artists," whereas both aspects of creativity are at best a plural creation derived from cultural notions, personal networks, financial and aesthetic judgment calls, particular routines, and socialization regimes (du Gay and Pryke 2002). To understand media work we must go beyond what McFall (2004, p. 15) calls "undoubtedly convenient" thinking in terms of clear boundaries between creativity and commerce, or between culture and economy. Indeed, if anything, the conflicts within media organizations can be better explained (and found) by looking at the often contested relationships between creativity – of producers, marketers, writers, technicians, and so on – and creative control, rather than between creativity and the market (Lampel, Lant, and Shamsie 2000).

Considering an emerging new logic inspired by convergence culture, a market sensibility in media work could foster new kinds of (co-)creative relationships between traditionally largely separate groups of producers and consumers. Beyond the boundaries of flexible firms and networked enterprises an earlier mentioned convergence culture of professional and amateur production must also be taken into consideration

here. Some call this the emergence of a "networked public culture" (Russell *et al.* 2006), which to some extent is non-market,
not-for-profit, and collaborative in character. The jury is out as
to what extent these trends influence the opportunities for
creative autonomy or innovative work in the creative industries, but it must be clear that the professional identities of
media workers are significantly disrupted, challenged, and
changed by the rapid developments in "glocal" markets and
technologies (Deuze 2005a).

Media Work and Media Logic

In order to describe and analyze adequately the various ways in
which practitioners in the different media professions under
investigation – journalism, advertising, public relations and
marketing communications, film and television production,
and game development – are affected by and give meaning to
the sketched developments in the production of culture, one
needs a holistic, integrated perspective on the nature of media
work. In this context I use the concept of "media logic" as
taken up and developed by Peter Dahlgren, where it refers to
"the particular institutionally structured features of a medium,
the ensemble of technical and organizational attributes which
impact on what gets represented in the medium and how it
gets done. In other words, media logic points to specific forms
and processes which organize the work done within a particular medium. Yet, media logic also indicates the cultural competence and frames of perception of audiences/users, which
in turn reinforces how production within the medium takes
place" (1996, p. 63).[13] Media logic can be medium-specific
because it primarily relates to production patterns within a
given technological and organizational context. Media logic is
an equally useful perspectival tool to overcome what may be
the most crucial problem in my discussion of what it is like to
work in the media: the notion, that what a journalist does is
guided by distinctly different ideas and factors of influence

than what informs the work of a game developer, television producer, or advertising creative – and vice versa. As argued before, one thing all these fields have in common is the fact that journalism, advertising, broadcasting, film, and game development are all examples of the production of culture. The stories told in the news, in the movies, and in games or advertisements all build upon and contribute to the collective memories, traditions, and belief systems of a community or society. This does not mean that a news report on CNN and a Nike ad produced for the soccer World Cup are equally important or valuable in informing and thus sustaining people's sense of community; it does mean that I wish to move beyond such normative concerns about the distinctions between different kinds of media content to focus on what people actually do when they work in the media, and how they give meaning to their actions and beliefs. In turn I presuppose that this process of giving and articulating meaning has consequences for the way media are made.

Each of the four main media professions is analyzed in terms of its media logic, which means each time that I will examine the institutional, technological, organizational, and cultural features of what it is like to work in, respectively, advertising (including public relations and marketing communications), journalism, television and film, and the game industry (see each separate chapter for details). First, I discuss each profession in terms of some of the particular developments in recent years in that sector, using media logic to flesh out more detail about what it is like to work in such an industry. After focusing on the four mentioned key professions, a synthesis of the issues, trends, and challenges these (and other) creative industries have in common is offered in the final chapter of this book, emphasizing how the issues and developments found in each can be seen as "bleeding" into one another, creating a spill-over effect within and between different sectors of the media. Please note: I am not saying that the different media or the work that media workers do are becoming similar or the same. I am arguing, however, that what typifies media professions in the digital age is an increasing complexity and ongoing liquefaction of the boundaries between different fields, disciplines, practices, and categories that used to define what media work was. In the concluding chapter I return to the general observations in the opening sections of the book to make sense of it all – of what it means to work (in the media) today.

CHAPTER FOUR

Advertising, Public Relations, and Marketing Communications

In a bold article in the *Journal of Advertising* in 1994, Roland Rust and Richard Oliver declared the death of advertising: "Mass media advertising as we know it today is on its deathbed, and its prognosis is poor. Advertising agencies are restructuring to accommodate a harsher advertising climate, agency income is flat, agency employees are being laid off, direct marketing is stealing business from traditional advertising, and the growth of sales promotion and integrated marketing communications both come at the expense of traditional advertising" (1994, p. 71). The demise of advertising has been predicted more than once, for different reasons, throughout the twentieth century. Interestingly, those foreseeing the death of advertising are not just critical academics or industry outsiders – sometimes the most successful among the practitioners themselves speak out in similar vein. Consider the case of Alex Bogusky, creative director of Crispin Porter + Bogusky (CPB), an American advertising agency based in Miami, Boulder, and Los Angeles. The agency started out in the 1960s as a tourism shop, only moving into advertising in the mid-1990s. Currently headed by Bogusky with Chuck Porter and Jeff Hicks, it is considered one of the most talked about innovative ad agencies to create "buzz" among its competitors, clients, and audiences – as exemplified by winning all the major awards in the advertising industry. In 2002, Bogusky was inducted into the American Advertising Federation's Hall of Achievement. One of the main reasons for the agency's financial success and critical acclaim is its reputation for staying away from "one-way show-and-tell" type of advertising in favor of viral, word-of-mouth and interactive marketing and advertising. An exemplary campaign of CPB was the so-called "Subservient Chicken" advertisement for client Burger King: a website featuring someone in a chicken suit you could order around, leading to communities online compiling their own "Subservient Chicken Request List."[1] Considering his success in breaking with established models of advertising in an interview with *Time* magazine (3 October 2004), Bogusky proclaimed: "The future of advertising is that it doesn't exist. The party is coming to an end for everybody."[2]

Advertising, marketing and public relations (PR) are industries that enable much of the production of content occurring in other commercial media. Although people in advertising can be among the most creative media workers and their work is sometimes more part of a community's collective memory than the information coming from politicians or journalists, they tend to be quite anonymous when compared to their colleagues in print journalism (who compete for a byline), television, film, or game design (who get their name on a credit roll). This kind of frustration has a tendency to creep into a practitioner's sense of professional identity. In the context of the emergence of a global convergence culture and increasing pressures on media workers to interact and co-create with their intended audiences, there is potential for an unprecedented new visibility for advertising practitioners – all the more reason to carefully map the media logic of the industry. Using this approach means investigating the institutional, technological, organizational, and cultural features of what it is like to work in the advertising industry.

Institution. On an institutional level, two developments run throughout the advertising industry: business fragmentation and concentration. These trends must be seen as co-constituent: many professionals in advertising, marketing, and PR start their own small-scale enterprises, while at the same time the existing conglomerates keep expanding their reach by acquiring certain successful or specialized smaller companies in the field. Large investment networks like Publicis, Omnicom, or Havas have been gobbling up agencies worldwide at an accelerated pace since the 1980s in an attempt to become transnational full-service companies: businesses that offer clients and advertisers a wide range of products and services, including advertising, marketing, and PR. Of the top twenty agencies in the 1980s – as reported by industry magazine *Advertising Age* – seventeen have been swallowed up by four major agency holding companies. Currently six large advertising companies account for sixty percent of the total advertising revenue. Of these vast networks of media agencies the originally British Wire and Plastic Product (WPP) group is the largest, with a reported market share of 17.5 percent and 60.5 million US dollars worth of accounts. The WPP group includes agencies and bureaus offering services in advertising, media investment management, consultancy, PR, and all kinds of marketing communications, employing close to 100,000 people in more than 2,000 offices in 106 countries.[3] Next to such networked corporations there exist several large media agencies, that in and of themselves reach clients and consumers worldwide. Of these agencies, according to the 2006 Report on Worldwide Media Agency Networks of the Recma-institute, US-based Starcom leads the pack with a market share of 7.4 percent and 25.6 million US dollars in accounts.[4] Starcom claims a network of 110 offices in 67 countries, employing nearly 3,800 professionals. However, the company is also a subsidiary of Paris-based Publicis Groupe – which in turn is a networked firm similar to the WPP Group, ranking second in global listings.

Facing increasingly bigger challenges in understanding and enacting the management of these big transnational corporations, the 1990s saw the emergence of a popular concept among practitioners as well as academics: integrated marketing communications (IMC). The IMC approach is largely aimed at breaking down the boundaries between different "above the line" (advertising, media planning and production) and "below the line" (sales promotions, public relations and other marketing services) disciplines within companies – largely in response to a worldwide shift in spending on traditional advertising campaigns to (new media-based) marketing services. Professionals would also use the traditional boundaries between advertising, marketing and PR as an instrument in articulating status, expertise, and allocating prestige within and between (divisions of) companies. Beyond such cultural turf wars, it is crucial to note that "each discipline had its own compensation structures that resulted in different objectives and practices, and there was generally little contact between the different disciplines" (De Mooij 2005, p. 234).

On an institutional level, IMC is a practice that seeks to coordinate the work practitioners do at different levels and disciplines within the firm. The assumption is, that by facilitating so-called "through the line" communication and cross-fertilization the traditionally insular and thus unwieldy nature of work within large full-service organizations becomes more flexible and, particularly, more consumer-focused. In doing so, IMC shifts the emphasis on what advertising, PR or marketing is from a producer point of view to a consumer point of view – in part motivated by research showing how media users do not see distinctions between advertising and promotions, PR, and other forms of marketing communications. De Mooij considers IMC in this context as a practice that puts the wants and needs of a carefully defined market segment – up to and including an individual consumer – first, which on a practical level means that much time and money gets spent on researching the consumer, developing databases, and coordinating contacts with the consumer. John Philip Jones (2004) suggests that such a "customer first" attitude does not necessarily mean that advertising and marketing professionals really pay all that much attention to consumers, as in everyday practice they tend to be more concerned with their competitor-colleagues. The mergers and integration practices of the 1980s and 1990s continue into the twenty-first century, leading however to quite different everyday realities for the media workers directly involved. As Joep Cornelissen (2003) summarizes, in some companies disciplinary integration has led to a strict emphasis on standardization and strong centralization of responsibilities for communication functions (advertising, product publicity, sales promotion, packaging, and direct marketing) with an individual marketing manager (i.e. brand manager, marketing communications manager, or advertising director). On the other hand, the same business practice inspired some corporations to decentralize their production and decision-making processes across individual managers of collaborative teams, each responsible for a project-based IMC plan.

The integration of companies, agencies, departments, and their practices is not a seamless process - especially considering the tensions between different disciplines, such as the work of creatives versus the activities of account planners and media buyers. The latter group is generally considered to be representative of the rational, quantitative, economic, and ever so slightly "dorky" side of the business, as their functional specialisms involve managing client relationships, providing consumer and product research, and the planning and buying of space and time across different media deployed in the advertising campaign. Lash and Urry (1994, p. 140) consider these professionals and their work "emblematic of the implosion of the economic, advertising as a business service, into the cultural, advertising as a 'communications' or 'culture' industry." Based on historical research on the emergence and growing importance of media planning, buying and account management, Liz McFall (2004) notes that these functional specialisms in advertising involve complex decision-making processes about how people use and understand media, what associations people have with certain brands or specific symbols, and about competing advertisements. Some of this work clearly involves rigorous and rationalized research based on quantifiable outcomes, yet much of it is also based on instinct, gut-feeling, casuistry (that is, whatever was decided last time a similar situation was encountered), and all kinds of other distinctly cultural factors – not least including the personal consumptive preferences of the professionals involved. Christopher Hackley (1999) further notes – based on depth interviews with practitioners in various departments at a leading UK advertising agency – how decisions about a campaign emerge through complex negotiations involving the client, account managers and creatives and other interested parties, each deploying their own highly subjective discursive tactics to accomplish their particular goals. This kind of complexity or cultural and economic fluidity contributes to making the work seem quite diverse and not so repetitive.

> No two days are ever the same. The thing about this business is that you can never rest on your laurels. its all about what you are going to do tomorrow, which is yesterday. Everything is constantly changing, and certainly technology is a huge part of that. (M, consumer research, US)

The ongoing consolidation of advertising agencies in large holding firms coincided on the workfloor with the ascension of the work of consumer researchers, media planners, and buyers in office hierarchies. "For decades the industry has been dominated by the creatives [. . .] who came up with ideas that were translated into television, print, radio, and billboard ads. Beneath them toiled the media buyers, who wore suits and purchased television and radio time, magazine pages, and billboard space for clients. Now the buyers are calling the shots" (Andrew Leonard in *Fortune* magazine of 28 June 2004).[5] Such departmental "King of the Hill" struggles have been further charged by the prospect of the disappearing media consumer. As Jones notes, the "clever and imaginative people" (2004, p. 12) working on the creative side in advertising are frustrated by the fact that they devote their skill and energy in coming up with advertisements that their intended audience does not really want to see or hear. With growing numbers of media consumers combining ad-avoidance behavior like zapping (channel surfing during commercial breaks) and zipping (fast-forwarding through ads in recorded media content) with spending their precious time making their own media, the power of the creative has shifted to the supposedly more economical, business-minded media buyer, planner, and account manager. This shift does not occur equally in all agencies, nor does it happen without a fight. Research among account planners in the US and the UK done by Hackley for example shows a distinct cultural distance between them and the executives in charge of certain campaigns, whereas the practice of account planning – which may involve anything from conducting or interpreting market research up to and including developing brand strategy – still elicits all kinds of feelings on the workfloor, ranging from passionate advocacy to open cynicism. Discussing how people responded to the restructuring of work in the organizations involved, Hackley notes how "changing the way people work in advertising agencies is a far from easy matter. Moving desks around is sometimes seen as tokenism, as likely to exacerbate differences as to dissolve them" (2003, p. 239).

The power shift from creative to planning in turn occurred in the context of a sharp decline in global ad spending at the start of the twenty-first century, during which time the largest agencies laid off almost of quarter of their workforce in the United States alone. This came after an initial internal reorganization process in transnational agencies, concentrating their services geographically in urban centers like New York and London, and cutting back or outright closing regional offices. Deborah Leslie documented the direct influence mergers and acquisitions have on the working lives of advertising professionals, signaling people's frustration about a growing emphasis in many newly "transnationalized" agencies on modifying and adapting campaigns from other branches for local application: "many creatives complained that they had less creative work to put in their portfolios" (1995, p. 415). Leslie found that the supposedly integrated and "glocalized" practices for many advertising professionals meant having to collaborate with colleagues across countries and disciplines, each informed by generally substantially different characteristics and histories of their respective local markets. She additionally noted how the managerial emphasis in this process tended to veer towards identifying and isolating similarities between consumers across the world rather than addressing each market's particularities.

In recent years, the focus in global advertising has shifted somewhat to an acknowledgement of cross-cultural complexities. McDonald's received the "Marketer of the Year" award in 2004 from trade magazine *Advertising Age* particularly because of the way it organized its *"I'm Lovin' It"* global marketing campaign.[6] The campaign was unique for the company in that it united and aligned all McDonald's enterprises around the world behind a single theme and brand direction, while at the same time allowing local agencies to create their own adaptations and interpretations of the campaign slogan. The McDonald's case can be seen as an example of contemporary transnational advertising and marketing practices, where local bureaus get more creative freedom while operating within certain parameters – like a key message, a specific slogan, or a target brand identity – set by the client or the advertising agency's head office. Considering the future of advertising, former world president of the International Advertising Association Joe Cappo (2003) sees a less rosy future for global holding firms and agencies, predicting that such companies cannot remain intact because of the fact that they are made up of dozens of different companies of different sizes, different cultures, and different personalities. Gernot Grabher (2002b and 2004) remarks how the affiliation of local advertising agencies with global holding firms tends to be limited to financial control only, which if anything suggests that situated work practices tend not to experience central steering, and experience and knowledge gathered locally does not seem to be flowing "upstream" (to corporate headquarters) or to other agencies in the network. The WPP group is one example of a global holding firm that started all kinds of programs and initiatives to encourage more inter-institutional exchange and learning by starting a company-wide training program called "SparkLab," a company-wide intranet facilitating so-called "Knowledge Communities" across and between the different agencies it owns, a world-wide partnership program called "Brandz", the publication of its own newspaper (*the Wire*) and magazine (*the Atticus Journal*), and online news bulletin (*e.wire*) to all companies worldwide. Similar, the Publicis Groupe of agencies organizes company-wide "Peak Performance" workshops for managers, whereas its agencies have separate staff training programs to introduce entry-level employees to what at Saatchi & Saatchi for example is called "the Saatchi way" of advertising.[7]

> We're one of those big bad corporations which has upsides and downsides. The upside is we have a lot of resources, we have proprietary information that isn't available to other companies. Not only are we working to create brand awareness for other brands but we have become a brand in a way ourself. However on a bad side, when you get into that corporate world, you get in that mindset that you are hiring this many people, you are going to put them through your training program, for the most part they are all going to think alike and it somewhat limits the way for creative thinking. (F, media planner, US)

The perceived and often celebrated variety of agencies and agency cultures within these groups limits the scope of attempts to either standardize the firm's practices, or effectively manage cross-agency collaboration. The reluctance and frustration experienced by creatives, planners, and managers in agencies that end up having to collaborate with agencies elsewhere within their owners' holding firm is not just an indicator of the limited and sometimes ineffective nature of such practices, it even gets celebrated by the practitioners involved as a sign of a (agency) culture's independence – which in turn is an unique selling point for the agency when soliciting new clients. This institutional arrangement reveals an ironic contradiction in the work of advertising, marketing and PR agencies in the context of the ongoing concentration of media ownership and the standardization that this process to some extent involves: "although agencies seek to differentiate themselves from their main competitors through a particular esthetic and a specific "way of doing things," they somewhat paradoxically also desperately endeavor to avoid a particular "house style". The aim is to be distinct and yet not predictable since this would inevitably limit the market" (Grabher 2004, p. 1498). It is safe to say the current changes in the industry are met with excitement as well as resentment on the workfloor – which response colors the success or failure of media concentration and integration as Mower (1999, p. 27) writes, "such processes require a collaborative – even collegial - workplace, where no single mode of communication is considered to be more desirable than another. Too often, advertising agencies do not accomplish this collegiality."

The second trend in advertising, in part inspired by the first, is one of increasing fragmentation and specialization. The recent history of the industry is rife with stories of both beginning as well as seasoned professionals branching off and starting their own agencies, initially positioning themselves against the bigger corporations by focusing on a specific niche (skillset, expertise or market), or simply by publicly stating they are different. Research by Sean Nixon (2006) into the workplace cultures of advertising agencies suggests that especially younger practitioners (such as art directors, writers, and creatives) can be seen as actively engaging in a Freudian "narcissism of minor differences" in which creative teams try to stand out in the advertising they generate.

> It is really important to have the tools you need. like if you are a writer then you should know proper grammar, the proper ways to set up an article, and the basic rules of writing. I

think you should also have an interesting and unique perspective as a creative. So, I think it is a foundation system, where have a bottom layer of tools that you use and then the next step is to refine them and say: how can I strategically break those rules to make my work different from someone else's? (F, creative, US)

Some professionals consider the increasing differentiation in the industry an example of "agency wars," where the ambition to be different and to stake a claim based on such different-ness can have dire consequences. Cappo suggests that the large holding firms experience splintering and defections as much as they are buying agencies. "Many of the largest clients in the business still assign various projects and products to smaller agencies as they look for new ideas and strategies [. . .] And, of course, there are thousands of small to medium-sized clients [. . .] that don't want to deal with a huge ad agency" (2003, p. 17). The smaller agencies tend to advertise themselves as non-traditional in their workstyles, particularly marking their criticism against the non-collegial, rigid, and frustrating practices of their large counterparts in the industry. Indeed, the trend of mergers has not deterred thousands of small and medium-sized agencies from setting up shop, and in fact acquiring some significant clients along the way.

A key motive for advertising professionals to break away from holding firms of large network companies such as Leo Burnett, Saatchi & Saatchi or JWT (abbreviating its name in 2005 from J. Walter Thompson) is their real or perceived lack of creative freedom in pursuing different, innovative or experimental forms of advertising, and what can be described as an increased emphasis on annual returns on investment and shareholder value. However, this does not mean smaller agencies do not benchmark their employees on a financial bottom line, nor does this suggest that small or medium-sized bureaus are conflict-free working environments. Indeed, international research clearly shows how conflict and rivalry are intrinsic if not essential ingredients in the way teams in agencies large and small do their work.

> I think that being able to communicate with co-workers is extremely important. Because we are on teams, and you have certain people to report to, and you can also have an angry client sometime, stuff like that. Keeping the lines of communication open is really important [. . .] In this profession especially you need to know how to leave work drama at work [. . .] you can be so stressed, but you have to be able to turn it off and turn it on. No crying. There is no crying in PR. You just have to do it. (F, account manager, US)

There is perhaps a significant difference in a company's ability to handle what Richard Edelman, president of one of the world's largest public relations firms (Edelman, with 2,000 employees in forty-five offices worldwide), described on his blog as today's era of profound and *"discontinuous change"* in media (posted on 21 November, 2005).[8] The institutional characteristics of smaller agencies allows them to position themselves more flexibly vis-à-vis new trends in the industry, for example regarding the emergence and adoption of new marketing techniques, new technologies, and new managerial styles. It must be clear that on an institutional level the experiences of practitioners in advertising, marketing and PR are influenced by similar processes in large and small businesses alike: a highly competitive work culture, characterized by discourses of integration and convergence (of media, of disciplines, and of divisions) in a context of ongoing power struggles and an increasing interdependence between the creative, managerial, client, and consumer sides of the industry.

Technology. As with all media work, advertising and technology are interdependent. According to Rust and Oliver (1994), technology is the skeleton around which advertising has formed, linking contemporary technological developments to transformations of advertising and marketing practices. Considering how technologies develop side by side social trends, and weighing the scholarly evidence that shows how new media tend to be used in organizations to fit or reproduce existing patterns of work, our understanding of the role of technology in shaping advertising must look at processes in the workplace where technologies reinforce or amplify organizational changes already underway. The popularity of IMC as a strategy for intra-organizatonal integration in the 1990s for example can partly be explained by the availability of interactive and networked communication technologies, leading to the establishment of video conferencing, company intranets, and other computer-mediated communication tools that enabled organizations to communicate across time and place. By implementing all kinds of cross-company software tools, technology serves as a standardization instrument in the industry, supposedly facilitating faster and more efficient media work as well as assisting top-down implementation of management strategies that privilege integration and central control (and environmental scanning) of workplace practices.

In her analysis of the diffusion of technologies in public relations, Melissa Johnson (1997) has noted that the introduction of all kinds of new technologies – desktop publishing, company intranets, computerized databases and file management systems, and so on – went hand in hand with a downsizing trend in the PR industry, forcing practitioners to be more productive and do more with less time and staff. Through a series of in-depth interviews with PR professionals, she also found how they saw themselves in the midst of a learning curve about new technologies: "all the respondents admitted to knowledge gaps about various technologies and their self-identity as a professional was dependent on reducing the gap. This attempt to live up to what one 'ought' to do and 'ought' to know caused considerable stress among practitioners. If they were not using certain technologies yet (particularly the Internet), they felt behind their contemporaries in other organizations" (1997, p. 226). Johnson's work shows how central (the mastery of) technology is in the everyday practice and professional self-perception of media professionals.

The production of advertising – particularly the work of art departments, creatives, brand managers and strategists – is changing because of new technologies too, as the internet increasingly becomes integrated in all kinds of networked devices, ranging from the desktop computer to a refrigerator, from a cell phone to your television set. This means that advertising, marketing, and PR are increasingly expected to be produced across different media platforms (with multiple tie-ins), while professionals in these industries additionally find themselves having to partly outsource their control over the advertising message to consumers online via viral, word-of-mouth, "buzz" and other types of interactive marketing techniques. This kind of interconnectivity – between different media, between media makers and media users, and between consumers among each other – tends to be seen as a direct exponent of the potential of new media. As more and more people immerse themselves in all kinds of networked, portable and personalized media, the consensus in the advertising industry is that the age of mass advertising is over. Campaigns consisting of a single medium (a magazine spread or a thirty-second television commercial) are considered to be less successful partly because of the "hyperfragmentation" of mass audiences across multiple media, and partly because of a credibility crisis advertising is experiencing, especially among those growing up in the media-saturated lifeworlds of the 1980s and 1990s. These generations not only tend to be quite media-savvy, they also are less likely to buy in to what marketers and advertisers are trying to tell them about their products and services. The new media environment certainly contributes to this trend, as people increasingly multitask and divide their time across different media and media use becomes highly individualized. This in turn weakens the appeal for mass marketed products and services, as market researchers conclude that consumers tend to look for items that are more particular to their wants and needs.

In a 2006 global industry overview based on consumer surveys and expert interviews, accounting and consultancy firm PriceWaterhouseCoopers (PWC) signals the rise of "Life Style Media" as "the combination of a personalized media experience with a social context for participation," which will create a media marketplace that is "a platform that connects media providers and media seekers through an organizational and technical infrastructure."[9] In its analysis, PWC implicitly refers to the blurring of the boundaries between media producers and consumers (which has organizational consequences) supercharged by the rapid appropriation of new media by people to produce, edit, share and distribute content themselves, on their own terms (which has a distinct technological dimension). Instead of reading this trend as the final nail in advertising's coffin, PWC (and a host of other industry observers) in fact sees all kinds of opportunities for new advertising practices: ads-on-demand, personalized ads, consumer activity ads, viral ads – all of which presuppose that consumers want to be involved in the advertising process, whether through voluntarily submitting their personal information to a company in order to receive customized communications and services, or by actively participating in the content of the ads.

The industry's framing of this "new" empowered consumer is not without problems. Joseph Turow for example considers the construction of twenty-first-century media users by marketers, advertisers and consultants as chaotic, self-concerned, and willingly contributing to a pervasive personal information economy as only serving an emerging strategic logic of mainstream marketing and media organizations "to present their activities not as privacy invasion but as two-way customer relationships, not as commercial intrusion but as pinpoint selling help for frenetic consumers in a troubling world" (2005, p. 120). Indeed, the audience has never been a given but must be seen as a socially constituted and institutionally produced category. Using interviews with advertising professionals in Finland, Liina Puustinen (2004) adds that the contemporary mainstream in marketing views the consumers and target groups as "unpredictable masses," which perspective allows marketers to both aim at taming the consumer mass into controllable segments, lifestyle groups, or sub-cultures, as well as interacting with consumers as active agents. In this context Puustinen and other researchers suggest that the primary function of advertising and marketing is to reduce the advertisers' anxieties, lack of knowledge, and imagination regarding the consumer.

Below I excerpt an interview (published 12 July 2004) by *Business Week* correspondent Michael Arndt with Larry Light, McDonald's global chief marketing officer, as it exemplifies the interdependent roles of technological and social change as these impact the advertising industry.[10]

> Q: It used to be pretty simple to market things in the US People bought things en masse. Goods were produced en masse. And the media were mass media. These days everything seemed atomized. Q: Do you think that the mass market is a thing of the past? A: The answer is yes. We're a global marketer. We're a big marketer. We're not a mass marketer. I don't think the mass market ever existed, but we didn't have the ability to reach the individual markets that did exist. What has changed is technology has facilitated our ability to reach people on a more customized, more personalized basis. That's a revolution. Q: But is this only a technological change? A: It's more than that. What has also changed significantly is the values of the market. If you go back 40 years, people wanted to be identified as normal. So they wanted the most popular car and the most popular color. From the consumer point of view, we've had a change from "I want to be normal" to "I want to be special."

The critical analysis of Turow, the industry enthusiasm of the PWC report, and the interview with Light effectively address a crucial issue in the debate about the impact of technology on media work: the application of new technologies is neither random nor inevitable, but always fits existing ways of doing things, the deliberate agendas of those using the technology, and wider social trends that influenced the initial diffusion and subsequent adoption of certain technologies in the first place.

The restructuring of business and management practices in large firms, the "glocalization" (combining global advertising with local adaptation and customization) of advertising production, the changing realities of the media marketplace and the reliance of the industry on technology to facilitate all of these processes cannot be seen separately. For the practitioners in the industry this particularly means that there are more options for advertising than ever before, to be produced using increasingly sophisticated devices, with growing pressures from both markets and clients to provide compelling content, engaging connectivity, platforms for participation, and, ultimately, significant returns on investments. However, such a conclusion perhaps misrepresents the growing creative interaction between media professionals and different individuals in society, which in the case of public relations has meant a shift from the idea of PR professionals as spin-doctors and "outsourcers of trust" towards what Michael Kent and Maureen Taylor (2002) coin a "dialogic theory of public relations." This theory presents a shift in thinking towards PR practitioners as facilitators and moderators of a dialogue between companies, consumers, interest groups, and other stakeholders in their clients' environment.

Particularly since the mid-1990s, scholars and practitioners alike have signaled a shift or rediscovery in PR of interpersonal channels of communication. In a panel study among experts in PR research and education across 25 European countries, scholars found that participants clearly favored developing two-way relationships in which parties adjust to each other as the main aim of PR, furthermore considering as most important PR tools: dialogue, networking, and communication skills (Van Ruler *et al.* 2004). In advertising and marketing theories and approaches regarding interactive ads and word-of-mouth marketing are also gaining currency. Advertising executives are increasingly attuned to the popularity of user-generated content and social networking online, and examples of collaborations between agencies, marketing services, and social networking sites such as *Facebook* or *MySpace* abound.[11] Although none of these trends are new in the sense that they were coined or introduced well before the 1990s, it is important to note that late twentieth century technological developments such as the World Wide Web and the multimedia cell phone have greatly contributed to their currency throughout the industry.

> Advertising is certainly not dead! Yet the role and appearance of advertising and the way we communicate brands are changing drastically. Everybody in the ad world agrees that we have to make the step from the traditional "30 second commercial" to integrated brand communication. You could say that the – in fact very conservative – advertising world experiences something of an identity crisis. We're not desperate, mind you, but it is clear that the ad world (and especially the classical agencies) has to reinvent itself. (M, strategy director, NL)

As this quote illustrates, the widely reported changes in advertising, marketing, and PR because of new technologies do not just neatly fit the corporate agenda, but also pose significant challenges to the way professionals do their work.

Organization. Advertising agencies tend to cluster in certain regions around the world. Among the top urban centers where creative talent and potential project partners are concentrated are cities like Tokyo, New York (home of the "adland" of Madison Avenue), Frankfurt (where the industry employs at least 5,000 advertising professionals), Paris, London (where Soho is a so-called "ad village"), Los Angeles, Milan, São Paulo, Amsterdam, and Madrid. The organization of work in advertising, PR and marketing firms centers almost exclusively on a project-by-project basis.

> We work project to project. We have two or three clients that are on a retainer system where we are their agency of record. We're only as good as the last thing we did for you. The client

> always will know where every dollar and every cent is going because we bring in the right team of writers, designers, producers of video if needed, and subcontracted photographers. The right team for that particular client for that particular job and in doing so it has meant historically now that a lot of clients come back to us for everything. (M, agency owner, US)

Project-based work has become the dominant feature in the new economy, as it is considered to possess the required flexibility to meet constantly changing customer needs, shifts in the composition of businesses, markets, and clients, and it provides a strategy to cope with a continual rearrangement of employers and employees within the firm. Additionally, a largely project-contracted workforce is cheaper, easier to control, and less likely to collectively organize or oppose increasingly transnational business practices.

The literature recognizes two types of project organizations relevant to the advertising industry, one within firms constituted by employees from different departments, and one based on temporary cooperative efforts across firm boundaries. Research in Denmark by Tina Brandt Husman (2006) suggests that interfirm projects are in fact quite rare, and professionals in such teams tend to get selected on the basis of agency ownership. This for example means that cooperative partners, if any, are to some extent forced onto the project team structure of an agency that is part of a larger holding firm. Several studies also conclude that in a project team between an advertising and media agency not much knowledge is transferred as they do not have the time nor strong incentives to learn what each other knows. Similar research in Germany by Caroline Jentsch (2004) reveals a slightly different picture, as she finds that agencies in Frankfurt – arguably the "hotspot" for the German industry – engage numerous external services and professionals in their projects, which selection process primarily is based on the activation of latent personal networks. These ties between different practitioners both within and outside of agencies and bureaus blur (or even hijack) the domains of work-life and private life, as the superficial yet intense networking that underscores such open project organization of media work is primarily driven by professional motivations while utilizing personal affinities. Grabher (2004) emphasizes that this kind of networking is instrumental in building "know-whom" rather than "know-how," which is indispensable for the relentless rewiring of ties and recombination of teams. Jentsch further notes how reputation and trust are key determining factors in selecting teammates and project partners, which in the case of small agencies means they tend to fall back upon a relatively stable set of professionals they have had good experiences with in the past. Larger firms generally rely on their own in-house specialists when assembling project teams. Jentsch additionally notes how this referring to known external partners contributes to the main difference between the adlands in London and Frankfurt, as the British agencies are much more likely to solicit the services of a constantly changing range and variety of professionals moving in and out of Soho.

The architecture of the work of large and small agencies can be best understood as one of what Gernot Grabher calls back-to-back (and, for some, simultaneous) "project ecologies." The concept of the project ecology, argues Grabher, comes closest to the lived reality of everyday work in the advertising industry, as it allows for "interdependencies between projects and as well as other more traditional 'permanent' forms of organization" (2002, p. 245). Based on rich empirical work done among advertising practitioners and agencies in New York, London, and Hamburg, Grabher finds that the organization of work in advertising indeed is project-based, but includes a wide variety of forms and templates, including agencies, firms, clients, and freelance talent, in which people are engaged in an almost constant and highly competitive dance around the table of media production in the advertising, marketing, and PR industries.

Key to understanding project ecologies in advertising is their heterarchic character: project teams are networks of professionals (temporarily) sharing common goals in which each participant shares more or less the same horizontal position of power and authority (Grabher 2001). This does not necessarily mean all participants in the team responsible for an advertisement, a campaign, or an integrated brand communications package are completely equal. Part-time, flexitime and freelance workers involved in these teams tend to have fewer securities and benefits than the professionals employed by the agency, firm, and client involved. When it comes to actual decision-making in the creative process, however, teams in project ecologies function on the basis of heterarchy. The project ecology of advertising involves:

- one or more marketing managers on the client side;
- account managers, planners, and creatives in an advertising agency or media bureau – sometimes with partnerships at one or more other agencies within the same group or holding firm; and
- a group of local or even international creative (such as: art and film directors, specialized photographers, graphic designers) and technical (offering services in audio and video processing, printing, lithography, IT) professionals that is hired on a project basis through largely personal network ties.

Project ecologies are different from a pure "projectization" of work – which implies a complete shift from stable firm-based work to flexible project-based work – as Grabher concludes, "project ecologies provide the organizational arena in which incongruent physical and organizational layers are 'stapled' for a limited period of time – just to be reconfigured anew in the context of subsequent projects" (2002, p. 259). An agency may start out being very flexible, open, and ever so slightly chaotic (especially in its biased self-representation), but could very well become a static organization over a short period time when previously rewarding practices sediment in a distinct way of doing things. As James Redmond and Robert Trager advise, "Organizational procedures develop themselves into entangled bureaucracies, which then lock up an organization when the world shifts" (2004, p. 30). Again I must emphasize that elements of chaos, bureaucracy, uncertainty, and procedural repetitiveness are all part of the organization of media work, which elements contribute to as well as are strategies to avoid stress factors in the workplace. The literature does not suggest a specific predictor of either one of such elements to dominate, whether it is working for a large or small agency, in Amsterdam or Johannesburg, providing integrated brand and marketing communications, or specialized services. The organization of work in advertising is context-driven, based on the specifics of the project at hand, which creates both opportunities and uncertainties for the workers involved – which tend to get articulated and negotiated through professional networks and clusters of contacts primarily based on previous experiences and personal affiliations.

Culture. The culture of advertising agencies, media bureaus, PR and marketing firms is first and foremost determined by the profile of people working there – which in terms of their own description of markets and consumers can be determined by looking at the demographics and psychographics of professionals in the industry. Unfortunately, the few studies among advertising practitioners in for example the United States, France, Finland, or England rely exclusively on qualitative interviews emphasizing cultural specificities, and therefore cannot be generalized across the industry. It is interesting to note that in the other media professions – game developers, journalists, workers in film and broadcasting – the situation is notably different. However, it is possible to get some idea of who advertising people are by looking at implicit references in the scholarly and trade literature, and by explicit figures mentioned in the annual reports of public holding firms like WPP or Publicis. In 2005 the Publicis Groupe reported 38,610 employees in 104 countries overall, with 8,900 employees specifically in their key advertising agencies such as Saatchi & Saatchi, Leo Burnett, and Fallon Worldwide, distributed across 251 offices in 82 countries. At the same time the WPP Group employed 70,396 people in more than 100 countries, including its flagship agencies Grey Worldwide, JWT, Ogilvy & Mather, and Young & Rubicam. In 2005 these firms shared almost the exact same figures regarding their workers: overall, 54 percent of all employees are female, although women are still a minority in executive positions and management teams (30 percent at Publicis, 33 percent at WPP).

The numbers of minorities are still extremely low in the industry. U.S.-based agencies owned by Publicis and WPP participate in the Minority Advertising Internship Program (MAIP) or the American Association of Advertising Agencies (AAAA), which program encourages African-American, Asian-American, Hispanic, and Native-American college students to strongly consider advertising as a career and places them at agencies throughout the country. In a study by New York City's Human Rights Commission, only two percent of the upper echelon of the advertising industry was found to be black. As reported in the *New York Times* (of 8 September 2006), "[f]aced with the findings, nearly a dozen agencies, including those owned by the Interpublic Group of Companies and the WPP Group, have promised to set numerical goals for increasing black representation on their creative and managerial staffs and to report on their progress each year [. . .] At the same time the companies have agreed to set up diversity boards and to link progress on the issue to their managers' compensation."[12] South Africa is one of the few countries that has an explicit Black Economic Empowerment policy, requiring companies to establish a 30 percent level of black ownership for advertising and communications companies. The 2005 report for the WPP Group in South Africa mentions its companies "are on track" (p. 112) to reach this percentage. As these firms are among the largest on the planet with a worldwide reach, there is no reason to assume these statistics are significantly different across the rest of the industry.

There are no specific entry-level requirements for the advertising, marketing or PR industry. Several reports suggest that professionals come from a wide variety of disciplines. Sean Nixon suggests that the various ways in which the creatives in advertising agencies give meaning to what they do is "built right into the kind of training these practitioners received en route to becoming advertising creatives" (2006, p. 95). Nixon identifies diplomas in fine art or graphic design as well as generalist humanities degrees as typical for creative work in advertising, which education was supplemented by all kinds of courses, workshops in and training within or sponsored by the company. Grabher (2004) finds that advertising practitioners in Germany and England are recruited from a broad range of educational and biographical backgrounds, claiming that further training seems to be the strongest influence on introducing discriminating effects between occupations in the industry. Differences in this pattern internationally tend to be seen as minimal, or waning. In his overview of advertising and public relations practices around the world, Doug Newsom (2004) notes regional differences, but also sees a growing role for the globalization and international cross-fertilization of standards and traditions. As the number of people employed in advertising and PR around the world increases, national and international professional organizations proliferate. Such organizations stimulate the development and upgrading of education and training, and employers increasingly turn to these programs to recruit graduates directly into their ranks as "there is little time today for on-the-job training" (2004, p. 96).

> The media industry on my side is very young, most of the associates and supervisors are all in their twenties, and, as far as higher management, they are very much in their early to mid-thirties, so. . . .(F, media planner, US)

Advertising professionals are generally described as an "atypical" occupational group: a "predominantly young, well-resourced, well-educated and fashionable, urban elite" (McFall

2004, p. 22). Advertising practitioners certainly seem like a youthful, fun bunch of people – who by all accounts work and live in a conflict-ridden, extremely stressful environment. "It's a job that comes with one form of rejection or another built into every day. You're either naturally resilient or learn quickly to become so, rolling with the punches" (Vonk and Kestin 2005, p. 163). The stress also relates to the phase before getting into the industry and becoming a known participant in professional networks. In a study among professionals working at Scottish advertising agencies Keith Crosier and colleagues (2003) found that the often mentioned rivalry between (and within) creative teams and those responsible for strategic planning was in fact seen as a productive tension, stimulating certain aspects of the work while still enabling some kind of pragmatic collaboration. If anything, the real conflict was felt between account planners and those in the parallel discipline of media planning. Although several authors confirm that rivalry and conflict are the key values and emotions that drive the work in the industry, this does not mean that anything goes and everything can be said. Using interviews with advertising practitioners at all levels in twenty-nine agencies in eight American cities, Minette Drumwright and Patrick Murphy (2004) found high incidences of what they describe as "moral myopia" and "moral muteness" across the board. Advertising professionals apparently only rarely talk about moral issues, and are particularly hesitant to actively question or critique the values and practices of clients. Drumwright and Murphy signal how "please-o-holic" tendencies and a general avoidance of criticism in fact keeps agencies in a subordinate position vis-à-vis their clients. Regarding the role of advertising in the lives of consumers, the interviewers found that informants were quick to shrug off ethical concerns, assuming the consumers are smart enough not to be fooled by persuasive communications. "It seems somewhat surprising that people whose professional raison d'être is to create advertising that works would simultaneously assert the powerlessness of their endeavors" (2004, p. 11).

According to John Philip Jones (1999), an agency's culture has important influence on its stability and productivity, and consists of a social culture – the type of people an agency recruits – and a philosophical culture – the agency's attitude toward the advertising enterprise. The best agency cultures, according to Jones, are successful because of their effective management and encouragement of the intuition and imagination of their workers. "Advertising agencies have a patchy record of success in producing effective campaigns, but good agencies get it right more often than they get it wrong. Their successes are due to their culture" (2004, p. 201). The culture of working in advertising, marketing and PR certainly differs from agency to agency, and from region to region (Taylor *et al.* 1996). However, it is possible to identify some key characteristics of the way people in these industries collectively work together, relate to each other and outsiders (clients, consumers, and critics), and give meaning to these competences. As mentioned earlier, the work of Gernot Grabher stands out in its rigorous and respectful analysis of the architectures of work in advertising. Grabher dissects the culture of the industry on three levels: the firm, the core team, and personal networks. On the level of the firm, over time the best ways of doing things get codified in certain tools providing menus for risk assessment, costing, project design, scheduling, and contractual agreements. The corporate culture in advertising is particularly colored by idiosyncratic personal constellations, focusing heavily on (stories about) the "stars" and agency founders – after whom many agencies are indeed named. If anything, argues Grabher, these kinds of stories and of more or less codified ways of doing things are among the few elements of an agency's culture that are repetitive. On the level of the core team within an agency – generally the only workers that enjoy permanent employment – Grabher signals a conscious cultivation of cognitive distance between the different participants in a project: the core team, the client, the external partners. By emphasizing each and everyone's particular role in the daily routines of working on a certain project, a delicate balance between the overlapping but at times different needs of clients, management and the creative process can be upheld. This careful dance leads the professional identities of advertising practitioners to "crystallize into 'creeds' whose distinctiveness is reiterated through organizational practices, professional styles, and distinct dress and language codes" (2004, p. 1495).

As argued earlier, it is crucial to note here how the personal and professional lives of practitioners in the field converge in the ways the work gets performed, organized, and evaluated. This in turn signals the important role personal networks play. Personal networks in advertising are ephemeral and powerful, formed through professional as well as private ties, and are governed by reputation. The focus of these networks is almost exclusively career-oriented, as they are constructed around what Grabher calls professional complimentarity: "relationships with practitioners who, potentially, could complement a core team or a supplier network in a future project" (2004, p. 1504). Jentsch (2004) finds that because of the high mobility of advertising practitioners both formal and informal professional networks extend across the country and cannot be seen to be particular to any specific city or region. She concludes that the personal networks so emblematic of the organization of work in these industries are indeed based on mutual sympathies, previous collaborations and word-of-mouth recommendations of friends – which process of networked hiring over time creates so-called "communities of practice" consisting of both part-time, fulltime and freelance workers located across the country and participating in many different projects throughout their careers. In order to stand out and get noticed, Sean Nixon notes, "young creatives would ally themselves with 'newness' in order to challenge more established colleagues. We might read into this pursuit of newness and creativity, then, a strategy of distinction and position taking by differently placed practitioners over the accumulation of recognition and status and its conversion into tangible economic rewards" (2006, p. 92). Again we must note the fascinating tension between the primacy of being different and unique versus the necessity of consistently participating in more or less cohesive networks that runs throughout the accounts of what it is like to work in advertising. On a final note I would like to add that none of these arguments and conclusions seem to be typical of the size of the company, agency or bureau people end up working for. In dispensing advice on how to get a job in advertising, Nancy Vonk and Janet Kestin (co-Chief Creative Officers at Ogilvy and Mather Toronto, one of the biggest agencies in the business) argue that the size of a company has little to do with its culture: "some big agencies (like ours) are nurturing and positive, while some of the smaller ones are the worst offenders" (2003, p. 70).

CHAPTER FIVE

Journalism

Journalism as it is, is coming to an end. The boundaries between journalism and other forms of public communication – ranging from public relations or advertorials to weblogs and podcasts – are vanishing, the internet makes all other types of newsmedia rather obsolete (especially for young adults and teenagers), commercialization and cross-media mergers have gradually eroded the distinct professional identities of newsrooms and their publications (whether in print or broadcast), and by insisting on its traditional orientation on the nation, journalists are losing touch with a society that is global as well as local, yet anything but national. Such are the key lamentations on the fate of journalism today. Is this indeed the end of journalism? Jo Bardoel and I (2001) asked the question in The Netherlands, where we argued it does not have to be – as long as a new "network journalism" adapted itself to changing social and technological realities. Writing mainly on the developments in US journalism, Michael Schudson considers the increasingly (and dangerously) critical or even outright cynical style of reporting and a growing role of entertainment values over sound news judgment in the field, signaling "an intrusion of marketplace values into the professionalism of journalists" (2003, p. 90). In Australia, Michael Bromley takes his answers to the same question – will journalism end – farthest. Pointing his finger at technological convergence as the main culprit, Bromley laments "the dismantling of demarcations between journalists and technicians, writers and camera operators, news gatherers and news processors, and between print, radio and television journalism" (1997,

p. 341) Bromley argues that the ongoing convergence of technologies undermines the basic skills and standards of journalism and fosters so-called "multiskilling" in newsrooms, which he sees as the result of economic pressures which cut back on resources while increasing workloads. Research in digital television newsrooms in Spain and the UK furthermore shows that, although especially the younger workers seem to embrace their digital, multi-skilled future, journalists in both countries are apprehensive about becoming increasingly computer-bound "mouse monkeys" required to keep up with the world of 24-hour news (Avilés *et al.* 2004).

Ultimately, journalism is not going to end because of cultural or technological convergence. There is however something to be said about the changing working conditions of journalists in different industries that are merging and to some extent collaborating in an attempt to reach new and especially younger audiences, while at the same time maintaining their privileged position in society. Journalism is attributed a seminal role in providing the collective memory and social cement of societies – both in the eyes of academics as journalists themselves, guided by "the modernist bias of its official self-presentation" (Zelizer 2004, p. 112). John Hartley additionally notes how news must be seen as "the primary sense-making practice of modernity" (1996, p. 32), contributing to a view of journalism as essential to con-stituting and maintaining social order and democracy itself. Modern journalism has consistently defined and legitimized itself as such, claiming to adhere to a social responsibility of public service regarding the democratic state, "informing citizens in a way that enables them to act as citizens" (Costera Meijer 2001, p. 13). For a media profession so central to society's sense of self, it is of crucial importance to under-stand the influences of changing labor conditions, profes-sional cultures, and the appropriation of technologies on the nature of work in journalism.

Institutions. Ownership in the news industry has traditionally been segmented by medium type. Often starting out as vehicles for political, religious, or corporate interests, newspapers, radio and television stations have gradually consolidated in large newspaper chains or broadcast news networks. Throughout the history of such chains or networks run concerns among journalists about media concentration, particularly fearing what some see as the inevitable consequences of being subsumed by a bigger company: downsizing, loss of editorial control over the creative process, and homogenization across the older and newly acquired titles. Although research does not suggest that either independent or corporate ownership is a significant predictor of quality in news reporting, one specific result of this wave of media mergers has been the implementation of job rotation practices – not just between different departments of a newspaper, but rather between different titles owned by the same firm.

> It is common here that you rotate every four or five years from department to department [. . .] On the one hand it's the destruction of cultural capital, because you just invested all those years in a network and then you have to move on again. Sure, you can take your address book with you and that usually happens, but you also have to establish new personal bonds with your contacts, and you have to become knowledgeable about a whole new subject. On the other hand, if you are stuck in one section for twenty years you will have become numb, you won't be able to do anything else. It's good to look with fresh eyes to the things that are happening around you. Well, there are pros and cons I guess. (M, newspaper, NL)

In the news industry rotation also means that the editors of large newspapers or directors of television stations in the bigger markets tend to prefer hiring reporters who first proved themselves working in "the provinces" for smaller papers and stations generally owned by the same company. In the last decades of the twentieth century, these companies were acquired wholly or partially by even larger media firms. Of these firms Rupert Murdoch's News Corporation is the largest, owning media properties all over the world. The company started out as a local newspaper chain in Australia, owning the *Adelaide News* and the *Adelaide Sunday Mail*.[1] After expanding his newspaper holdings across Australia, Murdoch moved into England in the 1960s and in the US in the 1970s. The company started Sky TV in 1983 – the world's first satellite television news and entertainment channel. Shortly thereafter, in 1985, Murdoch became an American citizen in order to be able to buy more media outlets in the US (next to his flagship paper the *New York Post*) – as only US citizens could own American television stations. In 1993, News Corporation became a majority shareholder of STAR (Satellite Television for the Asian Region) TV, broadcasting news and entertainment across the continent (but particularly relying on its dominant market share in India). In 1996, News Corporation's subsidiary Fox established the Fox News Channel in the US, a 24-hour cable news station. The company also owns or participates in numerous other, non-news franchises, such as sports teams, film studios, record companies, book publishing houses, and social networking websites – most notably the extremely popular social networking website *MySpace*.

After the start of the war in Iraq in 2003, British newspaper The *Guardian* reported that not only did Murdoch personally came out strongly in favor of the war – so did all the editorials of his 175 newspaper holdings across the world.[2] A 2004 television documentary called *Outfoxed* (by director Robert Greenwald of Brave New Films) painted a grim picture of what it is like to work for Fox News, using interviews and statements made by former Fox news producers, reporters, bookers and writers.[3] The filmmaker argues how these former employees were forced to push a politically conservative "right-wing" point of view or risk losing their jobs. The film for example shows daily internal memos that outline specific talking points to be covered that particular day by the channel's main news shows. Although there are many accounts of the role and influence of Murdoch – who if anything is a political opportunist and a self-proclaimed "libertarian" – on the way news gets reported across all of his media outlets, his presence in most of his newsrooms exists mainly through reputation. In a case study on the newspaper holdings of News Corporation, Timothy Marjoribanks (2000) concludes that while Murdoch is a strong influence on decision-making processes throughout the company, the daily management of specific organizations within the corporation allows for some degree of autonomy. Considering News Corporation as the perfect example of the contemporary networked enterprise form of cultural production, Eric Louw affirms: "we find multiple (and proliferating) styles of control and decision-making being tolerated in different parts of the network, so long as those at the centre of the web can gain some benefit from allowing a particular practice and/or organisational arrangement to exist in a part of their 'networked empire'" (2001, p. 64).

> There are too many influences on our work sometimes. People outside the media think media owners, such as Murdoch, exert undue influence, but this is almost never the case. Sometimes a newspaper will have an editorial line that it runs and will require its reporters to follow that line, but even this does not affect the stories too often. Often the influences are more subtle – sponsors, spin doctors, public relations people, or friendship with the subjects of the story. This is the time when a reporter shows his or her worth by rising above other factors to write fairly and bravely. (M, newspaper, NZ)

The process of accumulation of media properties accelerated in the 1990s, resulting in a market where there are more media (and thus: news) outlets owned by a smaller number of companies. This institutional trend has been supercharged by increased worldwide government deregulation on the one hand, and the rapid diffusion of digital media technologies on the other. The liberalization of national and global markets by governments during the second half of the twentieth century has had particular consequences for countries with a history of dual media systems, where commercial operators (mainly in broadcasting) worked side by side to government-protected public service stations. The case of the British Broadcasting Corporation (BBC) as a state-owned entity next to commercial enterprises like ITV is considered the textbook example of such a system. Public media organizations such as the BBC (or the ABC in Australia, ZDF in Germany, SABC in South Africa, and NOS in The Netherlands) are increasingly operating like commercial ones, whereas commercial companies have begun to offer competitive programs and titles similar to their public counterparts. By opening up the media market to transnational ownership, foreign investments and cross-media mergers in local markets, the formerly quite stable news companies started to shift towards what became an industry-wide buzzword in the 1990s: convergence. The institutional characteristics of convergence can be summarized as: companies developing partnerships with other (journalistic and non-journalistic) media organizations to provide, promote, repurpose, or exchange news, and the introduction of cross-media (integrated) marketing and management projects (Deuze 2004b).

It is important to note that the concentration of media ownership with the deliberate goal to integrate different departments and sections of the industry into cross-media enterprises is and always has been a top-down strategy. Studying the institutional and cultural contours of innovation at two Dutch newspapers owned by publisher PCM, Sierk Ybema (2003) typified management strategies in this context as "postalgic," noting how the industry's executives tend to come up with all kinds of far-reaching plans and futuristic ideals that are primarily interpreted by the journalists involved as unfair criticisms on their work. The direct result is the cultivation of some kind of nostalgia about the "good old days" among reporters and editors, which in turn leads to resistance to the proposed changes in the newsroom. A recent survey among hundreds of managers and journalists at US daily newspapers about change initiatives showed that the implementation thereof caused conflict and hurt morale (Gade 2004). Studies among processes of innovation and change in broadcast and Net-native newsrooms are rare, but suggest that the more teamwork-oriented, technology-dependent, and project-based nature of work in broadcast and online media facilitate more successful employee cooperation and buy-in (Quinn 2005). Ultimately, however, journalists tend to be cautious and skeptical towards changes in the institutional and organizational arrangements of their work, as lessons learnt in the past suggest that such changes tend to go hand in hand with downsizing, lay-offs, and having to do more with less staff, budget, and resources.

Catherine McKercher (2002), documenting the effects of convergence on media workers, argues that technological convergence and corporate concentration must be understood as part of the strategy of media owners to acquire new sources for profit, extending their control over the relations of production and distribution of news, and aiming to undermine the collective bargaining position of journalists through their unions by shifting towards a model of individualized and contingent contracts. Gregor Gall (2000) further notes that the introduction of such personal contracts in the news industry, though allowing individual journalists some freedom to negotiate their own terms and conditions of employment, in fact resulted in a deterioration of the working conditions of journalists: lower wages, less job security, and more contingent labor relationships (variable hours, job rotation, and flexitime). Similarly, Marjoribanks (2003) notes that the contemporary organization of work in transnational and converged news enterprises has allowed for the creation of a more flexible, multi-skilled and highly moveable – at least in the eyes of management – workforce.

A structure of convergent multimedia news organizations has been emerging since the mid-1990s, with companies all over the world opting for at least some form of cross-media cooperation or synergy between formerly separated staffers, newsrooms, and departments. According to a survey commissioned by the World Association of Newspapers (WAN) among 200 news executives worldwide in 2001, in almost three-quarters of these companies integration strategies were planned or implemented at that time. Perhaps the pioneering example is US-based Tampa Bay Online (TBO), a convergent news operation combining WFLA-TV (an NBC affiliate station), The Tampa Tribune, and a news website that provides original content plus material from print and television. The three media are housed in a special building called The News Center, where the different departments work together though a central multimedia newsdesk. After a couple of years of planning and development, in 2000 the reporters and editors of all the different media started moving in. Jane Stevens covered the transition for the *Online Journalism Review* and noted in 2002 that the gathering of breaking and daily news on all three platforms did not happen "without a lot of angst, complaints, missteps and aggravation. Some employees quit rather than change their way of doing journalism. Many more grumbled and went along. And a few rode the bull into the ring with equal parts fear and exhilaration."[4] The work at the Florida-based news organization is not completely integrated, but rather must be seen as an ongoing process of inter-firm collaborations. Michael Dupagne and Bruce Garrison (2006) for example note that the business and management operations of TBO remain separate, with staffs cooperating rather than working for a single converged organization. After spending a week at the News Center in 2003, Jane Singer (2004) found that although they were not universally enthusiastic, most journalists perceived convergence as having a number of advantages relative to the long-standing system in which each news organization is independent and, in the case of the newspaper and television station, competitive. At a personal level, the journalists seemed to agree that the ability to work in more than one medium can be seen as a career booster or at least an useful addition to their resume. William Silcock and Susan Keith also spent some time interviewing journalists at TBO (in 2002), focusing on the problems and challenges of convergence for everyday newswork. One of the issues they found was the lack of a common language in which to discuss, negotiate, and carry out more or less integrated news coverage. Instead, the journalists of the different media simply adopted a few words of each other's jargon, with print newsworkers (of whom there are 300+ in the newsroom on any given day) feeling in particular that they had to learn more about their ten or so colleagues in television than vice versa. "As a result, having a TV journalist write for one of the newspapers usually was, with a few exceptions, considered a waste of resources. So there was little need for TV reporters to learn the lingo of print journalism. However, in cases where print offered a dominant action, print terminology prevailed [. . .] The few television reporters who did write for print also had to adopt print's style conventions" (2006, p. 617).

> It is necessary to be multiskilled, because employers take that journalism as a whole, tv, radio, papers . . . if you write for radio you must also be able to write for the paper. When they say write a 200-word report you must produce it otherwise your chances of employment are limited. You have to have close relationships with people you work with, like with the tv people for example. [. . .] If you have a good relationship, life becomes easier. (M, freelance radio, SA)

All the researchers involved in studying and observing the ongoing operations at TBO and indeed other similar convergence journalism ventures around the world note how the biggest obstacles to seamless integration always boil down to cultural clashes. This goes especially for the print reporters, citing their deep distrust of broadcast journalists' work routines, scepticism about the quality of newswork of them having to do stand-ups for television or write blurbs for the Web, and their critical view on the quality and level of experience of their television and online counterparts. On the other side, television people reportedly feel their print colleagues to be conservative, slow, and oblivious to the wants and needs of their audiences (for instance as expressed through market research, sales figures and daily ratings). Kenneth Killebrew (2004) even reports how news managers charged with implementing the convergence process often seem skeptical and ill-prepared for the job. These kind of mutual stereotypes are not just the products of a stressful and confusing convergence experience, but are exponents of the historical separation of different professional identities and work cultures – which also suggests that interpersonal relationships and communication across the different media may resolve some of these clashes. Singer indeed emphasizes that cultural compatibility problems are not permanent. A number of journalists at TBO told her that anticipated problems had either not materialized or vanished with seeing the quality or successes of the work of their colleagues, eventually gaining respect for journalists in other parts of the news organization as a result of convergence.

The implementation and consequences of convergence differ from organization to organization. These different approaches can be explained by several factors. In an overview of new media innovation efforts in five European countries (Sweden, Denmark, The Netherlands, Switzerland, and Austria) we found a general lack of consensus or even vision regarding the nature of changes brought about by convergence among the editors, reporters, and managers involved (Bierhoff et al. 2000). Although several authors suggest that multimedia integration does not get realized across the board because of issues like (the remaining limitations on media ownership) legislation and the role of unions, ethnographers of the industry invariably note how traditional, carefully cultivated differences in organizational structures and work practices in specific news institutions correlate with critical perceptions of former competitors who are now supposed to be colleagues. Furthermore, convergence efforts tend to be seen as forced onto the reporter's plate (on top of everything else she is supposed to do), and the technology driven enterprise frustrates and confuses many of the newsworkers involved. Observers note that multimedia production processes generally are seen as time consuming and inefficient, and technical support is portrayed as insensitive to the reporters' needs. On the other hand, journalists that are among the earliest adopters and those leading the charge of innovations in their organization tend to be excited about the ongoing changes in the way they do their work. The point remains that from an institutional perspective convergence comes in different shapes and sizes, strongly influenced by both internal (practices, rituals, routines, cultures) as well as external (regulation, competition, stakeholders, publics) factors. Overall, convergence occurs throughout the news industry, affecting most if not all practitioners in the way they work.

A second feature of work on an institutional level is described by Schudson as a growing inter-institutional and intra-institutional news coherence, a development running parallel to processes of concentration and convergence in the news media. "Newsmagazines and newspapers preview their next editions on websites that reporters and editors at other news institutions examine as soon as they are available. Newspapers advertise the next day's stories on cable news stations. The result is interinstitutional news coherence" (2003, p. 109). It is important to note that this kind of streamlining of the news agenda is not a kind of working behavior caused by media concentration or convergence. Scholars have noted in the past how newsworkers tend to mirror each other closely, always treading a fine line between attempts not to miss out on important or breaking news stories covered by competitors, and the quest for the "scoop": to be the first to report an unique event, to uncover something nobody else reported on before. Convergence of different media organizations operating in the same local or regional market thus effectively solidifies news coherence (or rather: news isomorphism) across the media, even though reporters working in different departments still aim to score with a scoop for their respective newsrooms. Intra-institutional news coherence happens when the departments of converging or newly converged organizations synchronize their news agendas, use a common story budgeting system (as in the case of the TBO example), and coordinate the workflow across departments using a single content management system – a piece of software that enables automatic transfers and design of text, images, video, and audio.

The ongoing concentration of media ownership does not just extend the ties between different news operations across different media – it is also an institutional trend that makes news departments part of larger, sometimes transnational corporations that seek to pull the work journalists do into other sections of the industry.

> I firmly believe that all major media companies should be looking into ways to expand into console, mobile and pc gaming. The hardest part is evangelizing this type of work to those who hold the purse strings. I feel strongly that any media company that is not exploring the game space right now is not only ignoring the future but the here and now. I'm rather shocked at the apathy I meet, and yet it reminds of me of the climate we all faced when we started our online sites ten years ago. (M, media manager, US)

Several examples can be found in Australia, Japan, and the United States where journalists have collaborated with game developers to tell news stories.[5] Jon Burton (2005) shows that in the online news industry, interactive graphics have become a viable way to explain complex information and contextualize reporting, while several games developers such as Uruguay-based game studio Powerful Robot with its site

Newsgaming.com produce games that reflect real world events, using elements of journalistic practice to inform their design. The bottom line of such initiatives is the additional resources they require in news organizations, and the impact convergence of media (including forms, genres, and cultures) have on the working lives of journalists.

On an institutional level journalists face many changes – although it is still possible to argue that the concentration of media ownership and the convergence of news operations do not fundamentally challenge the fundamentals of basic news reporting (such as gathering and selecting news, interviewing sources, and fact-checking stories). However, as reporters and editors increasingly have to do their work in a context of individualized (and often contingent) contracts, cultural clashes, and increased economic pressures, it is safe to say that newswork for its practitioners has become more uncertain, stressful, and market-driven than in the past.

Technology. The success of journalism in reporting news across all media has always been influenced if not determined by technological advances: from manual typesetting to desktop publishing, from bulky cameras to handheld devices, from analog recording to digital editing, from single-medium to multimedia. At different times in the history of the profession, technology was (and still is) heralded as the bringer of all kinds of new threats and possibilities. However, technology is not an independent factor influencing the work of journalists from the "outside," but rather must be seen in terms of its implementation, and therefore how it extends and amplifies previous ways of doing things. "The new technologies make possible changes in news production and news outputs, but there is no reason to expect that the impact of the new technologies will be uniform across all news providers. Rather we might expect to find that there are differing impacts, contingent upon different technological applications which in turn are contingent upon the goals and judgments of executive personnel and any political regulators" (Ursell 2001, p. 178). I would like to extend Gillian Ursell's argument to include any and all workplace actors into the process of adopting and adapting to new technologies – including those who do not work physically in the newsroom and who are quickly becoming the majority in the field of newswork: freelancers, stringers, correspondents, and other non-permanently employed journalists. In an April 2006 survey on the changing nature of work in the news media in 38 countries, the International Federation of Journalists for example concludes that these "atypical" media workers make up around 30% of the membership of IFJ affiliates.[6]

Several studies have noted how the introduction of new technologies in newsrooms such as a content management system, desktop internet access, and the increased emphasis on so-called "multiskilling" (often involving retraining programmes or expectations of reporters in one medium to be schooled in the production techniques of other media) leads to increasingly pressurized production arrangements, to higher stress levels and burn-out rates, an ongoing recasting of specialists into generalist reporters, coupled with a widely shared sense among newsworkers that the newly introduced technologies translate into more work without providing added value for them. However, these reports are generally based on interviews with fulltime employees who in fact work inside newsrooms of provincial, national and global broadcast organizations and newspapers. Two important caveats must be made. First, that there is a significant cross-section of reporters and editors (in any organization) who can be considered to be enthusiastic early adopters of new technologies. Often these reporters are among the recent arrivals in the industry, and seize the chance for exploration and promotion the relatively "unclaimed" terrain the online environment offers to them (Deuze and Dimoudi 2002). A second caveat must be made regarding the role of the fastest growing segment of journalists: the freelancers, stringers, correspondents, and otherwise contingently employed newsworkers. For many of them, networked technologies, standardized software systems and the integration of newsflows across different media has potentially increased their chances of finding work, securing albeit temporary assignments, and working "on the go".

Even though the impact of new technologies in the news industry is varied, two general conclusions can be drawn: the process increases demand for and pressures on journalists, who have to retool and diversify their skillset to produce more work in the same amount of time under ongoing deadline pressures for one or more media. A second conclusion must be that technology is not a neutral agent in the way news organizations and individual newsworkers do their work – hardware and software tend to amplify existing ways of doing things, are used to supplement rather than radically change whatever people were already doing, and take a long time to sediment into the working culture of a news organization. The contemporary drive towards some kind of convergence across two or more media thus tends to offer little in terms of radically different forms of journalism or ways in which to gather, select, or report the news.

Jim Hall (2001) and John Pavlik (2001) place news and journalism in the social context of an evolving information society best typified by the dismantling of carefully cultivated hierarchical relationships between (mass) media consumers and producers. Hall for example emphasizes "the reciprocal links between news providers and readers" (2001, p. 25) in this "new" journalism environment, whereas Pavlik boldly states how "technological change is fundamentally reshaping the relationships between and among news organizations, journalists and their many publics, including audiences, competitors, news sources, sponsors and those who seek to regulate or control the press" (2000, p. 234). Contemporary journalism will have to come to terms with their audiences as co-authors or co-producers of the news (Bruns 2005). Instead of having some kind of control over the flow of (meaningful, selected, fact-checked) information in the public sphere, journalists today are just some of the many voices in public communication, including but not limited to professionals in public relations and marketing communications, advertisers, and citizens themselves through weblogs, podcasts, and using all kinds of other online publishing tools. Disintermediation removes the journalist as the traditional intermediary between public institutions – notably business and government – and news consumers. Although it is safe to say that this trend is not unique to the last few decades – people distributing their own neighborhood newsletters or broadcasting so-called "pirate" radio have been around for quite a while – new technologies like the internet propel such activities to the same (or even bigger) limelight as the work of professional journalists. In this context, technology indeed can be seen as severely disruptive, challenging the foundations on which work in journalism (and indeed, in the media as a whole) is built: media are made for audiences. Once the audience disappears or has gone off to make its own media (while freely and illegally copying, pasting, editing, and remixing the work of professional media producers), the professional identity of the media worker gets significantly undermined.

In a telling conclusion to three years (2004–2006) of closely monitoring the American news media, researchers at the US-based Project for Excellence in Journalism signaled "a seismic transformation in what and how people learn about the world around them. Power is moving away from journalists as gatekeepers over what the public knows. Citizens are assuming a more active role as assemblers, editors and even creators of their own news. Audiences are moving from old media such as television or newsprint to new media online. Journalists need to redefine their role and identify which of their core values they want to fight to preserve - something they have only begun to consider."[7] The same report also signals how news outlets have been reducing their newsrooms in an effort to cut costs, adding fuel to the argument that the current situation in many news organizations is one of having to do more with less (or only freelance) staff. In June 2006, the World Association of Newspapers released a strategy report called "*New Editorial Concepts*," exploring the ways in which affiliated news companies around the world are coming to terms with the changing media landscape. The report mentions six trends that are influencing newsrooms worldwide:

- The explosion of participative journalism, or community-generated content;
- The rise of audience research by media companies to learn new patterns of media usage;
- The proliferation of personalized news delivered online and on mobile devices;
- The reorganization of newsrooms optimized for audience focus;
- The development of new forms of storytelling geared toward new audiences and new channels;
- The growth of audience-focused news judgment and multimedia news judgment.[8]

What all the mentioned changes, challenges, promises, and problems of new technologies and convergence culture mean for the individual journalist differs widely across different news outlets and media organizations. Overall, journalists tend to embrace technology as long as they perceive it to enhance their status, prestige, and the way they did their work before. Resistance to a wholehearted embrace of innovative communication technologies as an instrument to foster community-generated content or connectivity tends to be grounded in a "reluctance by management to lead toward adoption, lack of resources to invest in new technology, lack of training, little or no access to the new technology, fear of lost time required to learn, and not enough time in the work schedule" (Garrison 2001, p. 234). The success or failure of journalists to deal with the role of technology in their work

must therefore also be set against the history of their professional identity, the changes in the institutional structure of the
industry, and the fragmentation and even disappearance of
their audiences (and thus advertisers).

Organization. Newspaper, magazine, television, radio, and
online media organizations, newsrooms, or individual
journalists tend to have quite different work practices. As a
rule of thumb, news outlets are located near the center of the
city or region their core audience is located. Broadcast
organizations are most likely to cluster together in a single
location, such as the "Media Park" in Hilversum, The
Netherlands (just south of Amsterdam). Even competing
newspapers sometimes occupy office buildings across the
street from one another. Since the introduction of news
websites in the mid-1990s, an ongoing debate in the industry
has been whether to integrate these online journalists into
the main radio, television or print newsroom, or to set up
separate office space for them. Although industry observers
tend to advocate integration – especially considering the
global trend towards convergence of multiple media
companies – most online newsrooms are located elsewhere
in the building, city or even country. Several larger news
organizations additionally operate specific bureaus –
geographically assigned crews that tend to be stationed near
government centers such as Brussels (to cover European
Union affairs), New York (United Nations), and Washington,
DC (US politics and the White House). Groups of smaller
organizations tend to pool resources and use the same
bureau, consisting of one or more correspondents and video
and sound technicians. Most news outlets have greatly
reduced the numbers of foreign correspondents in an effort
to cut costs. Instead, they rely on the services of two global
multimedia information conglomerates that dominate world
news, particularly regarding video footage of events and
happenings across the globe: Reuters and the Associated

Press (AP) – both primarily based in New York and London. Considering the dominance of these global agencies in the field of international reporting, Oliver Boyd-Barrett and Terhi Rantanen (2001) go as far to say that they should be seen as "news instructors," setting the standards of (western) news values across the globe during the twentieth century. Chris Paterson (2003) correspondingly argues that fewer major news providers are informing more people and doing so from fewer sources. Reuters, AP, and other smaller news agencies such as the French Agence France Presse (AFP), or United Press International (UPI) take advantage of the ongoing convergence within the news industries primarily through the formation of strategic alliances that increase their news gathering and distribution reach.

Newsrooms, whether in print, broadcasting or online, look remarkably the same all over the world.[9] Between 1999 and 2003 I have visited the offices of newspapers and television stations in places as varied as Lisbon, Helsinki, Amsterdam, Hilversum, The Hague, Johannesburg, Windhoek, Los Angeles, San Diego, and Perth, and found similar circumstances everywhere. Newsrooms tend to be quite open, with separate cubicles per reporter or per department (or "news beat"). The workspaces tend to look a bit chaotic: papers everywhere, cell phones and regular phones scattered across the desk, with a constant hum of desktop (and, increasingly, laptop) computers in the background. Comparing newspaper newsrooms and editorial structures in Germany, Great Britain, and the US, Frank Esser (1998) found that centralized newsrooms with a high division of labor were more particular to the Anglo-Saxon companies he visited. Continental European newspapers maintain many more branch offices which produce complete sections or localized versions of the paper. Although Esser reported that American and British journalists were more likely to be specialized and limited in the range of their responsibilities and range of tasks, later studies suggest – as noted earlier – that the trend toward media convergence in these and other countries puts increasing demands regarding the multiskilling of journalists involved.

Although journalists, much like other professionals in the media industries, like to think of themselves as autonomous and creative individuals, in fact most of the work at news outlets is based on a set of routine, standardized activities. Summarizing the ways in which journalists generally report the news, Lance Bennett (2003, p. 165ff) suggest they confront three separate sources of incentives to standardize their work habits:

- Routine cooperation with (and pressures from) news sources, such as public relations officials, spokespeople for organizations, celebrities, and politicians;
- The work routines (and pressures within) news organizations that especially newcomers learn about by having to adapt themselves to mostly unwritten rules and conventions about the "house style" way of doing things;
- Daily information sharing and working relations with fellow reporters, which in the case of certain beats results in journalists moving as a pack from event to event, encountering their competitor-colleagues at the same places, covering the same issues.

As the number of media outlets and sources of information increases, journalists tend to spend more of their time at their desks than in the past. This can contribute to newsroom socialization on the one hand – as reporters spend more time with each other indoors – as well as it facilitates telecommuting and other flexible work practices for "wired" correspondents and freelancers on the road. With wireless internet-enabled laptops, high speed telecommunications networks, and other portable communications devices, many employees today can work almost anywhere at least some of the time. In broadcast and converged news operations this has for example led to the growing importance of so-called "one-man-bands" or the less gendered "backpack journalists"

(Stevens 2002). These reporters are sent out on assignments alone, being solely responsible for shooting video, recording audio, writing text and putting it all together in a coherent news package. Although this practice is not new – in the 1960s and 1970s newspaper journalists would for example also at times take photographs for their stories – new technologies and the flexibilization of work have propelled this kind of individualized reporting into the news mainstream.

The organization of newswork follows certain rules, contributing to the effective management of information overload. Different news genres have established conventions and deadline structures, newsroom hierarchies tend to be based on seniority and status, and the majority of news is prescheduled (press conferences, business budget reports, or sports events) or delivered to the reporters through press releases. Conventional wisdom suggests that at least 80 percent of all the information that flows into a news organization gets discarded instantly. This includes pitches of freelancers and struggles at editorial meetings between different departments or individual reporters to get their story into the broadcast, paper, magazine or onto the site. Stuart Allan (1999, p. 50) suggests that the capacity of a particular news organization to present a wide range of information and viewpoints to some extent is preserved by the ongoing clash and discordancy of interests which exist between owners, managers, editors, and reporters. In an overview of the ways in which organizational and professional constraints influence the agency of individual reporters, Liesbet van Zoonen (1998) argues that journalists working for less institutional and more audience-oriented outlets – such as popular magazines, local news stations, human interest, and infotainment genres – experience more room for their personal interests and opinions when deciding on what to report. Studies among journalists consistently show how social and cultural competition, peer criticism, and even conflict within and among news organizations are a vital part of doing newswork. "This is a competition centered around an ethos which holds that it is right and inevitable to measure one's performance consistently against that of others and that one should thrill in victory and agonize in defeat" (Ehrlich 1997, p. 314). Competition in the newsroom is generally not perceived by journalists as a source of conflict, and indeed sometimes is seen as part of a professional team spirit.

> My time in print coincided with my years as a junior reporter. The media is mercilessly hierarchical and being at the bottom of the pile always comes with frustrations and heartache. So I am not sure I experienced as many joys as a print journalist., but I think that was largely an age and status thing. But TV was terrifically exciting. It was great to be part of a close knit team, (camera, editor, reporter) and, to be honest, good fun to be working for a medium that is so powerful. (F, tv news, NZ)

Although rivalry, creative conflict, and competition do play an important role, the professional socialization and generally quite bureaucratic structure of most mainstream news organizations in fact prevent any major deviancy. With the ongoing proliferation of niche markets and corresponding hyperfragmentation of audiences across different media titles, channels and forms, it is possible to argue that more spaces are opening up for individual journalists to get their stories out. On the other hand, these developments must be seen in the context of increasing commercial pressures and an overall problematic economic situation for most news outlets, thus limiting their cultural and financial potential to experiment with different, alternative, minority, or otherwise marginalized voices.

Culture. The twentieth century history of (the professionaliza-tion of) journalism can be typified by the consolidation of a consensual occupational ideology among journalists in differ-ent parts of the world. Journalism's ideology serves to continu-ously refine and reproduce a consensus about who counts as a "real" journalist, and what (parts of) news media at any time can be considered to be examples of "real" journalism. These evaluations subtly shift over time, yet always serve to maintain the dominant sense of what is (and should be) journalism (Deuze 2005b). An occupational ideology develops over time, as it is part of a process through which the sum of ideas and views of a particular group about itself is shaped, but also as a process by which other ideas and views are excluded or marginalized. In this context Barbie Zelizer (2004, p. 101) refers to ideology as the collective knowledge journalists employ in their daily work. The key characteristics of this professional self-definition can be summarized as a number of discursively constructed ideal-typical values. Journalists feel that these values give legitimacy and credibility to what they do – they talk about them every time they articulate, defend or critique the decisions they and their peers make, or when they are faced with criticisms by their audience, news sources, advertisers, or management. The concepts, values and elements said to be part of journalism's ideology in the available literature can be categorized into five ideal-typical traits or values that are generally shared among (or expected of) all journalists:

- Public service: journalists provide a public service (as watchdogs or "newshounds," active collectors and disseminators of information);
- Objectivity: journalists are impartial, neutral, objective, fair, and (thus) credible;
- Autonomy: journalists must be autonomous, free, and independent in their work;
- Immediacy: journalists have a sense of immediacy, actuality, and speed (inherent in the concept of "news");
- Ethics: journalists have a sense of ethics, validity, and legitimacy.

One has to note that these values can be attributed to other professions or social systems in society as well, and that these values are sometimes inevitably inconsistent or contradictory. To journalists this generally does not seem to be a problem, as they integrate such values into their debates and evaluations of the character and quality of journalism. In doing so, journalism continuously reinvents itself – regularly revisiting similar debates (for example on commercialization, bureaucratization, "new" media technologies, seeking audiences, concentration ownership) where ideological values can be deployed to sustain operational closure, keeping outside forces at bay. Randy Beam (2006) for example finds that "[r]ank-and-file journalists are more dubious about the business goals and priorities of their organization than are their supervisors" (2006, p. 180), showing that journalists in general tend to be more satisfied with their jobs if they perceive that their employer values "good journalism" over profit. Research by Tracy Russo (1998) additionally suggests that journalists identify themselves more easily with the profession of journalism than for example with the medium or media company that employs them. She especially notes how socialization and largely similar work-group demographics contribute to this identification process, through which journalists adopt the current and dominant way of thinking about the profession, its role in society and in the community it serves.

Comparing results from surveys among journalists in twenty-one countries, David Weaver (1998) found support for claims that the characteristics of journalists, including their demographics, are largely similar worldwide. Weaver however concludes there is too much disagreement on professional norms and values to claim an emergence of universal occupational standards in journalism. In earlier work (Deuze 2002) I had the chance to compare the findings from recent surveys among journalists in five countries: The Netherlands, Germany, Great Britain, Australia, and the United States, all similar Western democracies with at least a century-old tradition of established media roles in society. The surveys in these countries were all conducted via phone or face-to-face interviews. The scholars involved worked together in constructing and wording the questionnaire, exchanging data and interpreting results. Interviews yielded data on three sets of characteristics: occupational characteristics (contract, salary, type of media organization, specialization, relationships with colleagues and the audience, daily practices on the job); professional characteristics (media role perceptions and views on ethics); and basic demographic characteristics.

In the five countries examined one finds median ages of 32 in Australia, 35 in Germany, 41 in the United States, 42 in The Netherlands and 38 years in Great Britain. Newcomers in journalism tend to start out in jobs in local media, or find temporary positions and internships at (commercial) broadcast and online media. In print and among the more prestigious titles, journalism tends to be dominated by forty- and fifty-somethings. In a recent interview with the *Listener* – a popular New Zealand weekly current affairs and entertainment magazine – Linda Clark, one of the most prominent news professionals in her country, explained why she was quitting journalism after an award-winning career of 22 years referring specifically to the issue of age: "I've begun to think that journalism is a job you do best when you're twentysomething, strangely. When you're twenty-something the world is villains and heroes, issues are black and white and that's how journalism works now. It's how the media has to see issues a lot of the time. So when you're 25 and you're full of energy and your worldview is monochromatic, journalism makes a lot more sense. When you get older and nothing is black and white, and you realise that even the people you hound have redeeming features and even the people you really like do terrible things, it becomes so much more complicated."[10]

Generally about one third of journalists are women. Among younger reporters in the Netherlands (those who are still in their twenties) the gender ratio is 46 percent male to 54 percent female. The situation is similar in Germany, where 42 percent of journalists under 30 are women. The gender balance is more equal in (commercial) television newsrooms and among those working for popular magazines – both professional groups dominated by part-time, flexitime, and freelance professionals.

> You know what is really good about being a woman? You can use it. No, I'm kidding, it is really a lot of fun. It just does not seem like such a men's world. Now when I think about it, most of the professionals I have contact with are men. But that does not bother me at all, men are easy-going. I think it is an advantage of being a women. At our organization there are more women who are difficult to work with than men. (F, online, NL)

Regarding the media careers of women in general and in (Western) journalism in particular, Romy Fröhlich (2007) warns against what she calls a "friendliness trap" in the cultures of news organizations. On the one hand, supposedly "feminine" skills are legitimized in the increasingly market-driven, project-based teamwork environment of contemporary global cultural production. Certain evolutionary expectations of women such as being better communicators, having a greater capacity for empathy and inclusiveness, and a talent for dealing with (difficult) people seem to open more doors into the media professions. However, argues Fröhlich, "sooner or later [. . .] the supposed feminine values, attributes, and behaviors will be associated with a lack of assertiveness, poor conflict management, and weak leadership skills. And suddenly, the apparent head start turns out to be a career killer" (p. 174). Indeed, research on the position of women across mass communication shows clearly how age-old inequalities remain firmly intact well into the twenty-first century: a glass ceiling, the wage gap, sexism and harassment on the workfloor, gendered divisions of labor, and an overall lack of professional development opportunities (Creedon and Cramer, 2007).

In all countries the percentage of ethnic or racial minorities is well below the respective national averages. In The Netherlands two percent of journalists explicitly indicated having a migrant background (coming mainly from Turkey, Morocco, and Surinam). The British survey reported 1 percent journalists with a black Caribbean or black African ethnic origin. The surveys in Australia and Germany did not ask about ethnic backgrounds. Weaver and Wilhoit reported 9.5 percent of US journalists in fulltime jobs having an African-American, Hispanic, Asian-American or Native American background. Education levels are particularly high among Dutch and US journalists (79 percent and 89 percent), both countries with a long tradition of formal journalism education programs. In Germany (65 percent), Great Britain (49 percent) and Australia (35 percent), journalistic newcomers predominantly flow into the newsrooms via on-the-job and in-house training, although that situation is changing with the rapid development of all kinds of schooling options in those countries. In general it seems clear that today a bachelor's degree is the minimum qualification necessary for entering journalism. In most countries around the world, journalists seem politically a bit more left-leaning that the population in general. Reporting on studies in the United States, Britain, Germany, Sweden, and Italy, Thomas Patterson (1997) concluded that journalists generally are mainstream progressive rather than radical liberals, whose political beliefs work to "shade" rather than "color" the news.

Most journalists still work for traditional print media, newspapers in particular, although reports over time show that the fields of broadcasting and new media are gaining ground in terms of new openings and jobs offered to newcomers. Magazine, broadcasting, and online newsrooms tend to be significantly smaller in staff size than newspaper newsrooms, and the work for these newsmedia gets done almost exclusively on a contract by contract, freelance or stringer basis. The mentioned "beat-system" in journalism tends to be quite gendered. Consider for example the situation in The Netherlands, where the specific beats mentioned show women most likely (64 percent) to specialize in health and lifestyle issues and men dominating the sports (96 percent), crime (86 percent), and new media (87 percent) beats. Additional analyses show that minority journalists are more likely to work in "minority beats" (such as news about their "homeland," asylum seekers, or minority youths in metropolitan areas). The surveys show that journalists in Germany, the United States, Great Britain, and Australia agree that their influence on (the formation of) public opinion is even greater than it should be. Such findings indicate a sensitivity among journalists about their impact on contemporary society, though the extent of that impact is unclear and one may wonder whether these answers might reflect a preference for a neutral role, or are an exponent of a rather negative image of a gullible audience.

One indicator of the way journalists see their function in society is to ask them how important they rate a number of possible roles journalists are supposed to play in society. Topping the charts in all countries is an orientation towards explaining the news and getting the news out quickly. More recent surveys in the US, The Netherlands, and Germany show that the interpretive role of journalists is becoming increasingly popular. Although most countries do not have a similar history of longitudinal surveys among journalists, the available publications suggest that this conclusion can be drawn for most countries.

What these overall findings and conclusions suggest, is that journalists in elective democracies share similar characteristics and speak of similar values in the context of their daily work, but apply these in a variety of ways to give meaning to what they do. Journalists in all media types, genres, and formats carry the ideology of journalism. It is therefore possible to speak of a dominant occupational ideology of journalism on which most newsworkers base their professional perceptions and practices, but which is interpreted, used and applied differently among journalists across media. These interpretations and applications of what it for example means to be ethical, to provide a public service, or to break the news as quickly as possible are largely determined by the culture of the newsroom of publication one works for. "Culture is a potent influence in any organization, but particularly so in media ones. It can act as a powerful constraint, limiting acceptance of new products and processes, but it can also be a motivator, an enabler, a liberator of organisational energy" (Kung-Shankleman 2003, p. 77). The culture of newswork is a crucial element in the way journalism operates, not in the least because of the relative stability of the news industry throughout much of the twentieth century, creating the conditions for a firmly sedimented "way of doing things" in many companies, newsrooms, as well as among senior reporters and journalism educators. It is through this culture that the values of journalism's occupational ideology get their practical, everyday meaning. By doing things a certain way and privileging certain rationales for those actions and editorial decision-making processes over others, reporters and editors at specific news outlets sustain what can be called operational closure: the internalization of the way things work and change over time within a newsroom or at a particular outlet. Outside forces are kept at bay primarily by the rather self-referential nature of newswork, as expressed through the tendency among journalists to privilege whatever colleagues think of their work over criteria such as viewer ratings, hit counts or sales figures. Another example of journalism's self-reference can be found in the way ethical and professional problems and critiques are channeled through self-appointed accountability mechanisms such as press councils, ombudsmen, and readers' representatives, and trade publications (Van Dalen and Deuze 2006).

After interviewing more than a thousand journalists in Germany, Siegfried Weischenberg and Armin Scholl (1998) have further pointed out that the more or less consistent and routine-based organization of newswork within specific outlets is realized mainly through internal circular communication, where reporters and editors constantly reinforce, reiterate, and thus reproduce certain ways of doing things. Following Niklas Luhmann (1990), it is possible to argue that the culture of journalism functions as an autopoietic or "self-organizing" social system. Newcomers are primarily expected to adapt themselves, and to adopt the dominant (ideological) perception of what journalism is. A specific implication of this mindset is addressed by Farin Ramdjan in her investigation of the role and position of ethnic minority journalists in the boardrooms and newsrooms of all the main news outlets in The Netherlands in 2002.[11] Ramdjan concludes that newcomers in general and minorities in particular suffer from an existing closed, and hard to penetrate Dutch newsroom culture, characterized by a rather homogeneous professional population, a relatively untransparent editorial hierarchy, and a lack of mechanisms to encourage and promote new talent. In an earlier study, researchers (Becker *et al.* 1999) found that the most likely explanation for the difficulties women and ethnic minorities experience to either get a job or keep their jobs at American news organizations is the fact that hiring decisions in journalism are primarily based on informal membership of existing self-similar networks of journalists.

It is important to note that this more or less oppressive news culture is not consistently nor necessarily wholeheartedly underwritten by all journalists equally. With the numbers of minorities slowly but surely growing in newsrooms, an ongoing fragmentation of titles, channels, outlets (and thus jobs), the emergence of new work practices in convergent journalism, the proliferation of all kinds of citizen's, alternative and community media both online and offline, and the growing importance of freelance and part-time work in the field, it is safe to argue that the culture of journalism is becoming more diverse, open, and dynamic all the time. Journalists today enter a workforce that is built on the heyday of the twentieth century era of omnipresent mass media, but that is expected to perform in a contemporary news ecology where individualization, globalization, and the pervasive role of corresponding networked technologies challenge all the assumptions traditional newsmaking is based upon.

CHAPTER SIX

Film and Television Production

"Strategists must today work amid fragmentation, divergence, and opposition in the market: to optimize across nascent and long-standing business models; across new and traditional release windows; with old and new content programmers; and with both IP and traditional supply chains. This is the beginning of the end of television as we know it and the future will only favor those who prepare today." Thus reads the conclusion of a study on the future of television by IBM of March 27, 2006, a report based on industry interviews across the television value chain in the US, Europe and Asia.[1] Amidst similar predictions, surveys show how the sales of tv sets as well as the time spent with television are still growing consistently every year. Nielsen Media Research reported in September 2006 that the average American home today has more television sets than people, and that "average American television viewing continues to increase in spite of growing competition from new media platforms and devices."[2] In countries such as the US, Germany, and The Netherlands, about one in three pre-teens has a TV in their bedroom. A study among 1,000+ American parents of May 24, 2006 by the Kaiser Family Foundation concludes that the most common reason parents give for putting a TV in their child's bedroom is to free up other TVs in the house so the parent or other family members can watch their own shows.[3] In the movie industry, a similar picture emerges: on the one hand, observers and professionals proclaim the end of the industry because of piracy (illegal distribution of movies through online filesharing or sales of DVD copies), declining ticket sales, a surge in the popularity of home theaters, and the ongoing fragmentation of audiences. On the other hand, the total revenue from movies (including but not limited to ticket sales, rentals, and VHS/DVD sales) is still relatively stable, with a few big blockbuster titles (which in the industry are called "tentpole movies") breaking new records every year.

All this does not mean the film and television industry is not experiencing significant disruption and change. In a column for *Variety* magazine's website (of June 25, 2006), Peter Bart summarizes the issues facing the American film industry: "In the beginning, the business model for Hollywood studios was clear-cut: They financed the development and production of a slate of movies, drawing on a roster of stars and filmmakers, and presided over their distribution to wholly owned theaters [. . .] These days, production costs increasingly are being outsourced to hedge funds and other financing groups. And overseas entities often cover marketing and distribution costs in distant territories. Essentially, every aspect of studio overhead is now under serious scrutiny by corporate numbers crunchers."[4] Bart notes how the studios' corporate owners continue to demand costs must be cut and staff trimmed, but that the industry is also trapped within long-established management structures. The age of the traditional studio, concludes Bart, seems to be over. A business analysis in the *New York Times* (of August 19, 2006) confirms this picture: a shift in perspective among the larger studios from making movies to making products and content, executives complaining about facing too many unknowns (including changing moviegoer habits, rising production costs, changing technologies, and digital piracy), and the replacement of high-profile creative positions with marketing specialists and brand managers. As *The Times*'s Laura Holson summarizes, "many here predict dark days ahead. Movie-making is no longer a growth business, and has lost its luster among investors. Even the most well-run large movie studios often return only 5 percent to 7 percent annually [. . .] Executives say the decline in DVD sales, which began in early 2005, is taking a toll on budgets. And to complicate matters, studios have not figured out a money-making digital strategy to deflect piracy while, at the same time, appeasing fickle consumers who want movies online."[5]

The film industries in the United States, Great Britain, France, India, and elsewhere have been considered by a number of academics to be the vanguard of future employment practices in the global information society (Lash and Urry 1994). Work in film and, increasingly, in television and video, can be characterized as extremely precarious, generally freelance, project-based, involving what Josephine Langham (1997) has called a "roller-coaster atmosphere" of continual transformation and shifting uncertainties. Such uncertainty includes having unpredictable income levels, negotiating complex networks of industry players (actors, agents and managers, directors, producers, writers, and all kinds of technical staffers), as well as constantly moving in and out of having a job as televisions seasons end, film projects are completed, or management changes and people get replaced.

> Especially at the beginning you are kind of a "just a day-player," you know, you work for a day and you are paid [. . .] We're all pretty much independent, none of us works, not many of us work on a salary basis. we're all pretty much freelance workers [. . .] There is a lot more work now than there was when I first started [. . .] There are very few people in this business that have a halfway family. It is very tough on family, very tough. (F, film/TV location scout, US)

Thomas Borcherding and Darren Filson suggest that the risky, project-based, extremely uncertain yet completely hit-driven nature of the business "creates an environment that can lead to exchanges of sexual favors of newcomers" (2000, p. 26), hinting at the so-called "casting couch" problem of alleged sexual exploitation of young men and women entering the movie industry. The authors however conclude that with the breakup of the large studio-system and the death of long-term contracts tying certain employees to these companies, their power to make or break the careers of newcomers has diminished.

However, as there are many more people wanting to get in to the film and television business than there are jobs available, tension runs high in finding, keeping, and consolidating jobs and, ultimately, a career. Scattered evidence from recent lawsuits in the entertainment industry (such as a long-running case in the US ending in February 2006 against the writers of the popular television series *Friends*), suggest that the courts are sympathetic to arguments from industry lawyers that because of the particular nature of media work a pervasive sexual atmosphere can be necessary for the creative process of producing adult entertainment in general, and comedy in particular.[6] Helen Blair is among those who warn against both an overtly romantic view of the glamorous nature of working in film and television, as well as against the notion that in these industries everything is unpredictable and uncertain. Blair (2001) considers the film and television industries to be in a state of "precarious stability," signaling the structural dependency of production houses and film studios internationally on foreign (especially US) financing and distribution, and emphasizing how many professionals experience some continuity in employment over time because of being hired as part of teams that have worked together successfully before, or through an assertive, self-policed work ethic vis-à-vis their superiors.

Another caveat regarding the perceived precariousness of work in these industries must be made regarding at times quite predictable and almost factory-like film- and television-making process in the industry, as is the case with the production of popular franchises and series like long-running soap operas (the BBC's *Eastenders* and ITV's *Coronation Street* in Great Britain, NBC's *Days Of Our Lives* in the US, Channel Ten's *Neighbours* in Australia), other popular television drama (crime shows such as *Law and Order*, cartoons like *The Simpsons*, situation comedies like the British series *Last Of The Summer Wine*), and serial movies (some examples between 1976 and 2006: *Rocky I* through *VI*; between 1979 and 2007:

Alien I through *IV*, and *Alien vs. Predator I* and *II*). Many of these serials are made with crews consisting of more or less the same team members, or with a least a core of permanently employed professionals. Furthermore, some workers in the industry are in fact under long-term contracts with modern multidivision talent agencies, such as US-based William Morris Agency, or both US and UK-based International Creative Management (ICM).

Although the film and television industries have different histories and traditions in different countries, they have some aspects in common. Films and television shows are produced on a project-basis, and the required resources – financing, materials, talent, marketing, and human resources – are often assembled for a single film or season and then disbanded when production is complete. "Members of film crews therefore work on a temporary basis for many different production companies [. . .] resulting in a fragmented labor market comprised predominantly of freelancers [. . .] In that context, individuals choose (and aspire) to coalesce into work groups, referred to here as semi-permanent work groups (SPWG). An SPWG comprises a group of individuals working in the same department (e.g. camera, art) who work as specialized project teams and move from project to project as a unit" (Blair 2003, p. 684). Blair concludes that the situation for media workers in film and television can best be described as "semi-permanent" – always moving between intensive employment and short or long periods of unemployment. Work in the film, television, and video sectors of the media thus involves dealing with structural job insecurity as well the relative certainty of having new projects to shop around for, and – in a best case scenario – to prepare for.

As discussed earlier in this book, some assert that different sectors of the economy are becoming more like those in the cultural or creative industries. Research among and about workers in film and television suggest that these industries display many of the same characteristics of a more or less traditional production model – largely operating on the basis of recurring, routined, and repetitive processes – while at the same time experiencing structural uncertainties and unpredictability regarding the success or failure of its products, the success or failure of securing new (temporary, project-based) employment, and combining commercial viability with creative control in a globalizing industry.

Institution. "The film industry is big, complex and strange. It is big, not just in terms of its self generated hype and self-aggrandizement, but in real monetary terms; and critically in terms of trade earnings [. . .] Significantly, the film (and the associated advertising and television industries) is a growth industry, comfortably outstripping most other industries. Moreover, its employment impact is localised" (Pratt and Gornostaeva 2005, p. 2). Television stations and film companies tend to be part of a relatively small number of corporate groups that own multiple media properties. For example, according to the Bureau of Labor Statistics of the US Department of Labor, in 2004 over four-fifths of the jobs in film and television were in establishments with twenty or more workers, even though most companies in the industry have fewer than five employees.[7]

> It's just not the same. When you are working for a national network I found that they just had greater vision and the people were just so bright. Of course I mean these are the best [media professionals] in the country. And if anything I found that these were people who were, they were brilliant people. They were just able to see the big picture. Yet there are other things. You felt totally isolated to a great extent. You feel more insulated, this is a huge corporation. (F, TV production, US)

Although most of the major studios and production companies consolidated their holdings into large corporate conglomerations in the 1990s, a parallel development of media deconcentration is going on at the same time. In an analysis of this trend for *Slate* (March 18, 2005), Jack Shafer suggests that infighting, slow decision-making, and a general lack of cooperation among different media properties within the same corporation are the main reasons for this lack of synergy: "[a]sk anybody who works for a big media company how much cooperation they get from their corporate cousins, and you'll be greeted by a horse laugh. The broadcast division won't give the record division a sweet advertising deal if it can sell the same air time for more to an outside client. At the bottom of the ledger, every subsidiary must stand for itself."[8] Beyond consolidation and deconcentration of ownership lies a complex web of mostly temporary connections, links, joint ventures and alliances between media companies in a wide variety of fields. A 2006 overview by business strategy firm Future Exploration Network shows for example how the media industry is becoming increasingly interconnected, especially regarding combinations of content (film and broadcasting companies) and distribution (new media firms like Yahoo!, Google, and Microsoft with telecommunications companies such AT&T) deals.[9] Together with these multifunctional as well as dysfunctional entertainment corporations and networks a mass of specialized firms under independent ownership operate in film and television, providing specific services – such as set design, rental equipment, scriptwriting, talent agencies, and technical support – or producing shows and films for different what Jeremy Tunstall (1993) calls "publisher-broadcasters": companies that are solely responsible for assembling, publishing, and transmitting content that was largely commissioned and acquired from outside producers.

Steven Phelan and Peter Lewin (1999) claim that the emergence and rapid growth of independent film and television companies is in fact a strategic outsourcing response by Hollywood studios to the market and other uncertainties. In doing so, the large conglomerates would distribute some of the risks of mediamaking away, while retaining their bargaining power by controlling the marketing, distribution, and exhibition of movies or television shows. On the other hand, Robert DeFillippi and Michael Arthur (1998) have argued that the emergence and rise of independents originally was not only vigorously opposed by the Hollywood studios, but that a lot of these companies were (and are) started by successful actors or producers in order to have more creative freedom and ownership rights. All agree that the complex pattern of production in film and television gets facilitated by the flexible model of temporary project-based enterprises. Analyzing the film industries in Paris and Los Angeles, Allen Scott (2000, p. 99) notes how the tendency to outsource and subcontract the making of films and television shows contributes to the ongoing vertical and horizontal disintegration of corporate entities. Similar conclusions can be drawn for the television industries in these and other countries, where "production is increasingly carried out by networks of agents (creative artists and technicians under contract to a producer or company), and not, as in the past, by rigid, bureaucratic corporates sourcing programmes almost exclusively from internal facilities" (Barnatt and Starkey 1994, p. 253). Scott (2004) concludes that the accelerating process of decentralization of television production activities intensifies competition in global markets. In this context the non-US film and television industries are sometimes described as "cottage industries," as opposed to a corporate model where the production, distribution, and exhibition activities of film making and screening are integrated. Indeed, the vertical disintegration of the corporate studio model is a permanent response to a changing economy and society, indicating a shift towards a new institutional situation where constant change, production flexibility and market unpredictability are the norm, where "interpersonal and interfirm networking and the leveraging of social capital promote a more disaggregated production system" (DeFillippi and Arthur 1998, p. 18).

All of this does not mean large corporations control all aspects of the production of television and movies, nor has the global market completely opened up to hundreds of thousands small or independent companies. This complex and symbiotic two-tier production system in film and television runs throughout the industry, where independent companies can be under long-term contract of corporations, and where the same multi-national companies can completely outsource production or acquire a show or movie after production elsewhere, and where ownership of different media properties has a tendency to change quickly.

As with other creative industries, the world of broadcasting and film is an uncertain one: markets are unpredictable and move fast, and the production process is characterized by high skill division and task complexity – consider for example the number of professionals involved in the making of a film or show by examining the credit roll. To give a rough indication: according to the Motion Picture Association of America (MPAA), in 2005 a total of 549 new films were made in the US, with the American motion pictures industry employing 199,000 people in production and services that year.[10] In the UK, a 2005 survey of workers in the British film industry showed that 71 percent of them were unemployed at least once per year, for periods up to ten weeks or more.[11] Industry employment trends further indicate that the total number of employees (especially in production and services) in film and television is constant or slowly increasing after rapid growth in the late 1990s. In New Zealand – home of Peter Jackson's *King Kong*, and his *Lord of the Rings* trilogy – in 2001 the number of people employed in film and video production was more than double that of 1996.[12] The institutional context of work in film and television therefore must be seen as a combination of a growing number of people coming into an industry that is increasingly fragmented and networked in the way it runs its operations. "The result is that product innovation is organized in projects to facilitate experimentation, and that these projects are carried out on the market rather that within firms. This results in a high degree of organization and management of the market, in the guise of active leaders/boundary spanners, social institutions and geographical clustering. Generally, however, all entertainment firms compete on product differentiation in terms of content, rather than price. Simply put, in order to entertain, they have to continuously come up with new and original products" (Lorenzen and Frederiksen 2005, p. 18).

The recent developments in the institutional arrangement of work in film across different places and countries can be typified by what Andy Pratt and Galina Gornostaeva (2005) call a "translocalism" of production, meaning that film and television are increasingly produced at different locations – often in different countries – at the same time. Doris Baltruschat (2003) notes how the surge of international co-productions throughout the 1990s can be seen as typical of the increasingly export-oriented television and film industries, which practice leads to more commercially viable "global" products based on entertainment values rather than the expression of (or critical reflection on) distinctly "local" issues. "The drive to compete internationally, on the one hand, and to protect regional markets, on the other, had led to increased co-production activity in Canada, Europe and Australia" (2003, p. 157). The rise of co-productions is practically facilitated by the growth of international networks and affiliations between small and large media organizations that are not necessarily part of the same corporation. The internationalization of production gets also expressed in what is known as "runaway production": the loss of jobs in television and film when a project, or part thereof, is outsourced to other countries.

> There used to be two locations for entertainment and that was New York and LA. Now, that is no longer the case – everything's pretty much moved to Los Angeles [. . .] but the entertainment industry in general, especially in film, has gone to Canada and that's because of tax breaks [. . .] and a lot of people in LA are really upset about that because they are not going to get citizenship there and they can't work in Canada [. . .] and also there's tax breaks in Mexico so a lot of productions are being moved outside of the United States right now. So it's a tough job market. (M, independent filmmaker, US)

According to a 2004 report by the International Labor Organization this "runaway" film and television production increased by 500 to 800 percent since the early 1990s. The jobs lost would be virtually all those available for stunt performers and background actors, technicians, costume, make-up and scenery workers, plus some even among leading actors.[13] A continuing study by the US-based Center For Entertainment Industry Data and Research (CEIDR) shows that the shift in production of theatrical motion pictures from the US keeps growing as countries all over the world introduced incentives and government subsidies – especially in the higher budget ranges. The CEIDR also notes a modest increase in California-based television and to some extent film production, most likely encouraged by the American Jobs Creation Act of 2004.[14] This piece of legislation consists of a number of (temporary) tax breaks for both businesses and individuals including a phased-in deduction for domestic manufacturing income. Local film industries have historical roots, with national and regional governments in many countries using tax incentives to make these industries popular for location shooting. Andy Pratt (2006) notes how this situation is typical for locations such as Canada, Australia, New Zealand, Slovakia, South Africa, France, in every major city and many rural districts. The CEIDR further notes how the production of feature films, made-for-television movies, broadcast and cable network made-for-television movies and miniseries worldwide increased substantially between 1998 and 2005 (especially in Canada, Ireland, Australia, New Zealand, Eastern Europe, and the UK), signaling a collapse in US production during that period – with the exception of scripted prime time one-hour and half-hour broadcast and cable television programs and reality programs. Although these data are split up between different countries, a lot of productions are organized and institutionally co-owned across geographical boundaries.

Considering the twin processes of international co-production and runaway film and television production, the institutional arrangement of these industries must be seen as a typical example of the global production network of the creative industries, as discussed earlier in this book.[15] Such networks of production in the creative industries consist of interconnected functions and operations through which goods and services are increasingly globally produced and distributed. This means that global production networks not only integrate firms (and parts of firms or even individual cultural entrepreneurs) into working structures which blur traditional corporate boundaries or alliances, but also integrate national economies (or parts of such economies) in various ways. Neil Coe emphasizes how for example the investors and subsidizing parties in the making of a film or television series may be territorially specific (primarily, though not exclusively, at the level of the nation-state), these production networks themselves are what he calls "discontinuously territorial": for every film and every new season or series, networks are assembled and reassembled, new alliances are forged, large numbers of media professionals move in and out of these projects that are organized, and funding gets organized under different conditions with partners both in government (through cultural subsidies) and in business – all of which ties places and people temporarily together across different countries.

Technology. John Pavlik and Shawn McIntosh note how the US movie industry boycotted television when it first arrived, refusing to provide movies that could be shown on television (in full screen format, with for example more close-ups than wide shots to accommodate the design of the average TV screen) and even blacklisting actors who went to work for television. "Studios felt that television would draw audiences away from theaters and thus ruin the movie industry. This resistance to technological change has become a common pattern among entrenched media entertainment industries" (2004, p. 132). This picture is perhaps a bit too simplistic:

technological development and product innovation are intrinsic elements of working in the media, and the film and broadcasting industries are no exception. Indeed, these industries are crucial in the introduction, development and popularization of certain technologies such as video standards and equipment.

Although technology is part of the everyday workstyle of people in film and television – from the preparation of sets, stages, and locations to shooting, editing, and other post-production work (including marketing and distribution) – research does not suggest it radically changes the way practitioners in these industries work. On the other hand, the computerization of work has had specific consequences for the industry, as exemplified by the widespread us of software applications such as the popular *Movie Magic*, standardizing script breakdown and shooting scheduling. Such programs, as well as the contemporary omnipresence of cell phones on the set, facilitate a production environment characterized by constant changes, tweaks, additions, and deletions communicated almost instantly across different levels of the crew and the production pipeline.

> When I was starting out, the 1st AD [assistant director, MD] did breakdown pages for every scene in the movie. Every element involved in filming the scene goes into the breakdown page. Back then, the 1st would do these by hand [. . .] When computers came along, a program called Movie Magic (which we still use) was created. It automatically generates all of those breakdowns [. . .]So now, instead of being on the set next to my 1st AD, I'm sitting in the production trailer staring at my computer and printing updated schedules for the producer. Instead of a producer just making a decision, they create a lot more work for me, much of it secretarial. (M, 2nd assistant director, US)

The crucial role of technology in the media industry provides a structural demand for specialized, highly skilled freelancers, which specialists are indispensable to media employers but tend to be in short supply: "[t]he reasons for lack of supply ranged from a technological advance that employers wanted but which was known, at that particular moment, to only a very few individuals in the industry, to a traditional skill known to a dwindling number of individuals" (Storey *et al.* 2005, p. 1041). In a study among freelancers in the UK media industry, Kerry Platman finds a paradox: on the one hand freelancers tend to be seen as equipped with latest "cutting edge" skills and technologies, providing immediate and ready-made solutions to the labor and product needs of media client-employers. "Yet, at the same time, employers expected freelancers to 'fit in' and to share their 'vision'. They were cautious of entrusting work to individuals who might find their methods questionable or alien. They needed to identify any mismatches or tensions in advance. Budgets had dwindled, technology had advanced and customers had become more demanding. The pressures of modern media management were such that employers could not risk intransigence or rigidity from their freelancers" (2005, p. 581). The industry thus finds in its project-based and freelance-dominated organization of work an answer to the distinct challenges new technologies pose to making films and television shows.

Beyond specialized labor in temporary and to some extent quite restricted contexts the International Labor Organization (ILO) suggests that new information and communication technologies reinforce the tendency for actors and other film industry workers to be freelance rather than salaried, and for a de-professionalization of their jobs. As is for example the case of digital cameras replacing film, their capacity for almost endless (cheap) shooting and recording erodes the position of the people who load, cut, and edit (expensive) celluloid film, and shifts more control to the post-production process in digital studios. One aspect that runs throughout the literature on the role of technology in media work in general, and film and television work in particular, is the almost complete lack of training on the job regarding the use of new hardware or software, equipment, and technological facilities. This situation is particularly noticeable in the Anglo-American world, whereas employers in countries such as Germany and Sweden reportedly feel more responsible for providing their workforce with up-to-date skills (Christopherson and Van Jaarsveld 2005). In the US, this effect is mitigated to some extent by the role of numerous film and television schools as the primary provider of skills in these industries (as well as providing internships and other unpaid apprenticeship opportunities to newcomers), whereas in Europe or Australasia the majority of skills training takes place on the job. Arne Baumann (2002) shows that in Germany and the UK the most common route for newcomers into the media production industry is through a learning-by-doing process where skills are picked up informally and without certification. This individualization of the responsibility for learning and (re-)training has important implications for the shape and size of the workforce, as several studies show how media workers tend to spend many hours of unpaid work-time each week for training in order to keep up with the latest technologies.[16]

Arguably the most discussed role of technology in film and television has to do with the distribution and usage mechanisms of movies and programs. The fast-paced developments in digital, networked, screen-based and portable technologies are considered a threat to traditional ways of delivering content to audiences. Even though big blockbuster movies still draw huge national and, especially in the case of US products, international audiences, and the hours people spend all of the world watching television hold steady or are increasing, the "buzz" in the industry is one of radical, sweeping change. However, it is far from clear what these changes exactly will be. The main concern of the industry seems to be the popularity of interactive visual media such as sites on the World Wide Web with downloadable and uploadable streaming video (*YouTube* in particular), and digital video recorders that allow viewers to record, store, and order content on demand while fast-forwarding through or completely skipping other programming (including advertising). Producers and academics alike have thus engaged in a debate about a potential future of interactive television, where content is produced that somehow gives the consumer more control over her viewing experience (examples are: different camera angles, multiple-choice endings, opinion polls, and other audience voting mechanisms, links between websites and television shows, advertising-free content for a price, and so on). After conducting a survey among 74 American, Asian, and European corporate experts of interactive television (ITV), Jan van Dijk and Loes de Vos found that their images of ITV are rather weak and imprecise, even though these executives were all desperately seeking a suitable and concrete business model of ITV – which search Van Dijk and De Vos typify as a quest for some kind of "Holy Grail" (2001). Their research shows how new technologies open up and disrupt the business processes of media organizations, even though the predicted radical shift does not happen, and technologies get appropriated largely to fit existing patterns of production.

This does not mean the technological context for work in television and film is not changing. Indeed, numerous industry and scholarly reports suggest new types of television emerging around the world: ITV, IPTV (personalized television channels online using the internet protocol for websites, such as *Mine TV* in The Netherlands or *Bud TV* in the US), SMS-TV and MMS-TV (television genres that include text or multimedia messages sent in by viewers). In the US, South Korea and Japan television has found another way of interacting with new technologies, as people can watch programs and shows (on demand) on mobile handsets (such as the iPod Video, handheld gaming devices like Sony's PSP, or next generation cell phones). Interestingly, the companies that are developing specific television content for these small screens are new media (Qualcomm, Microsoft), technology (Intel, Texas

Instruments), and phone businesses (Nokia, Motorola) rather than traditional broadcast organizations.

What all of these formats, genres, and channels have in common is a growing role for the (individual) consumer in the process of producing television. As television users increasingly grow accustomed to having some kind of influence on the programs they are watching, producers have to consider interactivity as part of their imagination and preparation of new shows, or the next season of existing programs. The combination of consolidation and networking of different media organizations, formats, and properties with the emerging participatory media culture online suggests that making television (or movies for that matter) is increasingly not just about making television anymore – it is about developing cross-media strategies, adapting formats and plotlines to user interactions, and providing sponsors (investors and advertisers) a wide variety of options to tie in with the program's content. This combination of technological, economical and cultural convergence has become an important part of everyday experience on the workfloor of film and broadcast firms.

Organization. Companies, services, and individuals in the film and television industries have "an overwhelming tendency to locational agglomeration" (Scott 2000, p. 83), of which Hollywood in Los Angeles is the best example. The 2006 figures of the Los Angeles Economic Development Corporation show that 130,000 people were employed in entertainment in Los Angeles that year, compared with 127,200 in 2005.[17] These locales tend to be very high cost, which suggests that there must be a strong need and benefit of such location patterns. The reputation or image of certain places as being conducive to the creative industries has particular clustering effects: talent, services, and auxiliary companies gravitate towards these places, transforming them into distinct areas where everybody seems to be involved in the industry in one way or another. This clustering allows the different creative industries quick and relatively cheap access to services, talent, and skills.

> You always have to be flexible in this industry because nothing is permanent, companies are always being bought and stations fold so you always have to be ready to move and change so if you are living in the middle of nowhere [. . .] there's always going to be more jobs in LA or New York, mostly in LA if you want to work in production so you always have to be ready and willing if you want to succeed to move to a bigger city. (F, TV production, US)

The dominant theme in the literature is a notion of media workers as free agents, constantly searching for new challenges and better guarantees for their creative autonomy – which combined with a view of the industry that organizes itself around temporary projects requires and results in an abandonment of traditionally hierarchical, top-down, and rigid organizational structures and practices. Considering the way film studios and television producers work, this does not seem to do justice to the situation for many media workers, who are hired under semi-permanent contracts partly because of the repetitive nature of the tasks they have to perform, and in part because sometimes it is in the best interests of a studio, an agency, or an individual department head to attract, retain, and motivate certain talent through enhanced terms and conditions of employment. As the immaterial labor of workers in the creative industries is in itself an unstable and unpredictable commodity, it produces a higher degree of uncertainty of outcomes. This for example means that although a majority of practitioners constantly moves in and out of project-based employment, the organization of work in these industries tends to be quite hierarchical, rationalized, and formal – and if we want to believe recent trade publications, increasingly so. "The shift to more hierarchical, fragmented work and organisation with creative industries maturity should not obscure the fact that much creative industry, as a production chain, has long been characterised by 'traditional' divisions of labour separating conception and execution, with the former derived from creative, high skill, high value-added workers and the latter undertaken by routine, low skill, low value-added workers" (Warhurst *et al.* 2005, p. 15).

Although the labor markets for film and television in for example the US, Europe, and Australia or South Africa have different histories, the situation is becoming increasingly similar worldwide. Employment relations in these industries have been transformed from the structured and clearly bounded state of European public broadcasters' internal labor markets into boundary-less external labor markets, where a growing group of skilled professionals and experts flexibly supplies an industry of a few big companies and many small producers. The health of the occupational market and economy in film and television in fact is dependent on the mobility of workers between organizations, as the industry constantly needs new professionals for a wide variety of tasks and services dependent on the project at hand. The uncertainty (about whether the new job is the right one for you, or whether your new hire is the perfect person for the job) that comes with this high mobility of workers across different sectors of the industry gets managed by the companies and professionals involved through what Arne Baumann calls "restriction of access" policies: a strategic reduction in the number of exchange partners (such as freelancers and other temporary employees) within a production network. "If transactions are concentrated on a restricted circle of partners, the number of transactions increases. As a function of the number of transactions, coordination is improved as the frequent interaction aligns expectations and goals of the partners. At the same time, the uncertainty about each other's capabilities will decrease because partners learn about each other's skills over time [. . .] The result is relational contracting between already familiar partners" (2002, pp. 31–32). It is quite common in the industry that department heads – such as executive producers, directors of photography, and people in charge of set design or makeup – take a specific group of employees under their wings as they get hired into new projects. These lower-ranking professionals then get to select their assistants, of which candidates they also tend to privilege those with whom they had good professional (and/or private) relationships before. The most relevant recruitment strategies for production companies (and, increasingly publisher-broadcasters) are a combination of this hiring of regular staff and the use of reputation-based networks of colleagues – where regular staffers for example function as intermediaries by recommending people from their personal networks for positions in new project teams.

> All departments like to feel like they have a "team". Early in your career, if you're, say, a grip, you are looking for a Key Grip or Best Boy to latch onto to take you from show to show. If you're a Production Assistant, you look for a 1st or 2nd Assistant Director. The more teams you're a part of, the more you work. Then, as you move up the ladder, you become the person whose team people are looking to join. (M, film assistant director, US)

Simon Cottle uses the notion of a "production ecology" in the organization of work in television (similar to Grabher's earlier mentioned concept of the "project ecology" of advertising), which can be characterized by "a set of competitive institutional relationships and co-operative dependencies" (2003, p. 170). Project work in the media is ecological in that it combines elements of severe competition between investors, studios, service companies, and individuals with aspects of cooperation and dependencies through formal and informal production networks, reputation mechanisms, and access restriction policies. In order to understand the complex work-style of television and film professionals, one has to include elements of repetition as well as structural change, the development of interfirm and intrafirm networks and loyalties, and an appreciation of their ongoing negotiations to achieve a delicate balance between competing for jobs and collaborating on projects. Similar to the advertising industry, film and television workers tend to see their activities in terms of "above the line" and "below the line" tasks. Above the line work is thought of as creative talent and is more visible and better paid. It mostly consists of acting, directing, producing (scheduling, budgeting, human resources, quality control), and scriptwriting. Below the line practices are placed at the end of a movie or show's credit roll as these consist of technical and supportive work as varied as (digital and analog) editing, lighting, set design and construction, wardrobe assistance, and camerawork. "The 'line' is an accounting demarcation used in developing the budget for production. Some above-the-line costs are incurred even before a film goes into the production stage. Above-the-line costs include the story rights, the screenplay, the producer, the director and the principal cast" (Blair *et al.* 2003, p. 631).

Making a film or television show is dependent upon a complex mix of variables, some financial, some speculative, some technological, and some artistic. This does not mean that the creative process is completely unpredictable or free-floating in a sea of uncertainty. "Even though cinematic, musical, and multimedia goods and services appear at the moment of final consumption in a form that usually masks the concrete circumstances of their production, they nevertheless originate in complex labor processes grounded in distinctive geographic conditions that almost always leave strong cultural traces in the end result" (Scott 2000, p. 82). This does suggest that the organization of production has a direct impact on what the film or program will eventually look like. As the film and television industries, like other (mass) media, face increasingly unforeseeable changes in viewer tastes and preferences, as well as confronting consumers that are becoming producers too, the organization of work has to strike an uneasy balance between flexible and innovative production on the one hand, and some kind of routinized, more or less reliable structure of the creative process on the other hand. This is brought about by organizing the process in temporary projects, which are not fixed organizational designs, but loose-fitting structures of individuals, teams, and companies that are temporarily connected through a specific motion picture, television pilot, or season. Such project structures tend to be capable of flexible, experimental, and customized production, as well as being able to adapt to changing circumstances. It must be noted however that project-based employment still does not guarantee work for each individual involved. Changes in department heads or the replacement of a key actor or producer may very well result in contracts to be cancelled, as the incoming "above the line" professionals want to bring in people from their own network of colleagues and friends.

In an age of translocal and transnational production and col-laboration, the organization of work in the media can increas-ingly be seen as the management of temporary market-based networks of skill-holders, some of whom may work together within the context of a specific firm, studio or company, but most of them hired individually to perform a specific task or service for the project at hand. The majority of workers in tele-vision and film production has now become freelance. Ursell (2000) puts the proportion of freelance workers in the produc-tion side at 60 percent of the total. Allen Scott (2000, p. 88) uses the doubling of the figure for permanent workers as a rule of thumb for determining the total number of temporary work-ers in the film and television industry. Even among public broadcasters in Europe (such as YLE in Finland, the VPRO in The Netherlands, the BBC in England, or ZDF in Germany), who traditionally employed most of their workers on a permanent basis and developed content largely in-house, the trend in recent years has been to cut full-time staff and rely more on contract and freelance labor. It is safe to say that on any given project the vast majority of workers are employed in a freelance capacity. The uncertainty experienced by freelancers is a direct consequence of their short tenure and high labor mobility, combined with doing their job with the knowledge that there are little or no guarantees in terms of continuation or extension. In the television industry crews that get hired on a series of multiple seasons will still all go "on hiatus" over the summer, at the end of which period they may or may not get invited back onto the set.

According to Lorenzen and Frederiksen, one of the main problems of managing complex projects in film and television is to maintain the motivation of the practitioners involved (2005, p. 12). People are either preparing for another project or handle multiple projects at the same time in an effort to spread the risk of surviving the inevitable "dry" period of not getting hired onto a new project or a next season for several months. An additional stress factor during such a phase – next to financial worries – is the fact that the longer such a dry spell lasts, the more it looks suspect to potential employers who check the resume of the professional involved. Based on a research project involving 51 freelance workers in British television, radio, newspaper, publishing, and new media, several tentative conclusions can be drawn about how professionals experience their largely freelance worklives in the media (Storey *et al.* 2005). Overall, freelancers are quite positive about the implications of being relatively independent and autonomous in the way they build and give meaning to their careers. They see their freelance assignments as allowing them to work in new ways, on a variety of projects, and for a range of clients. "In theory at least, they were in a position to refuse unattractive assignments, walk away from difficult clients and renegotiate impossible deadlines" (p. 1051). The practice of identifying, applying for, and securing employment in the highly competitive media marketplace can be quite daunting, though. For one, labor markets in the creative industries are not completely free and open, as much work gets assigned through personal networks (deliberately limiting access to outsiders). On the other hand it can be in fact too easy to enter these markets, which can lead newcomers or those desperate for work to accept low fee rates, poor working conditions, or make them otherwise vulnerable to potentially exploitative situations. Freelancers have to come to terms with the fact that their sources of work could dry up at any time, and without warning. In doing so, the researchers found they deployed distinct coping strategies, consisting of:

- Trying to maintain a diverse range of clients and networks;
- Avoiding dependence on one employer or source of employment
- Pursue contracts for clearly defined and at times limited periods that would allow them to keep an eye open for other artist- or income-related opportunities;
- Developing and cultivating networks (through formal structures like talent agencies, guilds, unions, and professional associations, and informally through personal networks) in order to extend their range of potential clients and to gain access to intelligence about current or future job options;
- Sensitizing themselves to market opportunities (even if that means doing things they are not specialized in or that would mean changing their portfolio);
- Trying to build a reputation for being able to stay within budget, complete on deadline, and meet specified job specifications;
- Supplement their incomes by holding jobs in other fields as media work-based income is erratic;
- Avoiding behavior which could be seen as awkward, inconvenient or confrontational.

It is important to note that freelancers despite these complex, time-consuming and at times problematic efforts (in terms of maintaining artistic integrity as part of their personal and professional identity), they can still fail to gain work.

Culture. Considering earlier comments about the uncertainty and vulnerability of those more or less desperate for work in film and television, the crucial point towards understanding the way film and television industries work is through informal, personal, and social networks and relationships, distinctly blurring the lines between the private and professional. In fact it could be argued that the informality of the labor market in film and television is not only a prerequisite in order to succeed, it is in fact privileged and favored by people in the industry as a necessary component to the creative process. This deliberate blurring of the personal and professional as a benchmark for the production of culture in film and television connects on at least three levels with the way practitioners give meaning to their work. Studies among media workers generally show how creative work is experienced as intensely personal because it is often an expression of self. Additionally, the deregulation and vertical disintegration of the film and television industries has further supercharged the prevalence of (largely informal) social networks and personal connections as predictors of (temporary) employment or some kind of semi-permanent job security. Finally, on a technological level, new media have increased the outsourcing of services and projects to specialized businesses or individual experts, while also facilitating translocal and indeed global production networks – which further fragment the formal relationships and hierarchies of employees and employers and thus contribute to a need for other, more informal, forms of cohesiveness and consistency.

Because of the dynamic and informal nature of employment and projects in film and broadcasting and the limited life of most businesses in the field, the defining characteristics of a culture of work are even harder to articulate than elsewhere in the media. On the other hand, labor markets in these industries are distinctly local, as businesses and individuals tend to converge at specific locations such as London, Paris, Los Angeles, Sydney, and Wellington, which in turn helps a certain localized culture to sediment in the ways in which professionals interact, establish the norms and values guiding work and network processes, and give meaning to their (and each other's) plight. The networks of practitioners in film and television to some extent conform to the broad classification of the three phases of filmmaking: preproduction, production, and postproduction. Preproduction is the planning phase, which includes budgeting, casting, finding the right location, set and costume design and construction, and scheduling. Production is the actual making of the film. This is where the bulk of the workforce is active, which in the case of motion pictures can mean that the project involves hundreds of people. Postproduction activities take place in editing rooms and recording studios, where the product is shaped into its final form. A 2005 survey of the British audio visual industries' workforce among 6,885 professionals shows that the balance between men and women in most aspects of television and film production is more or less equal, with the exception of studio or equipment hire and postproduction, where the percentage of women is less than one-third, with an overall representation of women in the workforce of 38 percent.[18] Nearly half (47 percent) of the British respondents was aged under 35 years. The Australian Film Commission reports that the proportion of male to female employees for the film and video production industry in 2003 stood at 60 percent male to 40 percent female.[19] In the United States, theatrical and television cast performers' employment statistics from the Screen Actors Guild (SAG) show that "the distribution by gender in 2004 continues the well-established patterns of the prior four years, whereby males garnered the lion's share of roles, however, the total percentage of roles for female actors increased marginally. With regard to age, previous casting trends prevail, with a majority of roles going to actors under the age of 40."[20] Annual surveys in the US by Martha Lauzen show that in 2005, women comprised 17 percent of all directors, executive producers, producers, writers, cinematographers, and editors working on the top 250 domestic grossing films.[21] Lauzen also did work on the television sector of the industry (and both sectors are deeply interconnected through cross-ownership and production networks), finding that women made up 25 percent of all creators, executive producers, producers, directors, writers, editors, and directors of photography working on situation comedies, dramas, and unscripted programs (such as reality television and game shows) airing on the broadcast networks during the 2004–2005 season.[22] Beyond percentages, it also seems clear that the distribution of labor tends to be quite gendered, with women specifically underrepresented in the technical (pre- and postproduction) aspects of film and television work.

> Honestly it hasn't been my experience that women have a harder time getting jobs than men [. . .] I will say that there are some professions that are typically held by women, and some by men, and it could be hard to cross over [. . .] Grips and electricians tend to be men, hair and make-up artists tend to be women. I did meet a female grip once, and was truly impressed. (F, film production, US)

Werner Dostal and Lothar Troll (2004), studying the representation of professionals working in the media on German television, similarly conclude that men outweigh women 2:1 in the industry, and particularly dominate in action-oriented entertainment genres. The researchers furthermore show how media workers are overrepresented in the age group of 20-39 year olds. The social structure and working conditions of the media workforce display significant global, that is not national or locally specific patterns. A common feature in most Western countries is an employment pattern in the creative industries of a relatively young workforce, a high inter-firm mobility with patterns of short-term employment and ubiquitous freelancing (Baumann 2002). Workers in the three different phases also have varying lengths of tenure. Film crews, including groups such as the camera and sound departments, are usually only employed for the period necessary to shoot the film. However, the middle management layer, heads of departments, and management support staff are employed during preproduction, as well as during the period of making the actual film. The result of these employment patterns is that people work almost exclusively on a freelance basis, moving from one short-term contract to the next. As noted earlier, there are numerous examples of working in film and television whereby groups of workers collectively move from one project or season to the next, forming what Blair (2003) calls semi-permanent work groups. The participants of SPWGs can develop close relationships and certain ways of doing things over time. Such groups of colleagues – usually assembled on the initiative of a department head such as a director of photography, sound mixer, or first assistant director – generally stay together for a couple of years or so, and professionals can be members of more than one SPWG at a time. Film and television workers especially need to secure membership of multiple teams, networks and work groups, as not all of them guarantee employment every year. Therefore, the existence of these SPWG's contributes to the distribution of practices, know-how, norms and values between people and fields of expertise across an otherwise extremely uncertain, dynamic, and individualized industry. As stated earlier, the movement within and between projects and SPWG's is largely dependent on connection through personal contacts and industry insiders. The majority of workers in film and television hear about potential new jobs from someone they worked with before, or through general word of mouth – emphasizing the crucial role (informal) networks play in the industry.

> Persistence and determination pay off [. . .] no one cares what school you went to, it's really just what you bring to the room when pitching your story or yourself that's what really counts. There's no real job security whatsoever – every job is temporary so you're constantly thinking about the next [. . .] as in every industry, you have to pay your dues, mostly to get your name out there and make contacts. It's all about relationships [. . .] kind of like how to oil the machine to get read, get heard, get bought. (F, TV screenwriter, US)

Several studies suggest that men and women network in different ways, noting how women are more likely to form friendship bonds with the people who make up their network, whereas men are more distant and instrumental. Both men and women tend to be ambivalent regarding their network relationships, arguing on the one hand how the intense and unpredictable working environment of the media draws people together, which informality at the same time can destroy friendships in the case of conflict and tensions that are quite common in the industry. The characteristics of the culture of work in the media – long hours, job uncertainty, lack of income stability, high stress levels, intense teamwork – have direct consequences for the work – life balance of the professionals involved. Single households and dual earner households prevail, with childless couples a vast majority – especially among freelancers. In the UK, 41 percent of people in the film production workforce are single, and just over three quarters (77 percent) has children. It can be argued that professional freelancing for women is an acceptable employment form only as long as they can and are willing to match the "male professional" ideal. Those who want to have children either rely on a partner willing to practice egalitarian sharing of parenting and housework or have to reduce their job aspirations to a short-term career.[23] In this context Dianne Perrons (2003) notes with some surprise how the vast majority of professionals in the media like their work, for example noting their deep personal involvement with what they do. Although this may be true, it does not mean the media workplace is an egalitarian or open system. Not only are there extremely few women in top-level or so-called "green-lighting" positions where they could affect investment and programming decisions, the numbers for ethnic minorities in these industries in for example Australia, the UK, Germany and the US are almost negligible (except perhaps among actors). Furthermore, (controlled) conflict is a key value in the culture of project-based work in film and television. Conflict may arise over many issues in the creative process, but one can single out three particular areas of problems and concern that run throughout the chain of production: time, governance, and communication (Lorenzen and Frederiksen 2005).

> Sometimes scripts get torn apart and ruined, other times they get better in the process. The most that a writer can do is to accommodate the other members of the production team without ruining the script. If you don't find a way to accommodate them they will fire you and hire another writer. Then you have no control of or even influence over the process. You may – probably will – get fired anyway at some point, but if you refuse to make changes or are not "cooperative" you will be fired off the project for sure and may get a reputation for being "difficult" besides . . . not good for your long term career. (M, TV screenwriter, NL)

With the increase in international co-productions and translocal production networks it becomes quite a challenge to allocate and complete the different tasks in the process at the right time. Governance issues ensue with the involvement of multiple departments (production assistance, camera, sound, technical, hair and make-up, and so on) that according to Tunstall (2001, p. 194) each have a tendency to think horizontally in terms of only their own speciality, and not only have different skills but also different sources of information, motivations, and often interests. To that one can add the at times different agendas, work practices and idea(l)s of freelance specialists and contracted or semi-permanent employees. Third, because of the extremely varied nature of the sometimes hundreds of participants in the production of a show, season or motion picture it is possible to imagine the coming together of many beliefs, expectations, languages, norms, and practices in a single project, leading to (potential) communication problems. The production process of film and television is complex and chaotic, and at the same time hierarchical and bureaucratic – it is therefore not surprising that professionals upon completion of a particularly taxing project look forward to spending some time "on hiatus," in between jobs, unemployed . . . even though that situation becomes problematic again within a couple of weeks.

CHAPTER SEVEN

Game Design and Development

Arguably the most anticipated and biggest international event in the computer and video game industry is the annual Electronic Entertainment Expo (E^3) in Los Angeles, organized by the Entertainment Software Association of America (ESA). The expo is only open to game industry professionals, journalists, and guests of the publishers, distributors, hardware manufacturers, and game development studios that pay hefty fees to exhibit their products and services. E^3 is usually held in the third week of May of each year at the Los Angeles Convention Center (LACC) in the United States. In 2005 and 2006 between 60,000 and 70,000 people attended the show, according to the ESA. The ESA – a trade group representing US computer and video game publishers – announced on 31 July of 2006 to significantly scale down their annual E^{3}Expo, stating that "the evolution of the video game industry into a vibrant and expanding global market has led to the creation of major events in different regions, such as the Games Convention in Leipzig, the Tokyo Game Show, and company-specific events held by Sony, Nintendo, Microsoft, and others around the world. As a result [. . .] it is no longer necessary or efficient to have a single industry 'mega-show.'"[1] Game journalists and industry observers alike went ballistic – some lamenting the loss of the show, others skeptical about the largely commercial motives of the ESA, several considering the future for smaller, independent game studios now that they lost a prominent international platform. If anything, the furor over the annual E^3 and the comments on its downsizing suggest that the computer and video game industry is not just about "fun and games" anymore – it is a multibillion dollar industry that has effectively challenged and recently fused with all the major other cultural industries.

Until the "slump" years of 2005 and 2006 (when the entire industry prepared for a transition to the next generation hardware and software requirements of game console manufacturers Microsoft, Nintendo and Sony), the game industry's revenues grew three times as fast as video rental and cinema box office. The revenue generated by games, although still much less than the film, television, or especially music industries, goes well into the billions of dollars. Numerous studies and surveys commissioned by industry associations show how playing computer and video games has become a family affair, and cannot be exclusively attributed to the typical young adult males or teenage boys demographic anymore. According to the Interactive Software Federation of Europe (ISFE), "By 2003, 60 percent of Sony's PS2 players were over 18 and women now consider video games as a credible pastime, thus adding up to a quarter of European players in the age group 15 to 35. Similarly in the US the average video game player is now a grownup person aged almost 30, his European counterpart being 28 years old."[2] The ESA claims that the average age of gamers is 33 years, with 35 percent of gamers under 18, 43 percent between 18 and 49 years, and 19 percent 50 years or older. According to these organizations, female gamers make up about 40 percent of the gaming population, with the ESA concluding that "Women age 18 or older represent a significantly greater portion of the game-playing population (30 percent) than boys age 17 or younger (23 percent)."[3]

One particular effect the omnipresence of computer games in everyday life may have is on the characteristics, attitudes, and beliefs of young aspiring professionals and recent graduates currently entering the media workforce. In a study among young American business professionals Adam Carstens and John Beck (2005) for example document how games are now pervasive among those in the workforce, with the vast majority of workers reporting they have significant gaming experience.[4] "Games reinforce certain beliefs about the self, how the world should work, how people relate to one another and finally, how the goals in life in general. Games create a self-centered universe where the player is running the show, and can manipulate other people and objects to his or her will (within certain rules, of course)" (p. 23). The researchers also found that gamers are more likely to believe that "winning is everything" and "competition is the law of nature" than non-gamers, and that traditional and seniority-based top-down office hierarchies are deeply distrusted by gamers, as Carstens and Beck argue that playing games all their lives teaches these young professionals to dispatch with those in authority as quickly as possible. Although it is highly unlikely that these attitudes and beliefs can be attributed solely to growing up with playing computer and video games, it is safe to say games have become a widely accepted and popular part of contemporary society.

The global popularity of computer and video games can be seen as a revolution in home entertainment, within which environment people are moving from a passive world to an interactive world. Computer and video games (hereafter: games) however are much more than media industries with impressive profit margins or powerful anthropological case studies of the (future) organization of society; the sector is also home to a distinct logic of media work, where game developers and designers, once envisioned as counter-cultural explorers steeped in the computer hacker ethos, are now part of a creative process with multimillion-dollar corporate budgets. Within this field, certain game designers have become like rock stars or celebrities, with a professional identity similar to the "auteur directors" in film (Chaplain and Ruby 2005, p. 4). Names like Will Wright (*SimCity* – 1989; *The Sims* – 2000; *Spore* – 2007), Shigeru Miyamoto (*Donkey Kong* – 1981; *Mario Bros.* – 1983; *Legend of Zelda* – 1986), Peter Molyneux (*Populous* – 1989; *Theme Park* – 1994; *The Movies* – 2005), John Carmack (*Wolfenstein* – 1992; *Doom* – 1993; *Quake* – 1996) and

"CliffyB" (short for: Clifford Bleszinski; *Unreal* – 1998; *Gears of War* – 2006) generate a level of interest and fame as well as notions of creative uniqueness and excellence among a growing worldwide audience of gamers in a manner that parallels the images of Stanley Kubrick, Steven Spielberg, and George Lucas a generation before them. These and hundreds of thousands of other gameworkers design games that are played on a bewildering variety of devices, and indeed contribute to the innovation of hardware as well as software throughout the computer industry.

Games are primarily played on consoles that account for more than half of all game sales – the Nintendo GameCube or Wii, Sony Playstation (1 to 3), Microsoft Xbox or Xbox 360; on handheld portables – Nintendo Game Boy Color and Game Boy Advance, Nintendo DS, Sony PSP, Nokia N-Gage; using any mobile phone or other handheld game device; on desktop computers – browser based games (running in Windows, Mac OSX, or Linux) and online multiplayer games (via computer portals like Battle.net or console portals such as Xbox Live); and in game arcades using coin-operated machines, which is how the industry got started back in the 1970s and 1980s. For game developers each of these platforms has pluses and minuses. The advantage of console development is that a team develops a game for a static system with properties that are known and remain the same as the console goes through its five to six-year production cycle, whereas designing for personal computers means having to take into account almost endless and continuous variations of processors, video and audio cards, memory specifications and operating systems. Handheld games usually have much shorter development cycles and smaller teams than either console or PC games, thus offering publishers a relatively high return on investment. In the following overview of the media logic of game design and development, my focus will be on teams and projects aimed at the mainstream mass market for consoles and PCs.

Institution. With the downsizing of E³, the transition to next generation consoles, the emergence of mobile gaming and an ongoing convergence of the business with other cultural industries – particularly film, television, and advertising (the blend of which with games is called "advergames") – the games industry is indeed coming of age. It continues to be something of a maverick field of production within the creative industries, while it at the same time converges with a media system that is dominated by a handful of corporations – which trajectory shapes what Jennifer Johns calls a global video games production network. "The video games industry has a history which accelerates from small firms, maybe even individuals programming software in their bedrooms, producing for a highly niche market, to an industry dominated by multinational hardware producers" (Johns 2006, p. 157). Kerr (2006) describes the early games software industry as a "cottage industry" based around individual programmers working from home on a commission basis, evolving into a multinational industry where games are made by teams often numbering more than 100 programmers, designers, testers, artists, composers, technicians, and writers.

> Until the mid-1990s the threshold to start your own game company was pretty low. At the time you could get together with a bunch of guys in an attic or garage somewhere and start making games. Now you need to make a big investment in order to be able to make a game, it has become much more difficult. So that is not only as an investment to start a company, but also for an individual who wants to work in the industry. (M, game designer, NL)

Hiro Izushi and Yuko Aoyama (2006) bring more nuance to the games industry's historical evolution in a detailed comparison of the UK, the US, and Japan. In Japan, corporate sponsorships in arcades and consumer electronics, coupled with creative talent from the comic book and animation sectors shaped the sector, whereas in the US personal computers and university laboratories played a more important role. The bottom-up narrative of a youth culture of self-taught "bedroom coders" primarily describes the British context. In recent years, the particulars of each country's industrial trajectory have started to converge. One of the features of the contemporary games industry is the continuation of the rather independent, dispersed and idiosyncratic structure of the early years into a contemporary corporate context, where three console manufacturers and a small group of global games publishers dominate the field. In September 2005 *Game Developer Magazine* published a ranking of the top game publishers by six factors: annual turnover, number of releases, average review score, quality of producers, reliability of milestone payments, and the quality of staff pay and perks.[5] The global top five of this list are firms that consist of numerous smaller game studios, specialist companies, and other service providers (such as outsourcing agents, marketing and public relations, technological assistance, software development, and product distribution):

(1) *Electronic Arts*: founded in 1982 in the US, with 6,500 employees worldwide including 4,100 in game developers (after cutting 5 percent of its global workforce in February 2006), based in five hub studios in Redwood Shores, Los Angeles, Orlando (all US), Vancouver (Canada) and Chertsey (UK), along with development studios in Chicago (US), Montreal (Canada) and Tokyo (Japan);[6]

(2) *Activision*: founded in 1979 in the US, with about 2,000 employees (after cutting its global workforce by 7 percent in February 2006), headquartered in Santa Monica, California with additional offices in the US, Canada, the UK, France, Germany, Italy, Japan, Australia, Scandinavia, Spain, and The Netherlands;[7]

(3) *Ubisoft*: founded in 1986 in France, employing 3,500 people of which 2,800 dedicated to game production, headquartered in Montreuil-sous-Bois, France with fifteen

studios in eleven countries (particularly in the UK, Germany, and the US), also founded the "Ubisoft Campus" in Montreal in February 2005, offering a series of college and university level training programs in video game development;[8]

(4) *Konami*: founded in 1969 in Japan as a jukebox rental and repair business, 5,127 employees of which 2,664 in its Digital Entertainment Business division[9], headquartered in Tokyo, Japan with key offices in Redwood City and Los Angeles (US), as well as in Germany;

(5) *THQ*: founded in 1989 in the US and exclusively producing video games since 1994, worlwide approximately 1,700 employees, headquarted in Calabasas, California and owning studios in the US, Canada and Australia.[10]

The other companies in the top ten (beyond Microsoft, Sony, and Nintendo) were listed as Sega Sammy Holdings (Japan, a holding firm including video game hardware and software company Sega Corporation), Take-Two Interactive (US and U.K), Namco (Japan and US), Vivendi Universal Games (France), and Atari (US, subsidiary of Infogrames Entertainment). Atari, like EA and Activision, came in the news early 2006 after announcing to cut 20 percent of its worldwide workforce and to sell off its internal studios. At the time, Atari listed 490 employees on its payroll.[11] On a sidenote, it is notable that all three companies reported cutting most of these jobs at their US offices.

Although this brief overview describes an industry that has its fair share of conglomeration and concentration, among game developers, journalists, and newcomers the different studios and "dev firms" tend to be described with specific reference to their particular identities and ways of doing things. Consider for example the way Texas-based game developer Id Software – responsible for popular and infamous games such as *Doom* and *Quake* – describes itself: "Taking its name from Freud's primal, instinct-driven face of the human psyche, id Software is, by general acknowledgement, the coolest game shop in the world."[12]

Another aspect of Id Software that refers to a background steeped in hacker culture (preferring free sharing of information and technology) was its introduction to the industry of the shareware distribution method. "The idea was that consumers could download the first section of the game for free from the Internet or order it by mail. If they liked the game, they could purchase the rest of it by contacting the publisher" (Kent 2001, p. 458). The shareware method became the business standard for marketing and releasing new games. Another game studio to be mentioned here is Edinburgh, Scotland based Rockstar North – credited with the development of the *Grand Theft Auto* (GTA) series who have cultivated an off-beat reputation in the industry. The studio was originally called DMA – short for "Doesn't Mean Anything."[13] Game magazine *1Up* considers their anti-authoritarian attitude typical of the way the studio operates, as "[t]he company's names and leaders have changed over the years, yet there's a subversive sense of anarchy that permeates its work – a streak of lighthearted mayhem."[14] In a detailed account of Atari's history, Steven Kent (2001) cites the experience of consultant Ray Kassar as he joined the studio in 1978 and encountered the embodiment of Atari's slogan "work smart, not hard":"The first or second week I was there, Nolan invited me to a management committee meeting. I arrived at his office at 3.00. Everybody was sitting around in jeans and T-shirts [. . .] there were about six or seven of them drinking beer and smoking marijuana. They offered me a joint" (p. 110). This kind of posturing and attitude is quite common and must be read between the lines of other narratives describing a multi-billion dollar global industry dominated by multinational corporations. Small-scale projects as well as big budget games are thus mythically fixed by their producers within a quaint and sometimes bygone development culture (Ruggill *et al.* 2004, p. 300). In an in-depth study of gameworkers, Stephen Kline and colleagues (2003) note how these professionals all refer to a sort of rebelliousness in studio culture. They argue how the anti-corporate culture and "work as play" ethos of many game studios serves multiple functions at the same time: it convinces workers that they are free to really do what they want to do, it contributes to a more effective recruiting and retention system (constructing a narrative that people want to work there because of the supposed "coolness" of the studio), as well as it facilitates subtle yet pervasive disciplinary mechanisms for keeping people at work all the time.

The game industry is indeed a multibillion dollar industry – taking in annual revenues estimated (by industry sources) at roughly around 30 billion US dollars worldwide. The industry is concentrated in three core regions: North America, Europe, and Asia Pacific (Johns 2006). Although the industry has particular elements in each country, several characteristics are shared across regions. Considering the increasingly translocal and sometimes global operations in game development, it is safe to say that from the perspective of the individual game worker several of their experiences with the structure and organization of the industry are similar across the world. The game industry is a perfect example of the contemporary post-Fordist "weightless" economy at work, typified by a metalogic of instantaneous, experiential, fluid, flexible, heterogeneous, customized, portable, yet also fashionable and stylish products and productivity (Kline *et al.* 2003, p. 74). One the one hand, as these and other authors argue, the industry operates similar as other cultural or creative industries. Johns in particular suggests that "the cultural industries are becoming further interconnected as media conglomerates seek to deliver concepts via an increasing number of forms of content delivery" (2006, p. 159). The game industry collaborates with the music industry (in the form of tracks on games), the film industry (concept and script development, voice-overs, and visual effects), and the advertising and marketing industries following the completion of both hardware and software production. Outside the United States the game industry has also become part of deliberate government policies in for example Korea, Japan, Ireland, France, and Canada to strengthen the international competitiveness of its software industries by aggressively protecting copyrights, stimulating the formation of local and global business networks, and offering subsidies and tax breaks for game publishing and development companies (for example to fund the development of game prototypes that put studios in a stronger position when lobbying for a publishing deal). Considering the fast-paced growth and youth of the industry, computer and video games have become powerful drivers of a new global economy driven by information and communication technology, cultural production, and media convergence.

Aphra Kerr (2006, pp. 54–5) identifies four particular segments of the game industry, each with its own market charactertistics, revenue models, and production processes. The first segment, console games, has a high level of market concentration with only three manufacturers. As the costs of this market segment are substantial, there is a high barrier of entry to newcomers. The production of these consoles in fact does not generate much revenue for Microsoft, Nintendo, and Sony – the sale of software and subscriptions to online multiplayer gameplay services does. Games developed for these devices – which have a turnover time of about five to six years – tend to be expensive to develop, and can take between one to two years from idea, financing, and contracting to delivery, marketing, and distribution. The second segment consists of games for handhelds, which used to be a Nintendo monopoly. So-called "mini" games for cell phones can also be included in this segment, as these type of games get increasingly sophisticated and have the potential to offer all kinds of community and multiplayer features. Games developed for handhelds or phones vary greatly in their time schedule – downloadable "casual" games for cell phones tend to be relatively cheap and can be made quite fast (within a couple of weeks even), whereas cartridge-based games are much more expensive and take on average nine months to complete. The fourth segment is that of PC games, where a relatively open playing field based on common standards (in terms of operating systems, audio and video hardware, and internet access) is conducive to a high level of competition among a wide variety of game developers. This segment includes massively multiplayer online games which are extremely expensive to develop and have significant ongoing costs – for example regarding server upgrades, maintenance, and customer support.

Considering the institutional features of the game industry a couple of characteristics stand out. First, it has a distinct hourglass structure with a few corporate hardware manufacturers (Microsoft, Sony, and Nintendo) and multinational publishers (such as EA, THQ, Activision, Ubisoft, and Konami) dominating. According to the UK-based Entertainment and Leisure Software Publishers Association (ELSPA) the top ten publishers internationally control about two-thirds of the marketplace.[15] On the other side of the spectrum operate tens of thousands of game development studios, teams, and even individuals worldwide. In the commercial arena, games only get developed when a publisher agrees to finance the creative process, as they control the financing and marketing aspects of gamemaking, and are in a position to negotiate pricing and placing with retailers. Publishers not only finance, market, and distribute games, they also acquire or participate in development studios. Game publishing houses are often multinational operations with development studios and marketing operations in every major global market, thus controlling – much like the Hollywood movie studios – the major distribution bottleneck of the industry (Dovey and Kennedy 2006). In addition to operating as so-called "first-party" developers by commissioning games through their own in-house development studios and additionally designing, producing, and marketing the platforms upon which the games are played, publishers contract "third-party" development studios to make games for their publishing label. This process works the other way around too, as independent development studios try to sell their projects to a publisher. These studios do not have to deal with the risk of actually designing and producing hardware, but are dependent on the publishers (especially in the console market) in different ways, from getting costly access to proprietary software development kits necessary and paying steep license fees that allow them to design the game for a specific console, to sharing editorial and quality control with the manufacturers.

Professionals in the industry sometimes experience the production of PC or console games differently. Johns, quoting a publisher, argues that "[p]roducing console games is more of a lifestyle than with PCs" (2006, p. 165). Kerr (2006, p. 82) adds that the relatively low barrier of entry into the PC market produces intense competition between developers for a relatively small market, where many more titles are published than there is shelf space at retailers available. Johns further suggests that game developers have variable bargaining power vis-à-vis publishers at different stages in the lifecycle of consoles. Only well-known developers with a strong reputation, pedigree, and history of success retain high negotiating power and are able to secure high levels of artistic and editorial freedom when designing their games. Most developers, however, are constantly struggling to secure a publishing deal among an extremely competitive field, let alone claiming some kind of control over the end-product. Overall, the bargaining power of game developers is highest around the introduction of a next generation console (when manufacturers and their publishers need many games to get consumers to buy their console), and lowest once the console is established and has a relatively stable and profitable library of games.

Another area of contested dependency exists between independent publishers and game development houses through their respective reputations (if any) of being reliable – the industry is rife with stories of publishers that pull out halfway or put a project on hold due to internal restructuring, merge with another company that deprioritizes the ongoing projects, or simply are unable or unwilling to see the development of a game through to the end (Kerr 2006, p. 96). On the other hand, developers are equally at risk of having key employees leave during the production process – the industry is notorious for having problems retaining talent and suffering from a high attrition rate (especially among smaller studios) – and of mismanaging temporal and financial budgets. The relationship between a publisher and the developers is moderated by an internal (in case of first party developers) or external producer. "While ultimately beholden to the publisher, the external producer must also be seen by the developer as a valuable ally and member of the team – not just a narc for the publisher [. . .] because the external producer has the considerable power to reject deliverables and hold back payment to the developer, an adversarial relationship can develop between the external producer and the developer" (Gershenfeld *et al.* 2003, p. 44).

In recent years, a phenomenon of "second-party" publishers has gained ground in the industry, as companies increasingly outsource or subcontract all kinds of elements in the creative process across multiple studios or service providers in different parts of the world. About one-half to two-thirds of game development occurs more or less exclusively under the ownership of a publisher (Williams 2002, p. 47). This example of integration and consolidation is where contemporary observers signal a significant problem emerging, as publishers that control such a crucial share of game development and production tend to avoid risks – that are already a matter of fact of cultural production in the creative industries – and thus limit the range of games, diversity of ideas, and therefore vibrancy of the market by focusing on developing franchises, sequels, and re-used properties of other media such as books, comics and especially movies. As an example of this, one could consider contemporary top ten best-selling games lists worldwide that generally contain mostly sequels and movie adaptations rather than original games. Most research suggests that the production of tested formulas of franchises and sequels are an important way for publishers to pay the bills for the other, often more original games, and overall reduce risk. It is perhaps not surprising that industry experts and leading designers generally plead for more, not less unique professional identity in the business, as that is precisely the environment from where game developers and their studios came, or what they have built their image on. It is also a sign of increased self-awareness of workers in a rapidly professionalizing industry complete with numerous regional and international trade organizations as well as independent non-profit representation as in the case of the International Game Developers Association (IGDA; formed in 1994).

Next to publishers and developers, some other significant players in the game industry include related industries where games (or tools for games) are produced, such as universities and research laboratories, specialist animation/graphics/video/film companies, middleware (as in: supporting software applications, servers, and content management systems) development and business services, the government and military. The US army for example develops a game series of its own called *America's Army*, intended to simulate combat and life in the military, thus primarily functioning as a public relations and recruitment tool. In 2006, the army claimed on its site that the online version of the game had over six million registered players, ranking it among the top five PC online action games.

The market for computer and video games has grown exponentially, with a corresponding increase in the scale and production budgets for games, as well as heightened expectations of worldwide success. Up until the mid-1990s most games were made by teams of developers working in the same room, with maximum budgets in the hundreds of thousands. This situation changed with the introduction and widespread uptake of consoles and handhelds, and the introduction of PCs as gameplaying devices into the home. Games started to include three-dimensional graphics, elaborate soundtracks, and moved from quite narrowly contained spaces to "game-worlds", where players could roam around for days instead of being restricted to simply getting from point A to B. This led to the formation of larger teams and the development of all kinds of specializations, with budgets sometimes in the million dollar range. At the time of writing, the industry produces games that are made by "megateams" often spread across different countries for computers and consoles that have advanced graphic and audio capacities, are integrated with the internet and operate with budgets in the tens of millions. However, this is but one side of the institutional coin. At the same time there are fewer and larger games produced, there is also a trend towards more small-scale casual game production, of companies securing funding beyond the traditional publishers (through advertising agencies or movie studios for example, but also through self-funding), and of developers taking their game directly to the consumer through online distribution. Industry observers note that these trends have made the process of development more stressful and lead to high rates of burnout.

An interview with game developer Cliff Harris of Positech Games on the weblog *GameProducer.net* (10 July 2006) effectively summarizes some of the key experiences of people working in the game industry either for large corporations or smaller independent studios:

> GameProducer.net: After working years and years both in a big company and as a self-employed, how would you describe your experiences? What have been the pros and cons in both ways of doing games? Cliff Harris: Pros of big company: You learn what artists, producers, marketers and animators all do on a big game project. You learn how to work on huge projects and to understand other people's code. You get a regular salary and get to play great LAN [Local Area Network, MD] games every lunchtime. You learn some great code techniques. Donuts. Cons of big company: Pay isn't as high as it should be. Pressured to work long hours. Working with very poor quality code in some cases. Internal office politics. Being told not to interact with the customers. Lawyers. Donuts. Pros of Indie: Set your own hours, work on your own game. Work wherever you like, even in the park. Play games

when you like, holiday when you like. Close connection with the customers, direct stake in the success of each game. No Donuts. Cons of Indie: No guaranteed money. Can be lonely work. Nobody to turn to for a second opinion. No regular LAN buddies for games. No Donuts.[16]

Technology. Technology is intrinsically tied to the work in computer and video games. Since its inception, game production shared a relationship with technology that simultaneously builds upon the creative process while using technological innovation to coax developers to higher levels of adaptation. Most predominant in this respect are the advancement of console generations and PC graphics cards that allow game developers to create rich, ornate worlds that require development companies to spend more resources on technology and hire more staff or outsource tasks to specialists (or, indeed, consumers) in order to meet new standards, protocols and capabilities (Jeppesen 2005). The market for technically advanced games further drives the market for advanced graphics cards and next-generation consoles as consumers must purchase the latest upgraded computers or new consoles to play games developed to meet the technological specification particular to the new technologies. As developers create content that exceeds the current standards, they are, at the same time, making their past work irrelevant and making their future work more challenging. But the exploitation of technology is not limited to the technical aspects of the games – it is also embedded in the way game developers give meaning to their work.

A first indicator of the central role technology plays in the gamemaking process is the abundance of technical designations of jobs in the industry: animators, modelers, texturers, video and audio editors, 2D/3D artists and technicians, technical directors, programmers, network and hardware engineers, coders . . . According to the annual salary survey of Game Developer magazine, in 2006 the average paycheck of these workers is significantly higher than their colleagues in art, design, production, and quality assurance (including product testing and debugging). Programmers are the ones that build the games, often from scratch. However, especially as the technology driving game development becomes ever more sophisticated, the costs of programming and related tasks rise significantly. In a 2005 report on the computer and video game industry, the Organization for Economic Co-operation and Development (OECD) signals how publishers and studios increasingly turn to external partners in so-called "middleware" development, who provide the software that runs the graphics necessary for game development, including code compilers, software libraries (to simplify control of hardware), entire game engines and multiplayer platforms. These kinds of middleware suppliers are both small- to medium-size firms, as well as departments of large companies such as Microsoft and EA that have entered the lucrative middleware market in recent years. "Generally applicable, interchangeable, interoperable middleware tools may be a solution to contain rising costs, allowing developers to focus mainly on the creative side of games and license middleware technology" (OECD 2005, p. 19). Kerr (2006, p. 91) indeed suggests that development companies are increasingly using middleware to cut time and reduce research and labor costs. Game developers on the other hand are reluctant to rely solely on software solutions produced by others. Game handbooks indeed encourage aspiring developers to become proficient in technological problem-solving, as this is a way to make themselves known in the industry as the first to add a specific functionality to game design. Developers often consider it as part of their professional identity to work on the underlying software – either to accommodate it better to their game or to update it.

The work of Jon Dovey and Helen Kennedy (2006) is of particular significance in assessing the status of technology in gamework. Dovey and Kennedy identify three aspects of the dominant role technology plays in the production of games: the effects of working within a distinct "upgrade culture," the effects of technology on different orders of realism at play within game representation, and the determining structures of game engines on production. As the global hardware manufacturing industry feverishly renews, and replaces its technologies – memory chips, graphics cards, processor speeds – the creative work of game developers (including, but not limited to the technicians) must be understood as taking place in a context of permanent change, looking for and exploring new capacities, discovery, and development. Second, Dovey and Kennedy suggest that each advance, renewal or replacement of technology gets framed by game developers as enhancing the possibilities of realism in their games – calling this drive toward naturalistic realism a central feature of game design culture. Third, the game engine. The game engine refers to code that controls the game world, defines its rules, determines what can and cannot be done by the players and their characters. Writing a game engine is expensive, requiring a team of programmers working initially for months and subsequently for years as new iterations of a game brand are released. Game engines are also licensed to development studios who then can use the code to build their own game on it, such as in the case of the *Unreal* game engine, which has become the most popular engine used by both professional and amateur developers. *Unreal* offers an entire suite of programs, including its own scripting language called UnrealScript, which spurred a large community online developing their own versions or "mods" (short for "modifications") in order to change or enhance gameplay.[17] Another popular example is the Source engine by Valve Software, which not only is available online, but is also supported by a Valve Development Community (VDC), encouraging developers and "modders" alike to use the software, share their experiences with it, and contribute to its overall development.[18] Valve's Source engine powers popular games such as *Half-Life 2* and *Counter-Strike: Source*. Valve Software has historically been extremely encouraging of mod developers, as its game *Counter-Strike* was initially developed by "modders," became extremely successful, and was subsequently acquired by the company.

The core appeal of *Counter-Strike* has been attributed to many factors, of which two are key to the work and professional identity of game developers: the emphasis on collaborative authorship over the game – involving fans, software developers, producers, and consumers in constantly evolving and shifting roles – and the element of (online) team play, influencing game developers and "modders" worldwide to focus increasingly on the participatory aspect of (online) gaming. Recognition of this culture of participatory authorship has become a crucial element of the production process in the game industry, as it has since the early 1990s acknowledged the necessity of viral marketing and user control in product development by pre-releasing game source code, offering product versions as shareware, including level builders and editors with games, and tapping customer communities for input (Jeppesen and Molin 2003). Another indicator for the quite "democratic" character of the industry is the consensus among game developers that one of the best ways to get a job in the industry is to get noticed as a talented or popular game "modder" or level editor. This in turn reinforces the interdependency and at times role exchange between those who make and those who play games. The developer/gamer relationship becomes even more fuzzy if one considers the developments in the specific – and immensely popular – genre of massively multiplayer online games (MMOGs), where the gameplay experience is almost exclusively shaped by the interaction between players (Pearce 2006). The developers no longer create the experience, but are primarily responsible for supporting the gameworld environment and rules-based context. The emergence of in-game marketplaces (as in the various auction houses in *World of Warcraft*) and community organizations (such as guilds and clans) – including in-game advertisements and news media (like *The Second Life Herald*) – additionally allow players to change the game to fit their needs, extending the game into "real" life, and making them part of the development process. In doing so, gamers supply the industry with massive amounts of free labor, as their play has become work. Nick Yee (2006) notes how players invest a great deal of time in their virtual careers, and argues that the playing of especially MMOGs for a lot of gamers becomes an obligation, which often is more stressful and demanding than their actual jobs. Castranova (2005) has further showed how the trade of in-game artifacts has in fact become a real job for many gamers who earn significant amounts of "real" money by acquiring and selling swords, shields, and all kinds of other "virtual" items. "Video games are changing the nature of both work and play. It is not so much that businesses will need to adapt to gamers as much as that work and play are starting to become indistinguishable from each other" (Yee 2006, p. 70).

Finally, the role of technology in establishing hierarchy in the industry must be considered. As Ellen Ullman (1997) has previously noted on the field of computer programming, the work involved with building the user interface or designing the gameplay in a MMOG tends to have less prestige or status in the industry than the practices of those "closest to the machine": the designers and programmers of game engines, unique software applications, or intricate (realistic) character textures. Ullman suggests that in this kind of low-level programming the operation of the system becomes paramount, and the needs of the users are forgotten. Although customer interaction and relationships are considered very important in the industry, the internal hierarchies among game developers are generally made up with those responsible for user-friendliness and usability at the bottom of the ladder – as exemplified by the job that everyone has to do (especially newcomers) but that nobody likes: quality assurance. In this final phase of development every aspect of the game is tested for problems ("bugs"), the reporting of which understandably creates tensions between the production team and the testing department. In a telling sign, several industry textbooks refer to this final phase of the production process as a "death march" towards the moment of the release of the final game code for manufacturing.

Organization. Even though many observers and scholars document (and lament) the conservative trend among publishers regarding financing new games, an equal number of authors offer into evidence the fact that the game developer population as well as the organization of gamework in large and small companies has enormous creative and innovative potential – even though this is hardly recognized by the rather anonymous crediting process of gamework. "Computer games tend to collapse questions of labor and authorship down to a particular designer, production company, platform, technical feature, or genre" (Ruggill *et al.* 2004, p. 299). According to the IGDA, crediting is increasingly important in the industry now that development teams grow bigger, and many tasks are outsourced or subcontracted. The organization signals the discrepancy between the largely informal nature of crediting – a relic from the industry's history of small-scale and independent organization – and the current global production process sometimes involving hundreds of people across different studios, departments, cities, and countries. This is but one example of various tension points in the organization of gamework that can be seen as growing pains of an industry that is making the transition from cottage to corporate at breakneck speed (when compared to other creative industries).

Development studios and publishing companies are the two interacting institutional entities that make up the basic organizational structure of the game industry. In game development, the main jobs include design, production, art, programming, audio, and quality assurance, all of which gets coordinated by a team lead (sometimes called producer or director). Designers (leads, associates, assistants) establish the basic game concept, characters, and play mechanics. Before any work gets done, these gameworkers first write up an often detailed design document – a blueprint outlining all aspects of the game – similar to a screenplay in film. Interestingly, the consensus is that the design document is a dynamic piece, and assistant designers tend to be responsible by keeping it up to date as it is often used in the phase of game testing to see whether all the promised facets of gameplay in fact are there, and work. Although game writers – those responsible for story structure, dialogue, plot, and character development – are part of the design team, their work is often done by freelancers. Art directors, artists, modelers, and animators develop characters, virtual worlds, animation, and special effects. Sound engineers and designers are becoming increasingly important in game development with the introduction of surround sound capabilities, as well as the cross-media franchising of popular music – indeed, a growing number of popular games today come with a separate soundtrack on CD. That said, sound design is one of the specialisms that often get outsourced. Programmers develop game engines or modify existing ones to fit the design document of the project at hand, and design the important artificial intelligence for the game (which AI has specific consequences for the level of difficulty and playability of the game). Finally, testers play the game to evaluate it for problems and playability.

At the end of a project – as the deadline draws near people in the industry have come to expect six- to seven-day workweeks and ten to sixteen-hour workdays, a period less than affectionally called "crunchtime" – a lot of team members are (often reluctantly) assigned to participate in quality assurance. The caveat for this summary of gamework is that every game development project can be organized quite differently, with most likely some more specific similarities in the games produced by large corporations such as EA or Sega, and more diversity among the smaller and independent developers. Generally speaking, the lifecycle for a console game takes about fifteen months, whereas PC games have somewhat shorter production times, and casual games, cell phone games, as well as games developed for handhelds can take less than a month to complete (Kerr 2006, p. 86). In pre-production the conceptual infrastructure for the game is designed, its look mapped, schedules created, and resources assigned. A large part of this work involves making sure everyone on the team understands the specific technological context (hardware/software) within which the game will be produced. In prototyping programmers create the tools that build the game, and the rendering tools which iterate animation or special effects, permitting artists to design, review, and edit their creations. Artists are working on two- and three-dimensional models, developing textures, and animation for characters and the game world, while software engineers code the game mechanics and the story. The third stage is production. Game engines are now complete, and characters and animation are embedded in a working game. Testers are evaluating levels, and returning them for correction to the development team. Finally, the product is shipped to the publisher, who will run its own tests before approving a game for release. Although job titles and descriptions vary throughout the industry, and in everyday work jobs, tasks and responsibilities are likely to overlap to some extent, each department tends to be quite hierarchically structured (with top-down relationships between leads, subleads and associates, "senior" and "junior" job descriptions, and assistants).

Kerr (2006) notes how there are specific differences between companies in Japan and Europe, noting that for example British companies tend to concentrate all the necessary skills and specialties within the existing team (which means that people sometimes have nothing much to do), whereas Japanese firms are more likely temporarily to assign specialist groups of professionals to complete a particular task, after which these workers move on to another project. On a final note, the creative cycle of a game involves the production (on deadline) of numerous assets, milestones, or deliverables: specific elements of a game that each get evaluated, tested, and often also paid separately – which can make or break the process of bringing a game to completion. This in turn produces an atmosphere of constant pressure to deliver. With the internationalization of game production networks the missing of even one deadline of a certain milestone can significantly delay or completely derail an entire project.

Jennifer Johns (2006) documents how since the early beginnings in the 1960s and 1970s the game industry has seen two major trends emerging in the organization and orientation of work. First, as documented earlier in this chapter, the game industry is and always has been highly dependent upon technological innovation, both from within and outside the industry. The second trend shows an industry that increasingly operates on a global scale, producing games in teams sometimes numbering in the hundreds of people that are dispersed across several studios around the world, each responsible for different elements of a game. These studios tend to be located in either the US (California, Texas, Washington State), Canada (Vancouver, Montreal), Europe (notably France, the UK, and Ireland), and Asia (primarily Japan and South Korea). Johns considers this consolidation in "supra-regions" of software production networks problematic in that "[a]s in many other cultural industries, the global domination of media conglomerates limits the ability of smaller firms to gain access to finance and distribution" (p. 177). In recent years the industry has been moving towards a model of distributed development by outsourcing parts of its developing activities to companies all over the world, while retaining some key production, management, marketing and distribution services under central control. According to a March 2006 management report by Screen Digest, outsourcing is already common among the largest companies in the game industry, estimating that 60 percent of games studios outsource some of their work to service providers (mainly in Eastern Europe, India, and Vietnam) today, with this figure projected to rise to 90 percent by 2008.[19] Outsourcing is part of a series of strategies companies

deploy to cut labour costs and flexibilize production of increasingly expensive and challenging game projects. Although
some of the larger studios have the financial muscle to keep
people on the payroll, outsourcing is a particularly attractive
model for independent developers, who cannot afford to have
large periods where certain parts of the company are not
doing anything.

The IGDA released an in-depth report on the quality of life
and organization of work in the game industry on April 20,
2004, based on a survey of 994 game developers through the
IGDA website. Among the conclusions reported were figures
suggesting that game developers spend a lot of time at work:
"sometimes by choice, sometimes because it's the only way to
ship the game on time and avoid a disaster, sometimes
because it's company policy. Most of the time, it is due to outside pressures."[20] The British union Bectu warned in July
2007 that the game industry "burns out talent" by regularly
demanding twelve to sixteen hours a day for three to four
months at a time of its employees – without paying any overtime.[21] This situation is similar elsewhere.

> The industry has really changed – it has gotten better as well
> as worse. The game industry is professionalizing, while on
> the other hand it is still very chaotic and unpredictable. It is
> extremely competitive: there are still a lot of people who really
> want to work themselves to pieces because they like it so
> much and they really drive the competition. Those are the
> people who like games so much that they are willing to put in
> 80 hours per week – and those are people you have to con-
> stantly compete with. It is an industry where you have to
> prove yourself all the time. (M, creative director, NL)

Kline, De Peuter and Dyer-Witheford (2003) document how
the organization of work in the game industry tends to get
expressed by game professionals as playful, and fun. The
organization of gamework is thus constructed on a foundation
of "work as play." This ideology is promoted by the industry as
it legitimizes the long hours – especially at crunchtime or in

situations of "perma-crunch" - and dedication so vital to keep up production, meet deadlines, and deliver milestones. Dovey and Kennedy (2006) warn that the largely informal occupational setting of gamework must be seen as a highly systematized form of a new kind of global media enterprise where the workers are drawn from fan communities, which culture is maintained within and through the workplace. In its study, the IGDA concludes that most game developers work in the industry because they love to make games – although this passion diminishes somewhat among those who work for companies that put staff on hiatus during "down time" – when no new games are lined up.

> So my take on that is, as someone who's spent a lot of time crunching on a lot of projects a lot of years ago is, I found I could tell the management "Oh, we're just not as effective if we're working full out. And we just can't maintain this and we need to start taking some time off. You know, a day a week, at least." Nobody would have it, but I just started doing it. Management be damned. And they couldn't fire me because I was too critical and at the end of the project, here I was with an empty task list and my peers were faced with tons and tons if bugs that came from the sloppy work under pressure. So you just need to back yourself off, at least in my opinion. (M, game developer, US)

A significant issue in almost all companies is so-called "feature creep," which refers to the tendency of development teams to add all kinds of fun or cool features to a game during the production phase that were not planned in advance nor outlined in the original design document, and thus delay the game's completion. The lack of effective management to some extent can be attributed to the fact that game development leads and producers are often promoted from within, and thus tend not to have received any formal training in management. "Indeed, few people combine the skills and personality types required to become an effective manager with those required by front-line game development. Thus, all too often do we see very good developers become unhappy leads, or professional managers/producers whose very useful skills are sneered at by non-developers who feel that the managers don't know what they're talking about because they have never programmed a game" (IGDA 2004, p. 49). As in other areas of media work and management, the creative process tends to some extent to feed off existing tensions within different groups of professionals in a team, firm, or networked enterprise. The game industry is no different, reporting competitive tensions between first-party and third-party developers, between game designers and producers (often framed as the perennial "artists" versus "suits" conflict), and a third uneasy tension can occur between the development team and a marketing department, with marketers concerned about audience appeal and developers prioritizing editorial autonomy and artistic control – in addition to generally considering the public less important than the judgments of peers and colleagues for product evaluation.

Culture. In a special by the international edition of German magazine *Der Spiegel* (of August 24, 2006), game designer Heather Kelly of Ubisoft Montreal is quoted about the difficulties the industry experiences in adapting to the new customer demographic of women: "Many so-called girls games have a bad reputation – and rightly so [. . .] Most producers are male and difficult to motivate. They can't really be bothered to develop a game for their niece or daughter. And when they do, the game is usually full of dumb clichés. The budgets are also often much lower than those for men's games."[22] Similarly, in a documentary on the history of the video game industry produced by American public broadcaster KCTS (out of Seattle), one of the game professionals interviewed mentioned how "back in the old days" the normal way to relax after a hard week's work was for a manager to take the entire development team to a strip club.[23] Indeed, the demographics of gameworkers suggest anything but a demographically representative environment.

In the UK the digital games industry employs more than 20,000 people across all sectors, with 6,000 employed directly in game development. According to Kerr (2006), there are 270 independent and publisher-owned studios employing on average twenty-two people, with the largest studios employing well over 100 people. In the US the industry employs approximately 30,000 people directly in game production tracks. In Japan game hardware and software companies employ an estimated 30,000 people. Based on a census of media professionals in the UK, the government and industry funded research organization Skillset reported in 2004 that the overall representation of women in the audio visual industries stood at 38 percent, with the lowest level of representation for women in electronic games: 8 percent.[24] In an October 2005 report on workforce diversity, the IGDA put – based on a Web survey receiving 6,347 responses from around the globe – women at 11,5 percent of gameworkers. A later informal survey among more than 6,000 professionals by *Game Developer Magazine* put the figure at 10 percent. The IGDA summarized its findings into a "typical" profile of a game development professional as: "white, male, heterosexual, not disabled, 31 years old, working in the industry just over 5 years, university/ college educated, is a programmer, artist or designer, [. . .] agrees that workforce diversity is important to the future success of the game industry."[25]

The division of labor in the game industry is quite gendered, with women most likely to work in human resources (47 percent), and to some extent writing (30 percent), marketing and public relations (25 percent). On the other hand, the survey shows how male workers almost completely dominate the core content creation roles (such as design, programming, and visual arts). Beyond a discrepancy in gender, a significant characteristic of workers in games is their relative youth and inexperience, with the vast majority of professionals in their twenties working less than five years in the industry. Interestingly, these numbers suggest that relatively few people work in a freelance capacity in the game industry (the British Skillset study for example showed a figure of 11 percent) with the possible exception of independent developers. However, as most developers change employers every two years or so, it is safe to say that their contracts are indeed dependent on the limited life of the projects their company is able to provide them with. The industry is also known for aggressively recruiting experienced team leads away from other studios – sometimes in the middle of a project.

As mentioned earlier, the game industry seems steeped in a history where workers must love what they do and this is accentuated by the extraordinary negotiations they are willing to make to be able to do it. Several examples can be found, from non-compete agreements that limit the number of places an exiting employee can work, to contracts demanding exclusive access to all the intellectual properties produced by an employee during their time of employment. The most common negotiation is the willingness to submit to workweeks that exceed a traditional 40-hour structure. In the aforementioned IGDA survey on quality of life issues, it was found that 35 percent worked 65 to 80 hours during "crunch weeks" (time near the end of the development cycle), and 13 percent reported average crunch weeks of over 80 hours. About half of all respondents reported that this overtime went uncompensated. These crunch weeks can average from a month to six months (and recur around every milestone deadline), and are generally described as the most grueling phase of the production process. When employees are dissatisfied with their jobs, be that work duties or working conditions, it is assumed that there is always someone out there who is willing to do the same job – and probably for less pay. A possible reason for this is the abundance of even younger workers – often graduates from the booming programs, departments and schools in game development all over the world – willing to build their portfolio by sacrificially "paying their dues" largely for free to make themselves known among the colleagues. Younger workers tend to be more willing to accept portfolio experience as additional compensation for longer hours and more responsibilities. In the same IGDA survey, about a third of workers anticipated leaving the industry within five years and 51 percent after ten years.

The IGDA sponsors specific quality of life sessions every year at the annual Game Developers conferences in the United States and Europe, signaling the importance of recognizing this aspect of the workstyle of professionals in the game industry. Greg de Peuter and Nick Dyer-Witheford (2005) signal three particular types at the dark side of gamework: passionate pay slaves, precarious global developers, and free networked labor. Their research showed that developers, initially delighted by their "work as play" jobs, often found that the very factors that first appear so attractive – individual autonomy, flexibility, a "cool" corporate context or even a distinctly anti-corporate culture – can be also seen as a smokescreen to hide the exploitation of the enthusiasm of young game workers/game fans. Such exploitation is also made possible by the unlikelihood of young urban professionals to be married and/or have child-rearing responsibilities – which considering the gendered nature of gamework seems to contribute to its masculine culture. "Those in long-term relationships, those who have children or want to start a family, or those who simply don't want to reduce the time of life to time spent at work, are ostensibly excluded from the game sector, or will find it tremendously difficult to commit to the ludicrous hours that can be expected of them" (p. 9).

As the larger publishers are increasingly controlling or even owning game development companies all over the world, and outsourcing becomes a common practice, the precarious status of gamework deepens. For most practitioners a persistent sense of job uncertainty and the threat of project cancellation is quite common. Finally, the inclusion of the free labor that gamers do – level editing, game modding, participating in user forums, submitting feedback in online product innovation roundtables – can be seen as generating additional rev-

enue for the publisher at little or no extra cost, extending the
shelf-life of certain games that came with authoring tools, and
informally train the game development workforce of the
future. On the other hand, modifying and exchanging player-
made levels, maps, artifacts or even entire games is extremely
popular among game players and this kind of sociality is an
important reason for many gamers to play (Kerr 2006, p. 118).
Furthermore, it is safe to say that a majority of people who use
a map editor or post a message on a game forum are perhaps
not interested in working for the game industry, but are in fact
extending and expanding their playing experience – turning
themselves from otherwise "passive" consumers of game
products into "active" co-creators of content.

De Peuter and Dyer-Witheford also found sources of enjoy-
ment in gamework, such as the ability to work in a creative
capacity despite risk-averse corporate pressures, a generally
cooperative and anti-bureaucratic way of doings things at the
studio, and an overall sense of having fun on the job. However,
there seems to be a paradox here: in the self-perceptions
of many gameworkers their job environment can be best
described as playful, relaxed, fun, and exciting, whereas industry trends and managerial practices tend to veer towards more
formulaic, systematic, and flexible productivity (Schilling
2006). These two elements are not necessarily anathema –
rules and routines can in fact be productive, creative expression
that drives content creation is not automatically anarchic. It
could perhaps be argued that the tension and conflict these two
dominant modes of giving meaning to the process of gamework produce are part of what drives the industry-wide discussion on quality of life issues. In this context it is interesting to
note the introduction of dedicated "Quality of Life Managers" at
some studios. These employees are not doing any of the actual
developing, but are responsible for the comfort, creativity, and
productivity of those who do. One of these is Kent Schuelke,
who joined *Pandemic* in Los Angeles in 2000. Sitting down for
a moment at the GDC of 2006, he explains his role in the firm:

It started as a bit of a lark to just try and create some fun things for our employees to do and, they responded, the response was overwhelming [. . .] And the effect of doing it, frankly, having a quality company culture is just as important as making terrific games. This industry over the last ten years has gone through tremendous growing pains [. . .] most developers don't know how to deal with that [. . .] in the old days they would work long hours, hard hours, long weeks they would work into the ground. And there was a sense of machismo about it where it would be like "we're game makers. We're tough. We're working around the clock making these great games." And companies now, during this incredible period of growth, having these growing pains, they don't know whether to hang onto that past model, or look to something new in the future."[26]

Schuelke signals how the current company culture in game development is finding its way between the residue of "militarized masculinity" and cultivated independence on the one hand, with a commercial climate of milestones, crunchtimes, customer relationship management and marketing on the other hand. In fact, this review of what it is like to work in the game industry shows how game development is fast-forwarding through a history of professionalization that took an industry such as journalism more than a century. In doing so, these professionals have to come to terms with a wide range of issues – and do it fast. This bewildering pace often leads to overly simplistic classifications, for example of gamers as either "hardcore" or "casual," of development occurring in either "corporate" or "independent" contexts, and of work either as a site of exploitation or a source of playfulness. If anything, the lessons learned from the other, somewhat older media professions suggest that these and other dichotomies are not only false – these are strategies workers use to make sense of an otherwise complex environment, within which everyone is struggling to define and articulate a professional identity. In the next, concluding chapter I will tie these lessons to the ideas, trends, and developments as sketched in the previous sections of the book.

CHAPTER EIGHT

Conclusion: Liquid Media Work

Change and insecurity, whether real or perceived, are part of most if not all workstyles. The attributes of liquid modern life are diverse and complex, and cannot be reduced to a single culprit – capitalism, the global economy, rampant consumerism. Disruptive technologies such as internet, social trends (especially worldwide demographic convergence), cultural transformations, political and societal developments all contribute to a pervasive sentiment of a runaway world, a world where letting go of control, history, and tradition are advertised as the new necessary survival skills. The media, in whatever shape or size, amplify and accelerate these trends – more so because nowadays we are not just using media in a digital age; we are in fact living in and through media. It is tempting to analyze this kind of media life in terms of the boundaries and parameters that have well-established meanings such as social institutions (the family, the company, the state), and corresponding conceptual categories (culture, economy, creativity). However, the overview of the lives and identities of people professionally employed as media practitioners if anything suggests that these analytical devices are not particularly helpful if we want to make sense of media work – and thus of the problems and solutions people in overdeveloped capitalist democracies increasingly face on a day to day basis. Culture, the economy, the family, work, and play: these and many others benchmarks for understanding life in the digital age at best can be characterized by their fragility, and their status or meaning must be seen as fluid – spilling over in and through the media. It is by scrutinizing the strategies, tactics, and processes of meaning-making by professionals in the creative industries that we catch a glimpse of the future that many assume lies ahead for most workers in the knowledge economy of the information age.

Regardless of one's apprehension about the implications of integrating creativity with the market and, in a broader sense, culture with economy, the review of what it means to work in the four key media professions – advertising, journalism, film and television production, and digital games – does offer a number of important and fascinating pointers towards a more complex society where individualized workstyles somehow find ways to retain a sense of the "zombie" categories of modernity while adapting to the conditions of contemporary liquid life. What makes the media as creative industries particular and special is not so much their awesome power to generate revenue and to entertain compellingly, but the ways in which commerce, creativity, content, and connectivity as purposes and goals of individuals, organizations, and transnational networks come together, blend, and produce a bewildering complexity of inputs and outcomes. Media work shows that the market does not rule with an iron fist, that informal networks exist side by side with sedimented structures and routines, that the production process includes as well as excludes both commercial aspiration and creative impulse, and that the democratic nature of convergence culture is both a bottom-up (user-generated content) as well as a top-down (cross-media marketing and franchising) trend. In what follows, I briefly synthesize my impressions of media work in ten key concepts. Let me reiterate a crucial opinion or warning underlying all of this: whatever the validity of a liquid modern context to social analysis, one should never be tempted to assume that the current chaotic context of work, life, and play will, at some point in the near or distant future, settle in consensual or otherwise collectively embraced ways of doing things. Again, whether real or perceived, a structural sense of constant change and permanent revolution is the strongest guide or predictor of the human condition in the digital age.

Inhabited Institutions. Overall, media work tends to take place in the offices and on the workfloors of specific institutions: production houses, development studios, corporate structures. However, much of this work is contingent, freelance, and temporary. People are constantly moving in and out of these institutions, continuously reconstituting the creative process – whether in the marketing department or in the newsroom for example. Furthermore, under conditions of convergence culture people across and within different institutions and media producers as professionals or amateurs are increasingly (expected to be) working together, to collaborate and co-create. This process, amplified by new media technologies, only accelerates the flow of people, processes, and ideas through these organizations. The media can thus best be understood as what Tim Hallett and Mark Ventresca (2006) call 'inhabited' institutions. Regardless of industry or discipline, media institutions "are not inert containers of meaning; rather they are "inhabited" by people and their doings" (p. 215). In order to understand these inhabited institutions, they argue, we must critically and reflexively look at their *embeddedness*, as in: everyday interaction rituals and formal organizational structures, and the ongoing construction and negotiating of *meaning* by the people involved – which process in turn has consequences for the situation (or organization) in question (p. 231).

Convergence Culture. Within a contemporary context of ongoing global conglomeration in the media industries and a parallel emergence of an increasingly participatory media culture, Henry Jenkins (2006) articulates a convergence culture as the default setting for media work. Organizations brace themselves for intra- and interinstitutional collaborations and cross-media production, while at the same time cautiously courting the consumer in her (historical yet only recently acknowledged) role as co-producer of commercially viable and creatively inspiring content and connectivity. In this context it is interesting to note that research among media workers directly involved with two-way interactivity and a more empowered role for the consumer suggests that they are often reluctant and at times outright hostile towards exploring ways to share control with members of the audience. The reason for this, argue Pyungho Kim and Harmeet Sawhney (2002), is that interactive media are catalysts for a power shift away from traditional telecommunications firms. Media companies are thus predisposed to integrate convergence culture into their historically familiar (and economically successful) protocols. The professional identity of media workers is still negotiating an answer to convergence culture, the first contours of which I consider to move beyond traditional (and dichotomous) market and editorial institutional logics of cultural production towards a more complex, culturally convergent logic. This is perhaps not so much a seamless blend of the previous logics guiding the production of culture, but rather must be seen as an emerging new way of giving meaning to one's work and career in the contemporary new media ecology.

Creative Industries. In a digital age where the social inevitability of the individualized society meshes with the powerful forces of the global capitalist project, a formal merger between the notions of creativity and commerce makes perfect sense. That does not mean this is necessarily a good thing, but it does offer new ways of interpreting and understanding what it is like to work in the media today. Under progressively more complex conditions the global media environment is the playground for interactions between enterprising individuals and global corporations, culture creators, and business profiteers – an ecology where people seem to wear all those hats at one or other point in their life.

Hourglass Effect. As Keith Hackett and colleagues (2000) note, the media as an industrial employer is not just home to six or seven huge global megacorporations, but also to tens or hundreds of thousands of small business enterprises, varying from organizations as individuals to companies and networks of talent. The history of the media shows how both types of media work need each other – the one perhaps for the outsourcing of specialized activities, the other at times for acting as powerful sponsors or clients. Although the field of mass media clearly privileges the international conglomerate, the networked production process, the internal function (or dysfunction), and the interinstitutional coherence (or lack thereof) of media companies are quite similar and multifarious for employees in large and small organizations.

Global Production Networks. As social theories about the network society suggest, the networked form of enterprise is quite typical for media work – especially considering the ongoing outsourcing, offshoring, and subcontracting of (specialized and flexible) parts of the creative process – from financing to distribution and usage – across the planet. The analysis of media production and consumption cannot do justice to its object without taking into consideration how these global production networks (GPN) are played out on an everyday basis. Furthermore, the work of GPN scholars (Coe *et al.* 2004; Johns 2006) clearly shows how these translocal processes do not just play into the hand of powerful global corporations, but at specific times and instances – which are quite masterfully exploited by media workers themselves – in fact favor the talented individual, the free agent, or the smaller (and thus more agile) enterprise.

International Division of Cultural Labor. As the production of culture becomes contingent on a global network of companies and talent, the responsibility for preparing, finding, and keeping employment not only shifts almost completely to the individual, she also is integrated in a new international division of predominantly flexible, contingent labor. The media have a tendency to cluster in specific (urban) areas, within which regions an ongoing exchange of labor, talent, and skills takes place between people and organizations. Newcomers, recent graduates, and other hopefuls flock to these areas – often called "creative cities" as a marketing tool by their local governments – further contributing to an at times rollercoaster atmosphere. However, migration patterns of the international division of cultural labor tend to be mostly regional or virtual, rather than global, which enables further labor exploitation by multinational corporations – in turn assisted by the deregulatory policies of governments (Miller and Leger 2001). People tend to remain firmly in place as their talent migrates to fulfill part of the production pipeline: a location for a film shoot, a particular asset of a digital game, the marketing and customer relationship management services of a news organization. Locational agglomeration and the global networked form of enterprise can thus be seen to reinforce each other, adding to the contingency of media work, while at the same time professionals in these industries are more connected than ever before.

Semi-Permanent Work Groups. Chris Bodnar (2006) documents a new kind of self-identification among cultural laborers: the rise of a social movement of precarious workers, emerging beyond the traditional institutional contexts of governments, employers, and even unions or guilds. The growing number of precarious and contingent workers in the creative industries is certainly cause for concern. Yet, as the work of Helen Blair (2003) shows, media workers and their organizations develop strategies to counter the precariousness embedded in their workstyles, especially by informally self-organizing into groups or teams that tend to move from project to project together for a certain period of time. These so-called semi-permanent work groups (SPWG) benefit employer and employee, as the first can outsource the hiring and firing of team members to those in charge of specific aspects of the production process (such as team leads in game development, magazine editors, or assistant directors in film and television), whereas the employees can secure future employment through their (largely informal) personal networks. Such SPWGs are not without power, as the creative talent of their – again: often informal – leaders can be an essential element in the production process, which allows them to make certain demands. SPWGs are not just teams of individuals; its definition within the international division of cultural labor of the creative industries must be extended to include local or global networks of firms and companies, as well as temporary lineups of the interests of consumers and producers in specific communities (such as in the case of citizen journalism projects) or contexts (as in the user discussion forums of television shows or computer games).

Heterarchic Project Ecologies. The management and organization of media work moves in generally unpredictable and often chaotic cycles, where according to Gernot Grabher[1] teams move from heterarchic to standardized work forms, from streamlined to flexible production processes, and from bureaucratic to dynamic modes of organization. The main paradox and key source of tension in the organization of media work lies between on the one hand quite hierarchically structured firms – as job titles such as "editor-in-chief," "team leader" or "creative director" clearly suggest – and on the other hand an as-mentioned rather chaotic, conflict-prone, often emotional, and unpredictable creative process. Not only does this process take place both within and between different firms and individuals at times located in different regions or countries all over the world, but the roles these various players have in the production of culture are extremely diverse and complex. Some are permanently employed, others only parachute in for a couple of weeks to work on a certain aspect of the project; several people move in and out of projects all the time, others get hired away by aggressive competitors looking for a particular skill or talent, and many – if not most – media workers swim in what David Hesmondhalgh (2002) considers a pool of underutilized talent. The project-based nature of media work thus functions primarily on a heterarchic basis, where people constantly adapt to changing (yet semi-permanent) work teams, clients, and sponsors. All these actors together form what can best be described as symbiotic, mutually reinforcing, and recombinant ecologies.

Manufactured Authenticity. Considering the undeniable importance of informal networks, a crucial question remains how aspiring as well as seasoned practitioners manage and give meaning to their professional identity in the process. On a final note, two key strategies stand out, both having to do with authenticity. Being authentic, original, talented, and unique is an essential ingredient of media work. Authenticity is a problematic category, however, as there exists a "dynamic tension between authenticity seen as an individual's creative voice – that is, their ability to resolve problems in unique and distinctive ways [. . .] – and claims to authenticity that are carefully crafted to create a personae of an artist with a view to attracting the attention of customers, critics, gatekeepers, and other artists" (Jones *et al.* 2005, pp. 893–4). Manufacturing authenticity is not necessarily something one can do or control – it is as much a performance as it can be a claim made by or for someone (Peterson 2005). This underscores the elements of networking, and often quite powerful social bonds that determine the workstyles of media professionals in tight-knit clustered communities of practice. It is, in other words, not only about being good at something – it is also about carefully cultivating that image of being good. The management of this image works in two, not entirely distinct yet vitally important domains: economic and artistic. In commercial terms, one needs to be perceived to provide investors, directors, editors, and other stakeholders with work that would (contribute to) generate revenue, while the media worker also benefits from a creative image of being seen among her peers as someone with an unique or otherwise special talent.

Narcissism of Minor Differences. In the day-to-day process of media work authenticity in all its complexity primarily gets meaning through what Sean Nixon (2006) calls a cult of creativity partly bound up with a narcissism of minor differences. The key to standing out and cultivating one's image and professional identity in media work is not so much being original, nor does it mean getting known as someone who has unique insight into what will work in today's fragmented media market. As Nixon argues, a significant part of the production process in the work of media professionals centers on drawing attention of competitor-colleagues upon completion of the project. In doing so, media work often boils down to emphasizing and cultivating what are generally only small differences between what one group of professionals does, and what another team generates. "In important ways, however, the rubric of creativity represented a way of dramatizing the desires and insecurities generated by needing to mark out these differences in order to succeed in an intensely competitive world of work" (p. 103). Time again, the analyses of media workers in the different disciplines show how their primary concern – for a variety of reasons – tends not to be the customer, nor the client: it is peer review and recognition. It turns out that this individual and group level tactic is not only a way to take responsibility for one's own professional identity, but also serves as both an economic and artistic survival tool in an otherwise complex, unpredictable, rollercoaster industry.

Of course, there is much more to say about the workstyles of media professionals and the implications of these conclusions for a life lived in media. As societies move towards culturalized economies, glocalized production and consumption, lifestyle politics and an ongoing immersion in media, the lessons we can learn from the experiences of workers in the creative industries are clearly critical. Beyond the convenient categories of culture versus economy, core versus periphery, content versus connectivity, creativity versus commerce or even flexibility versus stability I would like to argue for a more complex and indeed liquid understanding of a life lived (and thus: worked) in media. A liquid life is, as Bauman perhaps underestimates, a media life. And this life is primarily shaped, and lived, by media workers.

Notes

PREFACE

1 See www.manpower.com
2 See http://corp.match.com/index/newscenter_press_glance.asp
3 Dawn Kawamoto and Greg Sandoval (March 31, 2006, 1:05 PM
   PST), *MySpace growth continues amid criticism*, CNET News, source
   http://news.com.com/MySpace+growth+continues+amid+
   criticism/2100-1025_3-6056580.html
4 See http://en.wikipedia.org/wiki/Zygmunt_Bauman

I LIQUID LIFE, WORK, AND MEDIA

1 In *Work, Consumerism and the New Poor* (Open University Press,
   2005), p. 5.
2 For a reference to developing a "workstyle," see the site of a
   British professional coaching agency called The Results Agency
   (at www.theresultsagency.co.uk); another reference is the website
   of Australian coaching agency MerryMentality
   (www.merrymentality.com.au/workstyle.html)
3 For Europe, see for example www.eiro.eurofound.eu.int
4 Source http://en.wikipedia.org/wiki/Cellular_telephone
5 Source: www.census.gov/ipc/www/img/worldpop.gif
6 Source: www.internetworldstats.com
7 See http://ourmayday.revolt.org/precarity.info/info.htm
8 See http://pewresearch.org/social/pack.php?PackID=5
9 According to a 2006 report by the World Institute for
   Development Economics Research (part of the United Nations
   University), in 2000 the richest 2 percent of households in the
   world owned half of global wealth. Report available at
   www.wider.unu.edu
10 See http://en.wikipedia.org/wiki/Tanya_Grotter
11 Source: www.blizzard.com/press/060228.shtml

12 Personal e-mail from Zygmunt Bauman to the author, Monday June 5, 2006
13 See www.worldinternetproject.net
14 See www.meetup.com/tour/
15 Statistics on the 'Global Top 500' websites from Alexa, source: www.alexa.com/site/ds/top_500
16 See http://huminf.uib.no/˜jill/archives/blog_theorising/ final_version_of_weblog_definition.html
17 See http://technorati.com/weblog/2006/02/83.html
18 See www.mmogchart.com
19 Although this insight to some extent also gets expressed by Lash (2002) and Silverstone (2007), I am indebted for this inference to Harmeet Sawhney, in personal e-mail communication of October 15, 2006
20 Phone interview with Craig Newmark, December 1, 2005
21 See for example the company profile at CBS '60 Minutes' at www.cbsnews.com/stories/2004/12/30/60minutes/ main664063.shtml

2 CREATIVE INDUSTRIES, CONVERGENCE CULTURE, AND MEDIA WORK

1 Source: www.sony.net/Fun/SH/1-35/h2.html
2 See media ownership chart (based on the situation in 2001) at http://www.mediachannel.org/ownership/chart.shtml
3 I take this critique from Heinz Steinert's (2003) reading and a reinterpretation of the foundational text for studying the culture industry by Max Horkheimer and Theodor Adorno, "*Dialektik der Aufklaerung*," which was originally published in 1944
4 See www.culture.gov.uk/creative_industries
5 See http://deuze.blogspot.com/2006/11/ remote-control-journalism.html
6 See www.earacheextrememetalracing.com
7 These remarks are drawn from a project I did with Mark Fonseca Rendeiro in 2003 when working at The Amsterdam School of Communications Research. A paper about that project can be downloaded from his weblog at www.bicyclemark.org/alternativemedia.pdf
8 Source: http://en.wikipedia.org/wiki/Big_Brother_(TV_series)
9 Source: www.ilo.org/public/english/dialogue/sector/techmeet/ tmmcgs04/index.htm

10 Source: www.generation-online.org/c/cimmateriallabour.htm

11 See www.vandusseldorp.com/publications/smstv.asp

12 Source: www.pewinternet.org/PPF/r/166/report_display.asp

13 Source: http://yhoo.client.shareholder.com/
    ReleaseDetail.cfm?ReleaseID=174993

14 Source: www.economist.com/surveys/
    displaystory.cfm?story_id=6794282

3 MEDIA PROFESSIONS IN A DIGITAL AGE

1 See summaries of EU research on employment in the cultural
   industries at www.mipc.mmu.ac.uk/conf/conf_pro.htm

2 For more info, see the working papers of the GPN research
   project, available at
   www.sed.man.ac.uk/geography/research/gpn/gpnwp.htm

3 View conclusions and full report of the ILO at
   www.ilo.org/public/english/dialogue/sector/techmeet/
   tmmcgs04/index.htm

4 See www.henryjenkins.org/2006/07/prohibitionists_
   and_collaborat.html

5 Source: www.ifj.org/pdfs/ILOReport070606.pdf

6 See www.gamewatch.org/phpBB2/viewtopic.php?p=227#227

7 See http://ea-spouse.livejournal.com/274.html

8 See www.gamewatch.org/phpBB2/viewtopic.php?p=94#94

9 See reports on US newspaper culture of the Readership Institute
   of Northwestern University at http://readership.org/culture_
   management/culture/main.htm

10 Source: www.igda.org/qol

11 For more detail on the Pareto Principle, see
    http://en.wikipedia.org/wiki/Pareto_principle

12 See http://longtail.typepad.com/the_long_tail/2005/05/
    the_origins_of_.html

13 Dahlgren in turn took his cue from the work of David Altheide
    and Richard Snow (1979).

4 ADVERTISING, PUBLIC RELATIONS, AND MARKETING COMMUNICATIONS

1 One such request list is at http://dev.magicosm.net/cgi-
   bin/public/corvidaewiki/bin/view/Game/SubservientChickenRe

questList. On an interesting sidenote, this site is based on the 'wiki' concept, which means anyone can edit, modify, and add information to the list. See the original chicken video at www.subservientchicken.com

2   See www.time.com/time/covers/1101041011/nextmarketing.html
3   See company info at www2.wpp.com/About/About_1_0.html
4   Reports available at www.recma.com; see agency overview for 2006 as reported in *Advertising Age*, 1 May, at http://adage.com/images/random/FactPack06.pdf
5   See http://money.cnn.com/magazines/fortune/fortune_archive/2004/06/28/374368/index.htm
6   See www.mcdonalds.com/corp/news/corppr/2004/cpr_12132004.html
7   See WPP annual report 2005 at www.wpp.com/WPPDocuments/WPP_AR_2005_How_we_behave.pdf; the Publicis annual report of the same year is at www.finance.publicis.com/en/60000/pdf/2005_annual_report_en.pdf
8   See www.edelman.com/speak_up/blog/archives/2005/11/is_public_relat.html
9   See the report in full at www.pwc.com
10 Quote taken from www.businessweek.com/magazine/content/04_28/b3891011_mz001.htm
11 Check for excellent and current examples of new media advertising and marketing the weblog Adverblog, at www.adverblog.com
12 See www.nytimes.com/2006/09/08/business/media/08ads.html

5 JOURNALISM

1   See News Corporation corporate timeline at www.cjr.org/_deprecate/newscorp-timeline.asp
2   See www.guardian.co.uk/Iraq/Story/0,2763,897015,00.html
3   See www.outfoxed.org/
4   See www.ojr.org/ojr/workplace/1017859157.php
5   See a discussion of some examples of *"gaming the news"* (in 2002) at the Pew Center for Civic Journalism, www.pewcenter.org/doingcj/spotlight/displaySpotlight.php?id=59
6   Report available at www.ifj.org/pdfs/ILOReport070606.pdf
7   See www.stateofthenewsmedia.org

8 See WAN report at www.wan-press.org/article11168.html

9 For an overview of international newsrooms (including pictures), see the entries titled "Real Newsrooms" at the *What's Next* weblog, www.innovationsinnewspapers.com

10 See www.listener.co.nz/issue/3429/features/5412/ a_new_morning.html

11 See Farin Ramdjan (2002), *Hoge Drempels*. Mixed Media foundation report, available (in Dutch) at www.miramedia.nl/media/files/hogedrempels.doc.

6 FILM AND TELEVISION PRODUCTION

1 See www.ibm.com/services/us/index.wss/ibvstudy/imc/ a1023172?cntxt=a1000062&re=endoftv

2 See www.nielsenmedia.com

3 See www.kff.org/entmedia/entmedia052406nr.cfm

4 See www.variety.com/article/VR1117945843?categoryid=1&cs=1

5 See www.nytimes.com/2006/08/19/business/media/ 19hollywood.html?_r=1&ref=business&oref=slogin

6 See for example coverage on the Friends case at CNN via www.cnn.com/2004/LAW/05/04/grossman.friends/

7 See www.bls.gov/oco/cg/cgs038.htm

8 See http://slate.msn.com/toolbar.aspx?action=print&id=2115066

9 The report is available at www.futureexploration.net/fom06/ Future_of_Media_Report2006.pdf

10 MPAA (2006), *US Entertainment Industry: 2005 MPA Market Statistics*, available (upon request) at www.mpaa.org/researchStatistics.asp

11 See www.skillset.org/film/business/overview/article_3444_1.asp

12 See www.stats.govt.nz/analytical-reports/employment-in-the-cultural-sector

13 Source: www.ilo.org/public/english/dialogue/sector/techmeet/ tmmcgs04/index.htm

14 See www.ceidr.org/CEIDR_News_3.pdf

15 See www.sed.manchester.ac.uk/geography/research/gpn/

16 See for example http://archives.cnn.com/2001/CAREER/trends/ 02/21/newmedia/index.html

17 See www.laedc.org/

18 Find these and other statistics on the British media industry at www.skillset.org/research

19 See www.afc.gov.au/gtp/mpallemployment.html

20 See www.sag.org (click on "Reports" under "Diversity")

21 Source www.moviesbywomen.com/marthalauzenphd/ stats2005.html

22 Source www.moviesbywomen.com/marthalauzenphd/ stats2005boxedin.html

23 This remark is taken from a 2003 report by Karin Gottschall and Daniela Kroos of the Zentrum für Sozialpolitik at the Universität Bremen, titled *Self-employment in Germany and the UK: labor market regulation, risk-management and gender in comparative perspective*. www.zes.uni-bremen.de/pages

7 GAME DESIGN AND DEVELOPMENT

The material in this chapter was partly gathered and analyzed with Chase Bowen Martin

1 See www.theesa.com/archives/2006/07/for_immediate_r.php

2 Source brochure available at www.isfe-eu.org

3 See www.theesa.com/facts/gamer_data.php

4 See also http://gotgamebook.com

5 As reprinted on the Wikipedia entry for video game publishers, where it additionally is noted that "this is not a ranking by revenue, but of the quality of experience of working with the publishers according to staff, and some video game development companies." See http://en.wikipedia.org/wiki/ Video_game_publisher

6 See www.ea.com

7 See http://investor.activision.com/background.cfm

8 See www.ubisoftgroup.com

9 Source www.konami.co.jp/en/ir/pdf/generalmeeting/34/ syosyu.pdf

10 See http://investor.thq.com

11 As reported by *Gamespot*, source: www.gamespot.com/news/ 6144510.html

12 See www.idsoftware.com/business/history

13 See for example http://en.wikipedia.org/wiki/Rockstar_North

14 Source: www.1up.com/do/feature?cId=3147750&did=1

15 See www.elspa.com

16 Source: www.gameproducer.net/2006/07/10/interview-with-positech-games-owner-cliff-harris-kudos-game-production

17 See http://en.wikipedia.org/wiki/Unreal_series

18 See http://developer.valvesoftware.com

19 See www.screendigest.com/reports/06outnextgames
20 See http://igda.org/qol
21 Source: http://news.bbc.co.uk/2/hi/technology/5202236.stm
22 See http://service.spiegel.de/cache/international/spiegel/
   0,1518,433347,00.html
23 More information: www.pbs.org/kcts/videogamerevolution
24 Source: www.skillset.org/research/census/article_1331_1.asp
25 Source http://igda.org/diversity (quote taken from pp. 9–10)
26 Personal interview with the author, March 23, 2006, San Jose

8 CONCLUSION: LIQUID MEDIA WORK

1. See www.giub.uni-bonn.de/grabher/publications/t_grabher.html

References

Aarseth, Espen (2006) The culture and business of cross-media productions. *Popular Communications* 4(3), pp. 203–211.

Altheide, David, and Snow, Robert (1979) *Media logic.* London: Sage.

Archibugi, Daniele, Held, David, and Köhler, Martin (eds) (1998) *Reimagining political community: studies in cosmopolitan democracy.* Palo Alto: Stanford University Press.

Aronowitz, Stanley, and DiFazio, William (1995) *The jobless future: sci-tech and the dogma of work.* Minneapolis: University of Minnesota Press.

Arthur, Michael (1994) The boundaryless career: a new perspective for organizational inquiry. *Journal of Organizational Behaviour* 15(4), pp. 295–306.

Avilés, José, León, Bienvenido, Sanders, Karen, and Harrison, Jackie (2004) Journalists at digital television newsrooms in Britain and Spain: workflow and multi-skilling in a competitive environment. *Journalism Studies* 5(1), pp. 87–100.

Bagdikian, Ben (2004) *The new media monopoly.* Boston: Beacon Press.

Baines, Susan (1999) Servicing the media: freelancing, teleworking and "enterprising" careers. *New Technology, Work and Employment* 14(1), pp. 18–31.

Baker, Wayne, and Faulkner, Robert (2005) Interorganizational networks. In Baum, Joel (ed.) *The Blackwell companion to organizations,* pp. 520–540. Malden: Blackwell.

Balnaves, Mark, Mayrhofer, Debra, and Shoesmith, Brian (2004) Media professions and the new humanism. *Continuum: Journal of Media and Cultural Studies* 18(2), pp. 191–203.

Baltruschat, Doris (2003) International film and TV co-production: a Canadian case study. In Cottle, Simon (ed.), *Media organisation and production,* pp. 181–207. London: Sage.

Banks, Mark, Lovatt, Andy, O'Connor, Justin, and Raffo, Carlo (2000) Risk and trust in the cultural industries. *Geoforum* 31, pp. 453–464.

Bar, Francois, with Caroline Simard (2006) From hierarchies to network firms. In Lievrouw, Leah, Livingstone, Sonia (eds), *Handbook of new media: social shaping and consequences of ICTs*, pp. 350–363. London: Sage.

Bardoel, Jo, and Deuze, Mark (2001) Network journalism: converging competences of media professionals and professionalism. *Australian Journalism Review* 23(2), pp. 91–103.

Barnatt, Christopher, and Starkey, Ken (1994) The emergence of flexible networks in the UK television industry. *British Journal of Management* 5(4), pp. 251–260.

Bauman, Zygmunt (2000) *Liquid modernity*. Cambridge: Polity.

(2002a) The twentieth century: the end of a beginning? *Thesis Eleven* 70(1), pp. 15–25.

(2002b) *Society under siege*. Cambridge: Polity.

(2003) *Liquid love*. Cambridge: Polity.

(2005a) *Work, consumerism and the new poor*. 2nd edn. Maidenhead: Open University Press.

Bauman, Zygmunt (2005b) *Liquid life*. Cambridge: Polity.

Bauman, Zygmunt, and Tester, Keith (2001) *Conversations with Zygmunt Bauman*. Cambridge: Polity.

Baumann, Arne (2002) Informal Labor market governance: the case of the British and German media production industries. *Work, Employment and Society* 16(1), pp. 27–46.

Beam, Randal (2006) Organizational goals and priorities and the job satisfaction of US journalists. *Journalism Quarterly* 83(1), pp. 169–185.

Beck, Ulrich (1992) *Risk society: towards a new modernity*. London: Sage.

(2000) *The brave new world of work*. Cambridge: Polity.

(2006) *Cosmopolitan vision*. Cambridge: Polity.

Becker, Lee, Lauf, Edmund, and Lowrey, Wilson (1999) Differential employment rates in the journalism and mass communication labor force based on gender, race, and ethnicity: exploring the impact of affirmative action. *Journalism Quarterly* 76(4), pp. 631–645.

Beniger, James (1989) *The control revolution: technological and economic origins of the information society*. Cambridge: Harvard University Press.

Benkler, Yochai (2003) The political economy of commons. *Upgrade* 4(3), pp. 6–9. www.upgrade-cepis.org.

(2006) *The wealth of networks*. New Haven: Yale University Press. www.benkler.org/wealth_of_networks.

Benko, Georges (1997) Modernity, postmodernity and social sciences. In Benko, Georges, Strohmayer, Ulf (eds), *Space and social theory: interpreting modernity and postmodernity*, pp. 1–27. Malden: Blackwell.

Bennett, Lance (2001) *News: the politics of illusion*. 4th edn. New York: Addison Wesley Longman.

Bierhoff, Jan, Deuze, Mark, and De Vreese, Claes (2000) *Media innovation, professional debate and media training: a European analysis.* European Journalism Center Report. www.ejc.nl/hp/mi/contents.html.

Bilton, Chris (2007) *Management and creativity: from creative industries to creative management.* Malden: Blackwell.

Blair, Helen (2001) "You're only as good as your last job": the Labor process and labor market in the british film industry. *Work, Employment and Society* 15(1), pp. 1–21.

(2003) Winning and losing in flexible labor markets: the formation and operation of networks of interdependence in the UK film industry. *Sociology* 37(4), pp. 677–694.

Blair, Helen, Culkin, Nigel, and Randle, Keith (2003) From London to Los Angeles: a comparison of local labor market processes in the US and UK film industries. *International Journal of Human Resource Management* 14(4), pp. 619–633.

Blanken, Henk, and Deuze, Mark (2007) *PopUp.* Amsterdam: Atlas.

Bodnar, Chris (2006) Taking it to the streets: French cultural worker resistance and the creation of a precariat movement. *Canadian Journal of Communication* 31(3), www.cjc-online.ca/viewarticle.php?id=1754.

Borcherding, Thomas, and Filson, Darren (2000) *Conflicts of interest in the Hollywood film industry: coming to America - tales from the casting couch, gross and net, in a risky business.* Claremont Colleges Working Paper 2000–07. http://econ.claremontmckenna.edu/papers/2000–07.pdf

Boyd-Barrett, Oliver, and Rantanen, Terhi (2001) News agency foreign correspondents. In Tunstall, Jeremy (ed.), *Media occupations and professions,* pp. 127–143. Oxford: Oxford University Press.

Brandt Husman, Tina (2002) *Organisational capabilities, competitive advantage and project-based organisations - the case of advertising and creative good production.* Frederiksberg: IVS.

Bromley, Michael (1997) The end of journalism? Changes in workplace practices in the press and broadcasting in the 1990s. In Bromley, Michael, O'Malley, Tom (eds), *A journalism reader.* London: Routledge.

Bourdieu, Pierre (1998) *Acts of resistance: against the new myths of our time.* Cambridge: Polity.

Bruns, Axel (2005) *Gatewatching: collaborative online news production.* New York: Peter Lang.

Burton, Jon (2005) News-game journalism: history, current use and possible futures. *Australian Journal of Emerging Technologies and Society* 3(2), pp. 82–93.

Bustamante, Enrique (2004) Cultural industries in the digital age: some provisional conclusions. *Media, Culture and Society* 26(6), pp. 803–820.

Canclini, Néstor García (2001) *Consumers and citizens: globalization and multicultural conflicts*. Minneapolis: University of Minnesota Press.

Cappo, Joe (2003) *The future of advertising: new media, new clients, new consumers in the post-television age*. McGraw-Hill.

Carnoy, Martin (2002) *Sustaining the new economy: work, family, and community in the information age*. Cambridge: Harvard University Press.

Carstens, Adam, and Beck, John (2005). Get ready for the Gamer Generation. *TechTrends* 49(3), pp. 21–25.

Castells, Manuel (2000) *The rise of the network society*. 2nd edn. Oxford: Blackwell.

Castronova, Edward (2005) *Synthetic worlds: the business and culture of online games*. University of Chicago Press.

Caves, Richard (2000) *Creative industries: contracts between art and commerce*. Boston: Harvard University Press.

Chan-Olmsted, Sylvia, and Chang, Byeng-Hee (2003) Diversification strategy of global media conglomerates: examining its patterns and determinants. *Journal of Media Economics*, 16(4), pp. 213–233.

Chaplain, Heather, and Ruby, Aaron (2005) *Smartbomb*. Chapel Hill: Algonquin Books.

Christopherson, Susan, and van Jaarsveld, Danielle (2005) New media after the Dot.com bust: the persistent influence of political institutions on work in cultural industries. *International Journal of Cultural Policy* 11(1), pp. 77–93.

Coe, Neil, and Johns, Jennifer (2004) Beyond production clusters: towards a critical political economy of networks in the film and television industries. In Scott, Allen, Power, D. (eds) *The cultural industries and the production of culture*, pp. 188–204. London: Routledge.

Coe, Neil, Hess, Martin, Yeung Wai-chung, Henry, Dicken, Peter, and Henderson, Jeffrey (2004) "Globalizing" regional development: a global production networks perspective. *Transactions of the Institute of British Geographers* 29(4), pp. 468–484.

Compaine, Ben (2005) *The media monopoly myth: how new competition is expanding our sources of information and entertainment*. New Millennium Research Council report. www.thenmrc.org/archive/Final_Compaine_Paper_050205.pdf

Cornelissen, Joep (2002) Academic and practitioner theories of marketing. *Marketing Theory* 2(1), pp. 133–143.

(2003) Change, continuity and progress: the concept of integrated marketing communications and marketing communications practice. *Journal of Strategic Marketing* 11(4), pp. 217–234.

Costera Meijer, Irene (2001) The public quality of popular journalism: developing a normative framework. *Journalism Studies* 2(2), pp. 189–205.

Cottle, Simon (ed.) (2003) *Media organization and production*. London: Sage.

Creedon, Pamela, and Cramer, Judith (2007) *Women in mass communication*. 3nd edn. Thousand Oaks: Sage.

Crosier, Keith, Grant, Ian, and Gilmore, Charlotte (2003) Account planning in Scottish advertising agencies: a discipline in transition. *Journal of Marketing Communications* 9(1), pp. 1–15.

Curran, James (ed.) (2000) *Media organisations in society*. Oxford: Oxford University Press.

Dahlgren, Peter (1996) Media logic in cyberspace: repositioning journalism and its publics. *Javnost/The Public* 3(3), pp. 59–72.

De Mooij, Marieke (2005) *Global marketing and advertising: understanding cultural paradoxes*. 2nd edn. London: Sage.

De Peuter, Greig, and Dyer-Witheford, Nick (2005) A playful multitude? Mobilising and counter-mobilising immaterial game labor. *Fibre Culture* 5. http://journal.fibreculture.org/issue5.

DeFillippi, Robert, and Arthur, Michael (1998). Paradox in project-based enterprise: the case of film making. *California Management Review* 40(2), pp. 125–139.

Deuze, Mark (2002) *Journalists in The Netherlands: an analysis of the people, the issues and the (inter-) national environment*. Amsterdam: Het Spinhuis.

(2004a) Global journalism education. In Merrill, John, de Beer, Arnold (eds), *Global journalism: survey of international communication*, 4th edn., pp. 145–158. New York: Longman.

(2004b) What is multimedia journalism? *Journalism Studies* 5(2), pp. 139–152.

(2005a) Towards professional participatory storytelling in journalism and advertising. *First Monday* 10(7). www.firstmonday.dk/issues/issue10_7/deuze/index.html.

(2005b) What is journalism? Professional identity and ideology of journalists reconsidered. *Journalism* 6(4), pp. 443–465.

(2006) Participation, remediation, bricolage: considering principal components of a digital culture. *The Information Society* 22(2), pp. 63–75.

(2007) Convergence culture in the creative industries. *International Journal of Cultural Studies* 10(2).

Deuze, Mark, and Dimoudi, Christina (2002) Online journalists in The Netherlands: towards a profile of a new profession. *Journalism* 3(1), pp. 103–118.

Dovey, Jon, and Kennedy, Helen (2006) *Game cultures*. Buckingham: Open University Press.

Drumwright, Minette, and Murphy, Patrick (2004) How advertising practitioners view ethics: moral muteness, moral myopia, and moral imagination. *Journal of Advertising* 33(2), pp. 7–24.

Du Gay, Paul (1996) *Consumption and identity at work*. London: Sage.

Du Gay, Paul, and Pryke, Michael (eds) (2002) *Cultural economy: cultural analysis and commercial life*. London: Sage.

Dupagne, Michel, and Garrison, Bruce (2006) The meaning and influence of convergence: a qualitative case study of newsroom work at the Tampa News Center. *Journalism Studies* 7(2), pp. 237–255.

Dutton, William, Kahin, Brian, O'Callaghan, Ramon, and Wyckoff, Andrew (eds) (2004). *Transforming enterprise: the economic and social implications of information technology*. Cambridge: MIT Press.

Ehrlich, Matthew (1997 [1995]). The competitive ethos in television newswork. In Berkowitz, Dan (ed.), *Social meanings of news*, pp. 301–317. Thousand Oaks: Sage.

Eisenmann, Thomas, and Bower, Joseph (2000) The entrepreneurial M-form: strategic integration in global media firms. *Organization Science* 11(3), pp. 348–355.

Ellul, Jacques (1967) *The technological society*. London: Vintage Books.

Elmer, Greg (2004) *Profiling machines: mapping the personal information economy*. Cambridge: MIT Press.

Esser, Frank (1998) Editorial structures and work principles in British and German newsrooms. *European Journal of Communication* 13(4), pp. 375–405.

Featherstone, Mike (1992) Postmodernism and the aesthetization of everyday life. In Lash, Scott, Friedman, Jonathan (eds) *Modernity and identity*, pp. 265–290. Oxford: Blackwell.

Felstead, Alan, and Jewson, Nick (eds) (1999) *Global trends in flexible labor*. Basingstoke: Macmillan.

Flew, Terry (2004) Creativity, cultural studies, and services industries. *Communication and Critical/Cultural Studies* 1(2), pp. 176–193.

Florida, Richard (2002) *The rise of the creative class*. New York: Perseus.

Fröhlich, Romy (2007) Three steps forward and two steps back? Women journalists in the Western world between progress, standstill and retreat. In Creedon, Pamela, Cramer, Judith (eds) *Women in mass communication*, pp. 161–176. Thousand Oaks: Sage.

Gade, Peter (2004) Newspapers and organizational development: management and journalist perceptions of newsroom cultural change. *Journalism Monographs* 6.

Gall, Gregor (2000) New technology, the labor process and employment relations in the provincial newspaper industry. *New Technology, Work and Employment* 15(2), pp. 94–107.

Garnham, Nicholas (2000) *Emancipation, the media, and modernity.* Oxford: Oxford University Press.

Garrison, Bruce (2001) Diffusion of online information technologies in newspaper newsrooms. *Journalism* 2(2), pp. 221–239.

Gershenfeld, Alan, Loparco, Mark, and Barajas, Cecilia (2003) *Game plan.* New York: St. Martin's Griffin.

Gershuny, Jonathan (2000) *Changing times: work and leisure in postindustrial society.* Oxford: Oxford University Press.

Giddens, Anthony (1986) *The constitution of society: outline of the theory of structuration.* Cambridge: Polity.

(2002) *Runaway world: how globalization is reshaping our lives.* London: Routledge.

Gopinath, Sumanth (2005) Ringtones, or the auditory logic of globalization. *First Monday* 10(12). www.firstmonday.org/issues/issue10_12/gopinath.

Grabher, Gernot (2001) Ecologies of creativity: the Village, the Group, and the heterarchic organisation of the British advertising industry. *Environment and Planning A* 33(2), pp. 351–374.

(2002a) Cool projects, boring institutions: temporary collaboration in social context. *Regional Studies* 36(3), pp. 205–214.

(2002b) The project ecology of advertising: tasks, talents and teams. *Regional Studies* 36(3), pp. 245–262.

(2004) Temporary architectures of learning: knowledge governance in project ecologies. *Organization Studies* 25(9), pp. 1491–1514.

Grabher, Gernot, and Ibert, Oliver (2006) Bad company? The ambiguity of personal knowledge networks. *Journal of Economic Geography* 6(3), pp. 251–271.

Graham, Phil (2005) *Hypercapitalism: new media, language, and social perceptions of value.* New York: Peter Lang Publishing.

Greenbaum, Joan (2004) *Windows on the workplace: technology, jobs, and the organization of office work.* New York: Monthly Review Press.

Hacker, Jacob (2006) *The great risk shift: the new economic insecurity - and what can be done about it.* Oxford: Oxford University Press.

Hackett, Keith, Ramsden, Peter, Sattar, Danyal, and Guene, Christophe (2000) *Banking on culture: new financial instruments for expanding the cultural sector in Europe.* www.artscouncil.org.uk/documents/publications/phpKKkKss.pdf.

Hackley, Christopher (2000) Silent running: tacit, discursive and psychological aspects of management in a top UK advertising agency. *British Journal of Management* 11(3), pp. 239–245.

(2003) Account planning: current agency perspectives on an advertising enigma. *Journal of Advertising Research* 43(2), pp. 235–246.

Hakim, Catherine (2003) *Models of the family in modern societies: ideals and realities*. London: Ashgate.

Hall, Jim (2001) *Online journalism: a critical primer*. London: Pluto Press.

Hallett, Tim, and Ventresca, Mark (2006) Inhabited institutions: social interactions and organizational forms in Gouldner's patterns of industrial bureaucracy. *Theory and Society* 35(2), pp. 213–236.

Handy, Charles (1998 [1989]) *The age of unreason*. Boston: Harvard Business School Press.

Hardt, Michael, and Negri, Antonio (2000) *Empire*. Cambridge: Harvard University Press.

Hartley, John (1996) *Popular reality: journalism, modernity and popular culture*. London: Arnold.

(ed.) (2005) *Creative industries*. Malden: Blackwell.

Herring, Susan C., Scheidt, L.A., Bonus, S., and Wright, E. (2005) Weblogs as a bridging genre. *Information, Technology and People* 18(2), pp. 142–171.

Hesmondhalgh, David (2002) *The cultural industries*. London: Sage.

Inglehart, Ronald (1997) *Modernization and postmodernization*. Princeton University Press.

International Federation of Journalists(2006) *The changing nature of work: a global survey and case study of atypical work in the media industry*. Research report. www.ifj.org/pdfs/ILOReport070606.pdf.

Ito, Mimi (2005) Technologies of the childhood imagination: Yugioh, media mixes, and everyday cultural production. In Karaganis, Joe, Jeremijenko, Natalie (eds), *Structures of participation in digital culture*. Duke University Press.

Izushi, Hiro, and Aoyama, Yuko (2006) Industry evolution and cross-sectoral skill transfers: a comparative analysis of the video game industry in Japan, the United States, and the United Kingdom. *Environment and Planning A* 38(10), pp. 1843–1861.

Jenkins, Henry (2004) The cultural logic of media convergence. *International Journal of Cultural Studies* 7(1), pp. 33–43.

(2006) *Convergence culture – where old and new media collide*. New York: New York University Press.

Jentsch, Caroline (2004) Projektorganisation in der Frankfurter Werbeindustrie. *Spaces* 2004–03, www.uni-marburg.de/fb19/personal/professoren/bathelt/forschung/spaces.

Jeppesen, Lars Bo (2005) User toolkits for innovation: consumers support each other. *Journal of Product Innovation Management* 22(4), pp. 347–362.

Jeppesen, Lars Bo, and Molin, Mans (2003) Consumers as co-developers: learning and innovation outside the firm. *Technology Analysis and Strategic Management* 15(3), pp. 383–383.

Johns, Jennifer (2006) Video game production networks: value capture, power relations and embeddedness. *Journal of Economic Geography* 6(2), pp. 151–180.

Johnson, Melissa (1997) Public relations and technology: practitioner perspectives. *Journal of Public Relations Research* 9(3), pp. 213–236.

Jones, Campbell, and Munro, Rolland (eds) (2005) *Contemporary organization theory*. Malden: Blackwell.

Jones, Candace, Anand, Narasimhan, and Alvarez, Josè (2005) Manufactured authenticity and creative voice in cultural industries. *Journal of Management Studies* 42(5), pp. 893–899.

Jones, John Philip (2004) *Fables, fashions and facts about advertising*. London: Sage.

(ed.) (1999) *The advertising business*. London: Sage.

Kalleberg, Arne (2000) Nonstandard employment relations: part-time, temporary and contract work. *Annual Review of Sociology* 26, pp. 341–365.

Katz, Harry, and Darbishire, Owen (2000) *Converging divergences: worldwide changes in employment systems*. Ithaca: Cornell University Press.

Kent, Michael, and Taylor, Maureen (2002) Toward a dialogic theory of public relations. *Public Relations Review* 28(1), pp. 21–37.

Kent, Steven (2001) *The ultimate history of video games*. New York: Three Rivers Press.

Kerr, Aphra (2006) *The business and culture of digital games*. London: Sage.

Killebrew, Kenneth (2004) *Managing media convergence: pathways to journalistic cooperation*. Malden: Blackwell.

Kim, Pyungho, and Sawhney, Harmeet (2002) A machine-like new medium - theoretical examination of interactive TV. *Media, Culture and Society* 24(2), pp. 217–233.

Kline, Stephen, Dyer-Witheford, Nick, and de Peuter, Greig (2003) *Digital play: the interaction of technology, culture, and marketing*. Montreal: McGill-Queen's University Press.

Kling, Rob (1996) *Computerization and controversy: value conflicts and social choices*. 2nd edn. San Francisco: Morgan Kaufmann.

Kung-Shankleman, Lucy (2003) Organisational culture inside the BBC and CNN. In Cottle, Simon (ed.), *Media organization and production*, pp. 77–96. London: Sage.

Lampel, Joseph, Lant, Theresa, Shamsie, Jamal (2000) Balancing act: learning from organizing practices in cultural industries. *Organization Science* 11(3), pp. 263–269.

Langham, Josephine (1997) *Lights, camera, action! Careers in film, television and video.* 2nd edn. London: BFI.

Lash, Scott, and Urry, John (1994). *Economies of signs and space.* London: Sage.

Lazzarato, Maurizio (1997) *Lavoro immateriale: forme di vita e produzione di soggettività.* Verona: Ombre Corte.

Leadbeater, Charlie, and Oakley, Kate (1999) *The new independents.* London: Demos. www.demos.co.uk/publications/independents

Leadbeater, Charlie, and Miller, Paul (2001) *The Pro-Am revolution.* London: Demos. www.demos.co.uk/publications/proameconomy

Leckenby, John, Li, Hairong (2000) Why we need the Journal of Interactive Advertising. *Journal of Interactive Advertising* 1(1). www.jiad.org/vol1/no1/editors/index.htm

Leslie, Deborah (1995) Global scan: the globalization of advertising agencies, concepts, and campaigns. *Economic Geography* 71(4), pp. 402–426.

Lessig, Lawrence (2001) *The future of ideas.* New York: Random House.

Levy, Pierre (1994) *Cyberculture.* Minneapolis: University of Minnesota Press.

(1997) *Collective Intelligence: mankind's emerging world in cyberspace.* New York: Perseus.

Lievrouw, Leah, and Livingstone, Sonia (eds) (2006) *Handbook of new media: social shaping and consequences of ICTs.* 2nd edn. London: Sage.

Lorenzen, Mark, Frederiksen, Lars (2005) *The management of projects and product experimentation: lessons from the entertainment industries.* www.cbs.dk/departments/ivs/wp/wp.shtml

Louw, Eric (2001) *The media and cultural production.* London: Sage.

Luhmann, Niklas (1990) The autopoiesis of social systems. In Luhmann, Niklas, *Essays on self-reference*, pp. 1–20. New York: Columbia University Press.

McChesney, Robert, and Schiller, Dan (2003) *The political economy of international communications: foundations for the emerging global debate about media ownership and regulation.* UNRISD Technology, Business and Society Paper 11. www.unrisd.org.

McFall, Liz (2002) Advertising, persuasion and the culture/economy dualism. In du Gay, Paul, Pryke, Michael (eds), *Cultural economy: cultural analysis and commercial life*, pp. 148–165. London: Sage.

(2004) The culturalization of work in the "new economy: an historical view. In Elgaard Jensen, Torben, Westenholz, Ann (eds), *Identity in the age of the new economy: life in temporary and scattered work practices*, pp. 9–33. Cheltenham: Edward Elgar.

McKercher, Catherine (2002) *Newsworkers unite: labor, convergence and North American newspapers.* Lanham: Rowman and Littlefield.

McLuhan, Marshall (1994 [1964]). *Understanding media: the extensions of man*. Reprint edn. Cambridge: MIT Press.

McManus, John (1994) *Market-driven journalism: let the citizen beware?* Thousand Oaks: Sage.

Manovich, Lev (2001) *The language of new media*. Cambridge: MIT Press.

Mantler, Janet, Matejicek, Amanda, Matheson, Kimberly, and Anisman, Hymie (2005) Coping with employment uncertainty: a comparison of employed and unemployed workers. *Journal of Occupational Health Psychology* 10(3), pp. 200–209.

Marjoribanks, Tim (2000) *News Corporation, technology and the work-place: global strategies, local change*. Cambridge: Cambridge University Press.

Marler, Janet H., Woodard Barringer, Melissa, Milkovich, George T. (2002) Boundaryless and traditional contingent employees: worlds apart. *Journal of Organizational Behavior* 23, pp. 425–453

(2003) Strategising technological innovation. In Cottle, Simon (ed.), *Media organization and production*, pp. 59–75. London: Sage.

Miller, Toby, and Marie-Claire Leger (2001) Runaway production, run-away consumption, runaway citizenship: the new international division of cultural labor. *Emergences* 11(1), pp. 89–115.

Miller, Toby, Govil, Nitin, McMurria, John, Maxwell, Richard, and Wang, Ting (2005) *Global Hollywood 2*. London: BFI Publishing.

Mitchell, William (1999) *e-topia*. Cambridge: MIT Press.

(2003) *Me++: the cyborg self and the networked city*. Cambridge: MIT Press.

Mower, Eric (1999) Agency management: some secrets. In Jones, John Philip (ed.), *The advertising business*, pp. 17–28. London: Sage.

Neilson, Brett, and Rossiter, Ned (2005) From precarity to precarious-ness and back again: labor, life and unstable networks. *Fibre Culture* 5. http://journal.fibreculture.org/issue5.

Newsom, Doug (2004) *This is PR: the realities of Public Relations*. 8th edn. Belmont: Wadsworth.

Nixon, Sean (2006) The pursuit of newness: Advertising, creativity and the "narcissism of minor differences." *Cultural Studies* 20(1), pp. 89–106.

Norris, Pippa (2002) The bridging and bonding role of online com-munities. *Harvard International Journal of Press/Politics* 7(3), pp. 3–13.

(1998) *Critical citizens: global support for democratic governance*. Oxford: Oxford University Press.

Papper, Robert, Holmes, Michael, and Popovich, Mark (2004) Middletown media studies. *The International Digital Media and*

Digital Arts Association Journal 1(1), pp. 1–56. www.bsu.edu/icommunication/news/iDMAaJournal.pdf.

Paterson, Chris (2003) *Prospects for a democratic information society: the news agency stranglehold on global political discourse.* Paper presented to the EMTEL: New Media, Technology and Everyday Life in Europe Conference of April 23–26 in London, UK.

Patterson, Thomas (1997) The news media: an effective political actor? *Political Communication* 14(4), pp. 445–455.

Pavlik, John (2001) *Journalism and new media.* New York: Columbia University Press.

Pavlik, John, and McIntosh, Shawn (2004) *Converging media: an introduction to mass communication.* Boston: Allyn and Bacon.

Pearce, Celia (2006) Productive play: game culture from the bottom up. *Games and Culture* 1(1), pp. 17–24.

Perrons, Dianne (2003) The new economy and the work-life balance: a case study of the new media sector in Brighton and Hove. *Gender, Work and Organisation* 10(1), pp. 65–93.

Peterson, Richard (2005) In search of authenticity. *Journal of Management Studies* 42(5), pp. 1083–1098.

Peterson, Richard, and Anand, Narasimhan (2004) The production of culture perspective. *Annual Review of Sociology* 30, pp. 311–34.

Platman, Kerry (2005) "Portfolio careers" and the search for flexibility in later life. *Work, Employment and Society* 18(3), pp. 573–599.

Phelan, Steven, and Lewin, Peter (1999) Paradox in project-based enterprise: what paradox? *California Management Review* 42(1), pp. 180–191.

Poster, Mark (2004) The information empire. *Comparative Literature Studies* 41(3), pp. 317–334.

Pratt, Andy (2006) "Imagination can be a damned curse in this country": material geographies of filmmaking and the rural. In Fish, Robert (ed.), *Cinematic countrysides.* Manchester: Manchester University Press.

Pratt, Andy, and Gornostaeva, Galina (2005) *The film industry re-considered: commodity chain analyses and beyond.* Paper presented at the RGS conference on September 1, 2005, London, UK.

Puustinen, Liina (2004) *The most desirable target group: an analysis of the construction of gender and age in advertising business.* Paper presented at the Crossroads in Cultural Studies Conference of 25–28 June 2004, Urbana-Champaign, Illinois.

Putnam, Robert (ed.) (2004) *Democracies in flux: the evolution of social capital in contemporary society.* Oxford: Oxford University Press.

Quinn, Stephen (2005) *Convergence journalism.* New York : Peter Lang.

Redmond, James and Robert Trager (2004) *Balancing on the wire: the art of managing media*. Boulder: Coursewise.

Reeves, Byron, and Nass, Clifford (1996) *The media equation: how people treat computers, televisions, and new media like real people and places*. Stanford: CSLI Publications.

Resnick, Paul, Zeckhauser, Richard, Friedman, Eric, and Kuwabara, Ko (2000) Reputation systems. *Communications of the ACM*, 43(12), pp. 45–48.

Rifkin, Jeremy (2004). *The end of work*. 2nd edn. Marston Mills: Tarcher.

Rorty, Richard (1999) *Philosophy and social hope*. New York: Penguin.

Rossiter, Ned (2006) *Organized networks: media theory, creative labor, new institutions*. Rotterdam: Nai Publishers.

Ruggill, Judd, McAllister, Ken, Menchaca, David (2004) The gamework. *Communication and Critical/Cultural Studies* 1(4), pp. 297–312.

Russell, Adrienne, Ito, Mimi, Richmond, Todd, and Tuters, Mark (2006) *Networked public culture*. http://netpublics.annenberg.edu/alternative_media/networked_public_culture.

Russo, Tracy (1998) Organizational and professional identification: a case of newspaper journalists. *Management Communication Quarterly* 12(1), pp. 72–111.

Saez, Emmanuel (2006) Income and wealth concentration in a historical and international perspective. In Auerbach, Alan, Card, David, Quigley, John (eds), *Public policy and income distribution*. New York: Russell Sage Foundation Publications.

Schiller, Dan (1999) Deep impact: the web and the changing media economy. *Info* 1(1), pp. 35–51.

(2000) *Digital capitalism: networking the global market system*. Cambridge: MIT Press.

Schilling, Melissa (2006) Game not over: competitive dynamics in the video game industry. In Lampel, Joseph, Shamsie, Jamal, Lant, Theresa (eds), *The business of culture: strategic perspectives on entertainment and media*, pp. 75–104. Mahwah: Lawrence Erlbaum.

Schudson, Michael (2003) *Sociology of news*. New York: W.W. Norton.

Schulze, Bernd, Thielmann, Bodo, Sieprath, Stephan, and Hess, Thomas (2005). The Bertelsmann AG: an exploratory case study on synergy management in a globally acting media organization. *International Journal on Media Management* 7(3 and 4), pp. 138–147.

Scott, Allen (1997) The craft, fashion, and cultural-products industries of Los Angeles: competitive dynamics and policy dilemmas in a multisectoral image-producing complex. *Annals of the Association of American Geographers* 86(2), pp. 306–323.

(2000) *The cultural economy of cities*. London: Sage.

(2004) The other Hollywood: the organizational and geographic bases of television-program production. *Media, Culture and Society* 26(2), pp. 183–205.

Sennett, Richard (1998) *The corrosion of character: the personal consequences of work in the new capitalism*. New York: W.W. Norton.

(2006) *The culture of the new capitalism*. New Haven: Yale University Press.

Shapiro, Andrew (2000) *The control revolution: how the internet is putting individuals in charge and changing the world we know*. New York: PublicAffairs.

Silcock, William, and Keith, Susan (2006) Translating the tower of Babel? Issues of definition, language, and culture in converged newsrooms. *Journalism Studies* 7(4), pp. 610–627.

Singer, Jane (2004) Strange bedfellows: diffusion of convergence in four news organizations. *Journalism Studies* 5(1), pp. 3–18.

Steinert, Heinz (2003) *Culture industry*. Cambridge: Polity.

Stevens, Jane (2002) Backpack journalism is here to stay. *Online Journalism Review*, April 2. www.ojr.org/ojr/workplace/1017771575.php

Storey, John, Salaman, Graeme, Platman, Kerry (2005) Living with enterprise in an enterprise economy: freelance and contract workers in the media. *Human Relations* 58(8), pp. 1033–1054.

Taylor, Richard, Grubbs, Mariea, and Haley, Eric (1996) How French advertising professionals develop creative strategy. *Journal of Advertising* 25(1), pp. 1–14.

Taylor, T. L. (2006) *Play between worlds: exploring online game culture*. Cambridge: MIT Press.

Terranova, Tiziana (2000) Free labor: producing culture for the digital economy. *Social Text* 18(2), pp. 33–57. www.uoc.edu/in3/hermeneia/sala_de_lectura/t_terranova_free_labor.htm

Thompson, John (1996) *The media and modernity: a social theory of the media*. Palo Alto: Stanford University Press.

Toffler, Alvin (1980) *The third wave*. London: Pan Books.

Tuchman, Gaye (1973) Making news by doing work: routinizing the unexpected. *American Journal of Sociology* 78(1), pp. 110–131.

Tunstall, Jeremy (1993) *Television producers*. London: Routledge.

(ed.) (2001) *Media occupations and professions*. Oxford: Oxford University Press.

Turner, Bryan (2003) McDonaldization: linearity and liquidity in consumer cultures. *American Behavioral Scientist* 47(2), pp. 137–153.

Turow, Joseph (2005) Audience construction and culture production: marketing surveillance in the digital age. *The Annals of the American Academy of Political and Social Sciences* 597, pp. 103–121.

Ullman, Ellen (1997) *Close to the machine: technophilia and its discontents.* San Francisco: City Lights.

Urry, John (2003) *Global complexity.* Cambridge: Polity.

Ursell, Gillian (2000) Television production: issues of exploitation, commodification and subjectivity in UK television labor markets. *Media, Culture and Society* 22(6), pp. 805–825.

(2001) Dumbing down or shaping up? New technologies, new media, new journalism. *Journalism* 2(2), pp. 175–196.

Vaill, Peter (1996) *Learning as a way of being: strategies for survival in a world of permanent white water.* San Francisco: Jossey-Bass.

van Dalen, and Arjan, Deuze, Mark (2006) Advocates or ambassadors? newspaper ombudsmen in The Netherlands. *European Journal of Communication* 21(4), pp. 457–475.

van Dijk, Jan, and De Vos, Loes (2001) Searching for the Holy Grail: images of interactive television. *New Media and Society* 3(4), pp. 443–465.

van Ruler, Betteke, Vercic, Dejan, Buetschi, Gerhard, and Flodin, Bertil (2004) A first look for parameters of public relations in Europe. *Journal of Public Relations Research* 16(1), pp. 35–63.

Von Hippel, Eric (2005) *Democratizing innovations.* Boston: MIT Press. http://mitpress.mit.edu/democratizing_innovation_PDF.

Vonk, Nancy, and Kestin, Janet (2005) *Pick me: breaking into advertising and staying there.* Mississauga: Wiley.

Warhurst, Chris, Thompson, Paul, and Lockyer, Cliff (2005) *From conception to consumption: myopic analysis of the creative industries.* www.hrm.strath.ac.uk/ILPC/2005/confpapers/Warhurst-Thompson-Lockyer.pdf

Wasko, Janet (2003) *How Hollywood works.* London: Sage.

Weaver, David (ed.) (1998) *The global journalist: news people around the world.* Cresskill: Hampton Press.

Weischenberg, Siegfried, and Scholl, Armin (1998) *Journalismus in der Gesellschaft: Theorie, Methodologie und Empirie.* Opladen: Westdeutscher Verlag.

Wellman, Barry, Quan-Haase, Anabel, Witte, James, and Hampton, Keith (2001) Does the internet increase, decrease, or supplement social capital? social networks, participation, and community commitment. *American Behavioral Scientist* 45(3), pp. 437–456.

Williams, Dmitri (2002) Structure and competition in the US home video game industry. *International Journal on Media Management* 4(1), pp. 41–54.

Wilson, Chris (2001) On the scale of global demographic convergence 1950–2000. *Population and Development Review* 27(1), pp. 155–171.

Ybema, Sierk (2003) *De koers van de krant*. Amsterdam: Vrije Universiteit.

Yee, Nick (2006) The labor of fun: how video games blur the boundaries of work and play. *Games and Culture* 1(1), pp. 68–71.

Zelizer, Barbie (2004) When facts, truth and reality are God-terms: on journalism's uneasy place in cultural studies. *Communication and Critical/Cultural Studies* 1(1), pp. 100–119.

Index